THE DIPAVAMSA

AN ANCIENT BUDDHIST HISTORICAL RECORD

THE DIPAVAMSA

AN ANCIENT BUDDIST HISTORICAL RECORD.

EDITED AND TRANSLATED BY

HERMANN OLDENBERG.

GYAN

Published by

Gyan Publishing House
5, Ansari Road
Daryaganj, New Delhi-110002
Phone: 011-47034999, 9811692060
E-mail: books@gyanbooks.com

Distribution Network
gyanbooks.com
India, USA, Canada, UK, Australia, France

ISBN : 978-81-212-3329-3 (PB)
First Published, 1879

2nd Impression 2020

Printed at: Gyan Press, Delhi.

The Dipavamsa
Author: Hermann Oldenberg

THE

DÎPAVAṂSA:

AN ANCIENT BUDDHIST HISTORICAL RECORD.

EDITED AND TRANSLATED BY

HERMANN OLDENBERG.

WILLIAMS AND NORGATE.

14, HENRIETTA STREET, COVENT GARDEN, LONDON;

AND 20, SOUTH FREDERICK STREET, EDINBURGH.

1879.

INTRODUCTION.

The **DÎPAVAṂSA**, an edition of which I here lay before the public, is a historical work composed in Ceylon by an unknown author. George Turnour, who first drew the attention of European scholars to the Dîpavaṃsa [1]), declared it to be identical with a version of the Mahâvaṃsa to which the Mahâvaṃsa Ṭîkâ occasionally alludes, the version preserved in the Uttaravihâra monastery. This is certainly wrong [2]). We must undertake, therefore, a research of our own as to the origin of the Dîpavaṃsa and its position in the ancient literature of the Ceylonese.

The Mahâvaṃsa Ṭîkâ, when commenting on the title

---

1) See the Journal As. Soc. Bengal, vol. VI, p. 790, 1054; VII, p. 919 et seq.

2) The arguments by which Turnour supports his theory are entirely founded on errors and inaccuracies. Turnour says, for instance, that the opening lines of the Dîpavaṃsa are quoted in that Ṭîkâ as contained in the Uttaravihâra-Mahâvaṃsa. The Ṭîkâ quotes those lines indeed (India Office MS. of the Mahâv. Ṭîkâ fol. ko'), but without the slightest reference to the Utt.-Mahâvaṃsa. The only passage referring to the Mahâvaṃsa of the Uttaravihâra which I know, is quite sufficient to show that this work was different from the Dîpavaṃsa. In the Mahâvaṃsa Ṭîkâ (India Off. MS. fol. gha') we are told, that the Uttaravihâra-Mahâvaṃsa contained a statement somewhat different from the usual one, with regard to the descendants of king Sîhassara: „Uttaravihâravâsînaṃ pana Mahâvaṃse Sîhassarassa rañño puttapaputtakâ caturâsîtisahassâni râjâno ahesuṃ, tesaṃ kaniṭṭhako Bhaggusakko (corrected to Bhagusakko) nâma râjâ. tassa puttapaputtakâ dvâvîsatisahassâni râjâno ahesuṃ, tesaṃ kaniṭṭhako Jayaseno 'ti vuttaṃ." The Dîpavaṃsa (3, 43. 44) in the contrary agrees with the statements of our Mahâvaṃsa (p. 9) which are in contradiction to the Mahâvaṃsa of the Uttaravihâra.

of the Mahâvaṃsa, contains the following important remarks [1]):

„Mahâvaṃsaṃ pavakkhâmîti mahantânaṃ vaṃso tantipaveniparamparâ 'ti pi sayam eva vâ mahantattâ ubhayattha paridîpitattâ vâ Mahâvaṃso, taṃ Mahâvaṃsaṃ. tesam pi buddhabuddhasâvakâdînam pi guṇamahantânaṃ Mahâsammatâdînam pi vâ râjamahâmattânaṃ (râjamahantânaṃ?) pavenidîpitattâ ca buddhâgamanâdipakârehi mahâdhikârattâ sayam eva mahantattaṃ veditabbaṃ.

anupamavaṃsaanuggahâdinaṃ (°dînaṃ Paris MS.)
sabbaṃ aññataṃ (aññâtaṃ Par. MS.) kataṃ suppakâsitaṃ
apariyâgataṃ (ariyâbhataṃ Par. MS.) uttamasabbhi vaṇṇitaṃ
suṇantu dîpatthutiyâ sâdhusakkatan ti (comp. Dîpav. 1, 5)

iminâ Aṭṭhakathânayen' ev' assa mahantattaṃ paridîpitaṃ (paridîpitattaṃ?) ca veditabbaṃ. — tenâhu porâṇâ:

dîpâgamanaṃ buddhassa dhâtuñ ca bodhiâgamaṃ (bodhiyâgamaṃ Par. MS.)
saṃgahattheravâdañ ca dîpamhi sâsanâgamaṃ
narindâgamanaṃ vaṃsaṃ kittayissaṃ suṇâtha me 'ti

(comp. Dîpav. 1, 1). imâya pana gâthâya nayena (gâthânayena Par. MS.) pi assa sakhyâ (saṃkhyâ Par. MS.) mahantattaparidîpitattaṃ ñeyyaṃ. evaṃ Mahâvaṃsan ti laddhanâmaṃ Mahâvihâravâsînaṃ vâcanamaggaṃ porâṇaṭṭhakathaṃ ettha Sîhalabhâsaṃ hitvâ Mâgadhikabhâsâya pavakkhâmîti adhippâyo."

As two stanzas are quoted here, the first of which is said to be taken from an Aṭṭhakathâ, the second from a work of the „Porâṇâ", and as immediately afterwards mention is made of the Sinhalese „Porâṇaṭṭhakathâ", the contents of which are expressed in the Mahâvaṃsa in Pâli, there can be very little doubt that this Aṭṭhakathâ and

---

1) I give this passage according to the India Office MS. (fol. ko'), together with the various readings of the Paris MS. (fol. ko') which M. Feer has kindly communicated to me. — Comp. Turnour's Introd. to the Mahâvaṃsa, p. XXXI.

that work of the Porâṇâ are identical with each other and with the Porâṇaṭṭhakathâ mentioned afterwards. If I am right in asserting the identity of the works alluded to under these various expressions, we learn from this passage the following important fact, viz.: there was an Aṭṭhakathâ handed down and probably also composed in the Mahâvihâra, written in Sinhalese, the introductory stanzas of which allude to a historical account of Buddha's visits to Ceylon, of the Councils, of Mahinda etc., intended to be given in that very Aṭṭhakathâ, and these stanzas are almost identical with the opening lines of the Dîpavaṃsa. There must, therefore, most probably be some relation between this Aṭṭhakathâ and the Dîpavaṃsa which will be of a sufficient interest to justify a further inquiry.

Let us see what results we may obtain as to the contents of this Aṭṭhakathâ and as to its literary form? Let us ask particularly in what way the Pâli stanzas quoted from this Aṭṭhakathâ were connected with its main substance which was composed in Sinhalese?

The Mahâvaṃsa Ṭîkâ, after the passage quoted above, goes on to give some details about the way in which the author of the Mahâvaṃsa made use of this Sinhalese Aṭṭhakathâ on which his own work is based. It is said in the Ṭîkâ: „ayaṃ hi âcariyo porâṇamhi Sîhaḷa[ṭṭha]-kathâ-Mahâvaṃse ativitthârapunaruttidosabhâvaṃ pahâya taṃ sukhaggahaṇâdippayojanasahitaṃ katvâ 'va kathesi". The work in question is called here, as repeatedly afterwards, Sîhaḷaṭṭhakathâ-Mahâvaṃsa. It is not difficult to account for this expression where the two at first sight contradictory elements of a (theological) commentary (Aṭṭhakathâ) and of an extensive historical narrative (Mahâvaṃsa) are combined together. If we look at Buddhaghosa's Aṭṭhakathâ on the Vinaya, we find that the author has there prefixed to his explanation of the sacred texts a detailed historical account of the origin of the Tipiṭaka, its redaction in the three Councils, and its propagation to Ceylon by Mahinda and his companions. Buddhaghosa's commentary is based, as is well known, on that very Sinhalese Aṭṭhakathâ of the Mahâvihâra, which we are now discussing, and we may assume almost with certainty, that to this Aṭṭhakathâ a similar historical introduction was prefixed which may have been even of a greater extent than that of Buddhaghosa. If our inference is correct, we have found in what way the title „Sîhaḷaṭṭhakathâ-Mahâvaṃsa" could apply most properly to this work: it is a historical account (Mahâvaṃsa) which forms a constituent part of a theological commentary (Aṭṭhakathâ), and which is composed in order to give to the dogmatical contents of the latter the indispensable historical foundation [1]).

We are not very likely to go too far astray, if we try to form an idea of the style of composition of this Sinhalese Aṭṭhakathâ-Mahâvaṃsa according to the analogy of what we have before us in Buddhaghosa's comment. According to this, the Aṭṭhakathâ-Mahâvaṃsa appears to have been written, in the main, in prose; it was intermixed, however, with a considerable number of stanzas in order to emphasize the more important points of the narration and to raise them above the level of the rest. The Pâli verses quoted above, which are taken apparently from the introduction to the whole work, render it highly probable that all these stanzas were composed in Pâli. It was necessary, of course, to convey to the Sinhalese clergy of that time the understanding of the sacred Pâli texts by a commentary written in Sinhalese; if, however, in the course of such a commentary the most important and remarkable points were to be expressed in a metrical form, we may easily understand, that for such a pur-

1) In order to show how an Aṭṭhakathâ could contain extensive and detailed historical statements, we may refer also to the quotations which the Mahâvaṃsa Ṭîkâ gives from the Aṭṭhakathâ of the Uttaravihâra, concerning the history of Susunâga (Turnour's Introduction, p. XXXVII), of the nine Nanda kings (l. l. p. XXXVIII), of Candagutta (l. l. p. XLII), of the descendants of Mahâsammata (l. l. p. XXXV). It we compare the last passage with the statements about the same subject given above (p. 1, n. 2) from the Mahâvaṃsa of the Uttaravihâra, we are lead to believe, that the Mahâvaṃsa also of the Uttaravihâra formed a part of the Aṭṭakathâ of that monastery in the same way as was the case in the Mahâvihâra.

pose the language of the sacred texts which contained so abundant a stock of models for metrical composition, appeared much more appropriate than the popular dialect of the Sinhalese.

A considerable number of verses ascribed to the „Porâṇâ“, i. e. taken from the ancient Sinhalese Aṭṭhakathâ, and quoted by Buddhaghosa or in the Mahâvaṃsa Ṭîkâ, present the same close resemblance and almost identity with passages of the Dîpavaṃsa, which we have observed in the two verses given above. In proof of this I give the following examples:

Samanta-Pâsâdikâ (MS. Orient. 1027 of the Brit. Museum) fol. ga': tenâhu porâṇâ:

Vedisagirimhi Râjagahe vasitvâ tiṃsa rattiyo
kâlo 'va gamanassâ 'ti gacchâma dîpam uttamaṃ. |
paḷinâ Jambudîpâto haṃsarâjâ va ambare
evam uppaṭitâ therâ nipatiṃsu naguttame. |
purato puraseṭṭhassa pabbate meghasannibhe
patiṭṭhahiṃsu kûṭamhi haṃsâ va nagamuddhanîti.

Comp. Dîpav. 12, 35—37.

Samanta-Pâs. fol. kâḥ' — kha: sâ panâyaṃ (i. e. the second Council)

yehi therehi saṃgîtâ saṃgîtesu ca vissutâ
Sabbakâmi ca Sâḷho ca Revato Khuddhasobhito |
Yaso ca Sâṇasambhûto, ete saddhivihârikâ
therâ Ânandatherassa diṭṭhapubbâ tathâgataṃ, |
Sumano Vâsabhagâmi ca ñeyyâ saddhivihârikâ
dve ime Anuruddhassa diṭṭhapubbâ tathâgataṃ. |
dutiyo pana saṃgîto yehi therehi saṃgaho
sabbe pi pannabhârâ te katakiccâ anâsavâ 'ti.

Comp. Dîpav. 4, 50—54.

Mahâv. Ṭîkâ fol. khau: tenâhu porâṇâ:

yakkhânaṃ buddho bhayajananaṃ akâsi,
te tajjitâ taṃ saraṇaṃ akaṃsu buddhaṃ,
lokânukampo lokahite sadâ rato
so cintayi attasukhaṃ acintamassa. |
imañ ca Laṅkâthala mânusânaṃ

porâṇakappaṭṭhitaṃ vutt[h]avâsaṃ
vasanti Laṅkâthala mânusâ bahu
pubbe va Ojamaṇḍavaradîpe 'ti.
Comp. Dîpav. 1, 66. 73.

Mahâv. Ṭîkâ fol. ṭâṃ: tenâhu porâṇâ:

Suppatiṭṭhitabrahmâ ca Nandiseno Sumaṇadeviyâ
putto mâtâ pitâ c' eva gihibhûtâ tayo janâ 'ti.
Comp. Dîpav. 19, 9.

Mahâv. Ṭîkâ fol. ḍhṛi': tenâhu porâṇâ:

Anulâ nâma yâ itthi sâ hantvâna naruttame
catumâsaṃ Tambapaṇṇimhi issariyaṃ anusâsitâ 'ti.
Comp. Dîpav. 20, 30.

These passages which we may almost with certainty pronounce to belong to the ancient Aṭṭhakathâ-Mahâvaṃsa of the Mahâvihâra, will suffice to show, to what extent the author of the Dîpavaṃsa borrowed not only the materials of his own work, but also the mode of expression and even whole lines, word for word, from that Aṭṭhakathâ. In fact, a great part of the Dîpavaṃsa has the appearance not of an independent, continual work, but of a composition of such single stanzas extracted from a work or works like that Aṭṭhakathâ; many of the repetitions and omissions [1]) which render some chapters of the

1) The most striking example of such repetitions is the account of the three Councils, each of which is described twice, the author, no doubt, having had before him two different authorities. The case is similar in the following passages:

(12, 51—53:)
samaṇo 'ti maṃ manussalokeyaṃ khattiya pucchasi bhûmipâla,
samaṇâ mayaṃ mahârâja dhammarâjassa sâvakâ
tam eva anukampâya Jambudîpâ idhâgatâ. |
âvudhaṃ nikkhipitvâna ekamantaṃ upâvisi,
nisajja râjâ sammodi bahuṃ atthûpasaṃhitaṃ. |
sutvâ therassa vacanaṃ nikkhipitvâna âvudhaṃ
tato theram upagantvâ sammoditvâ c' upâvisi.

(17, 27:)
puṇṇakanarako nâma ahû pajjarako tadâ
tasmiṃ samaye manussânaṃ rogo pajjarako ahû.

An instructive example of the abrupt and fragmentary character of some parts of the Dîpavaṃsa is contained in the account of the conversion of young Moggallâna (5, 55—68), which would be almost unintelligible if we did not possess the same narrative in the Mahâvaṃsa (pp. 28—33).

Dîpavaṃsa almost illegible, we may account for not by the inadvertence of copyists, but by this peculiar method of compilation.

The results we have obtained regarding the connexion between the Dîpavaṃsa and the ancient Aṭṭhakathâ of the Mahâvihâra, furnish us with a clue for gaining an insight into the relative position of the Dîpavaṃsa and the second important historical text of the Pâli literature, the Mahâvaṃsa. The two works are, indeed, in the main nothing but two versions of the same substance, both being based on the historical Introduction to the great Commentary of the Mahâvihâra. Each work represented, of course, their common subject in its own way, the Dîpavaṃsa following step by step and almost word for word the traces of the original, the Mahâvaṃsa proceeding with much greater independence and perfect literary mastership. The Dîpavaṃsa, as regards its style and its grammatical peculiarities, betrays the characteristics of an age in which the Sinhalese first tried to write in the dialect of the sacred texts brought over from India; there are passages in the Dîpavaṃsa which remind us of the first clumsy attempts of the ancient German tribes, to write Latin. The Mahâvaṃsa is composed very differently; its author masters the Pâli grammar and style with a perfect ease which cannot have been acquired but after many fruitless attempts, and which may be compared with the elegant mastership of Latin composition by which the Italian poets and scholars of the *renaissance* excelled. The turning-

---

A careful consideration, however, of this passage shows that the boundary-line between what is said and what is omitted does not present those signs of capricious irregularity which inevitably characterize gaps caused by a copyist's carelessness. The omissions are governed by a certain principle. The important and interesting parts of the story are fully told; the less prominent events which form only the connecting links between the chief points of the narrative, are altogether omitted. I think that both these omissions and those repetitions are to be accounted for, in the main, by the extremely awkward method in which the author compiled his work, though I do not deny, of course, that many of the gaps which are found throughout the whole work, are to be referred to a different origin, viz. to the misfortunes to which the tradition of the Dîpavaṃsa has, from then till now, been exposed.

point between the ancient and the modern epoch of Pâli literature in Ceylon, is marked, no doubt, by the great works of Buddhaghosa, which were not less important from a literary than from a theological point of view.

Both Mahâvaṃsa and Dîpavaṃsa finish their records at the same point, viz. with the death of king Mahâsena. This coincidence is, of course, nothing but a consequence of the two works' being derived from the same source. We may find in this a new confirmation of our opinion that this source is the Aṭṭhakathâ-Mahâvaṃsa of the Mahâvihâra Monastery. The reign of that very king Mahâsena was a fatal time to this monastery. A hostile party succeeded in obtaining king Mahâsena's sanction for destroying the Mahâvihâra; during a period of nine years the monastery remained deserted by its former inhabitants; afterwards, after long and violent ecclesiastical struggles, it was reconstructed. We may easily understand, therefore, why historical writers belonging to the Mahâvihâra fraternity should stop just at the epoch of Mahâsena's reign, where the past destinies of their spiritual abode were divided from the present.

After these remarks about the relation of the Dîpavaṃsa to the ancient theological commentaries and to the Mahâvaṃsa, we now proceed to collect the data which throw a light on the question, at what time the Dîpavaṃsa was composed. Turnour infers its anterior origin, compared with the Mahâvaṃsa, from the fact of the first line's, as he says, of the Dîpavaṃsa being quoted in the Mahâvaṃsa Ṭîkâ, the authorship of which he ascribes to Mahânâma, the author of the Mahâvaṃsa itself. But apart from Turnour's opinion on the age of the Mahâvaṃsa Ṭîkâ being totally wrong, we have seen, that those lines are quoted in the Mahâvaṃsa Ṭîkâ not from the Dîpavaṃsa itself, but from the Aṭṭhakathâ on which the Dîpavaṃsa is founded. So we lose the date on which Turnour's opinion is based. What remains, are the following data:

1) The Dîpavaṃsa cannot have been written before A. D. 302, because its narrative extends till that year.

2) Buddhaghosa was acquainted with a version of the Dîpavaṃsa which, however, differed in some details from that which we possess[1]).

3) The continuator of the Mahâvaṃsa (p. 257, ed. Turnour) tells us, that king Dhâtusena (A. D. 459—477) ordered the Dîpavaṃsa to be recited in public at an annual festival held in honour of an image of Mahinda.

4) These data being given, it is only of a secondary importance, that the Mahâvaṃsa Ṭîkâ, which was composed in much later times, mentions an Aṭṭhakathâ on the Dîpavaṃsa[2]).

The result is, that the Dîpavaṃsa — be it in that very version which we possess or in a similar one — was written between the beginning of the fourth and the first third of the fifth century. We do not know as yet the exact date of the composition of the Mahâvaṃsa[3]), but if we compare the language and the style in which the two works are written, there will scarcely be any doubt as to the priority of the Dîpavaṃsa. The words, besides, by which Mahânâma characterizes the works of his predecessors:

> porâṇehi kato p' eso ativitthârito kvaci
> atîva kvaci saṃkhitto anekapunaruttako,

apply so extremely well to those peculiarities of the Dîpavaṃsa of which we have spoken above, that they appear to have been written most probably with reference to this very work.

---

1) Some lines from that version of the Dîpav. are quoted in the Samantapâsâdikâ. They partly agree with our text; partly they differ in such a way that they cannot be reconciled with it. See my notes on Dîp. 11, 17; 12, 1. — The Dîpav. is also quoted in the Aṭṭakathâ on the Kathâvatthu; see the note on 5, 30.

2) fol. ṇe (with reference to the ecclesiastical quarrels in Mahâsena's reign): ye keci bhikkhû vâ ussâpitanikâyantaraladdhikâ vâ tath' eva amhâkaṃ âcariyâ akaṃsû 'ti vadeyyuṃ, tesam pi taṃ parikappitavipphanditam eva, tesaṃ abhilâpamattaṃ vâ 'ti Dîpavaṃsaṭṭhakathâyaṃ vuttaṃ.

3) The arguments of Turnour who brings it under the reign of Dhâtusena (Introd. p. LIV), are extremely weak.

I have made use in editing the text of the Dîpavaṃsa, of the following MSS.:

I. MSS. written in Burmese characters.

1) [illegible]: MS. belonging to Major Fryer who brought it to England from British Burmah. About the third part of the Dîpavaṃsa (6, 87 — 15, 91) is wanting; instead of this the MS. contains a fragment of the Thûpavaṃsa. The MS. has been written Sakkarâj 1190 = A. D. 1828.

2) *N*: A Collation of the MS. presented by the late king of Burmah to the Colonial Library in Colombo. This MS. was collated by Gombadde Watte Dewa Aranolis with the MS. M (see below), for the use of Mr. Rhys Davids; its readings are indicated, for the most part in English characters, sometimes in Sinhalese writing, at the margin of M. If the reading of N is not expressly indicated by Dewa Aranolis, but if we are, from the silence of the collation, to draw the conclusion, that N agrees with M — a conclusion which is, of course, by no means always a safe one —, I designate such readings by *n*. If only a part of the single words is indicated, I include in brackets those parts which we are to supply from M.

II. MSS. written in Sinhalese characters.

3) *G*: MS. of the Paris National Library (collection Grimblot; fonds Pâli 365). Although this MS. is written in Sinhalese characters, its readings agree at a good many passages with the Burmese MSS. The text of G has been corrected from a MS. very similar to B.

4) *A*: MS. of the India Office (Pâli Collection no. 95).

5. 6) *B*. *C*: Copies of two MSS. of the Dadalle Wihâre, made for Mr. Rhys Davids, now in the Cambridge University Library (Add. 945. 946). In the five first Bhâṇavâras there are frequent corrections in C made from another MS. than that from which C has been copied. I designate these corrections by *c*.

7) *M*: Copy made by Gombadde Watte Dewa Aranolis for Mr. Rhys Davids from a MS. of the Busse Wihâre. Written on paper. Now in the Cambridge University Library (Add. 944).

8) *R*: MS. of the Cambridge University Library (Add. 1255). This is a copy of a MS. belonging to Mr. James d'Alwis.

9) *D*: MS. in the possession of Mrs. Childers, London; it is a copy made for the late R. C. Childers.

10) *E*: MS. of the Paris National Library (Coll. Grimblot, fonds Pâli 366).

11) *S*: A copy written on paper, which the priest Subhûti of Vaskaḍuve was kind enough to send me. There are some good corrections, written with pencil, on the first leaves, which I designate by *s*.

I have used, besides, the following abbreviations:

X = all Burmese MSS.
Y = all Sinhalese MSS.
Z = the class of MSS. represented by CDEMRS.

All our MSS. are derived from the same original source which was very incorrectly written in Burmese characters, as we may infer from some of the blunders common to all of our MSS.[1]). Perhaps this was the MS. brought in 1812 from Siam to Ceylon by the Modliar George Nadoris[2]).

The way in which the single MSS. are derived from their common source, will be shown by the following table:

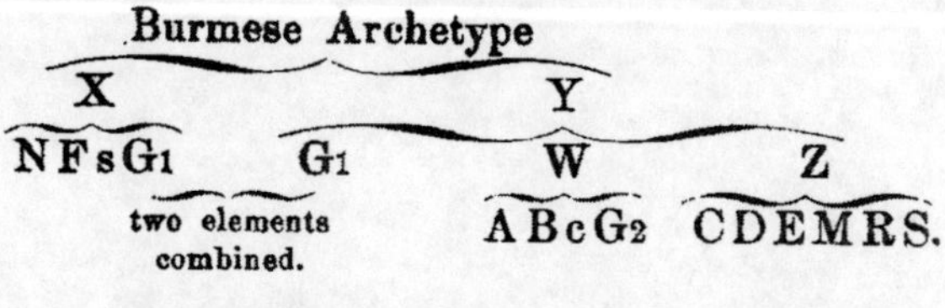

As to their critical value, the Burmese MSS. (X) deserve to be classed first; least is the value of Z, the

1) See, for instance, 1, 6. 55; 4, 45; 11, 3; 22, 18.
2) See Journ. As. Soc. Bengal VI, p. 790.

apparent correctness of which is owing not to real ancient tradition, but to arbitrary attempts of emendators.

It appeared desirable to print not the text corrected as far as possible, but the text of the *codex archetypus*, and to give in the footnotes my own emendations as well as those tried already in the MSS. In many passages I have refrained from correcting manifest grammatical blunders, errors in numbers of years etc., because I was afraid of correcting not the copyist but the author himself. Many passages also appeared to me too hopelessly corrupt for me to try to correct them. Of the various readings I could give, of course, only a selection, or the work would have increased to its threefold extent.

I cannot finish without having expressed my sincere thanks to the librarians and owners of MSS. who very liberally lent them to me or allowed me to collate them. My special thanks are due also to Dr. R. Rost who aided my undertaking from its beginning to its end with the greatest kindness in many various ways, and to my learned friends Dr. G. Bühler and Mr. Rhys Davids, but for whose kind and indefatigable assistance I should not have been able to add to the Pâli text of the Dîpavaṃsa a translation written in the language of a foreign country.

Berlin, September 1879.

The Editor.

Namo tassa bhagavato arahato sammâsambuddhassa.

Dîpâgamanaṃ buddhassa dhâtu ca bodhiyâgamaṃ
saṃgahâcariyavâdañ ca dîpamhi sâsanâgamaṃ
narindâgamanaṃ vaṃsaṃ kittayissaṃ, suṇâtha me. |
pîtipâmojjajananaṃ pasâdeyyaṃ manoramaṃ
anekâkârasampannaṃ cittikatvâ suṇâtha me. |
udaggacittâ sumanâ pahaṭṭhâ tuṭṭhamânasâ
niddosaṃ bhadravacanaṃ sakkaccaṃ sampaṭicchatha. |
suṇâtha sabbe paṇidhâya mânasaṃ, vaṃsaṃ pavakkhâmi
paramparâgataṃ
thutippasatthaṃ bahunâbhivaṇṇitaṃ etamhi nânâkusumaṃ
va ganthitaṃ, |
anûpamaṃ vaṃsavaraggavâsinaṃ apubbaṃ anaññaṃ tatha
suppakâsitaṃ
ariyâgataṃ uttamasabbhi vaṇṇitaṃ suṇâtha dîpatthuti sâ-
dhusakkataṃ. | 5

Those readings of the MSS. which the Editor thinks to be correct, are spaced out, as well as his own conjectures.

I, 1. This verse is quoted in the Mahâvaṃsa Ṭîkâ (Turnour's MS.). dhâtu ca ABGX, dhâtuñ ca Z, Mahâv. Ṭ. dhâtu may be the genitive; compare some examples of similar genitives and locatives at 15, 21. 27; 16, 82; 17, 53. — 4. °âbhataṃ ABcG2, Mahâv. Ṭ., °âbhabhataṃ F, °âgataṃ NG1Z. — nânâkusumavarabhûtagaṇṭhitan N, nânâkusumaṃ varabhutagaṇhitaṃ F, nânâkusumavadasutapaṇḍitaṃ G1, etaṃhi nânâkusumaṃ va ganthitaṃ Y, Mahâv. Ṭ. — 5. This Çloka which is quoted in the Mahâvaṃsa Ṭîkâ, runs there thus: anupamavaṃsaanuggahâdinaṃ sabbaṃ aññataṃ kataṃ suppakâsitaṃ apariyâgataṃ uttamasabbhi vaṇṇitaṃ suṇantu dîpatthutiyâ sâdhusakkatan ti.

Âsabhaṇ ṭhânapallaṅkaṃ acalaṃ daḷham akampitaṃ
caturaṅge patiṭṭhâya nisîdi purisuttamo. |
nisajja pallaṅkavare narâsabho dumindamûle dipadânam uttamo
na chambhati vîtabhayo va kesarî disvâna Mâraṃ sahasenavâhanaṃ. |
Mâravâdaṃ bhinditvâna vitrâsetvâ sasenakaṃ
jayo attamano dhîro santacitto samâhito |
vipassanâkammaṭṭhânaṃ manasikârañ ca yoniso
sammasi bahuvidhaṃ dhammaṃ anekâkâranissitaṃ. |
pubbenivâsañâṇañ ca dibbacakkhuñ ca cakkhumâ
sammasanto mahâñâṇî yâme tayo atikkami. |
tato pacchimayâmamhi paccayâkâraṃ vivaṭṭayi
anulomaṃ paṭilomañ ca manas' âkâ sirîghaṇo. |
ñatvâ dhammaṃ pariññâya pahânaṃ maggabhâvanaṃ
anusâsi mahâñâṇî vimutto upadhisaṃkhaye. |
sabbaññutañâṇavaraṃ abhisambuddho mahâmuni
buddho buddho 'ti taṃ nâmaṃ samaññâ paṭhamaṃ ahû. |
bujjhitvâ sabbadhammânaṃ udânaṃ katvâ pabhaṃkaro
tad' eva pallaṅkavare sattâhaṃ vîtinâmayi. |
samitasabbasantâso katakicco anâsavo
udaggo sumano haṭṭho vicintesi bahuṃ hitaṃ. |
khaṇe khaṇe laye buddho sabbalokam avekkhati,
pañcacakkhu vivaritvâ olokesi bahû jane. |
anâvaraṇañâṇan taṃ pesesi dipaduttamo,
addasa virajo satthâ Laṅkâdîpaṃ varuttamaṃ |
sudesaṃ utusampannaṃ subhikkhaṃ ratanâkaraṃ
pubbabuddhamanuciṇṇaṃ ariyagaṇasevitaṃ. |
Laṅkâdîpavaraṃ disvâ sukhettaṃ ariyâlayaṃ
ñatvâ kâlaṃ akâlañ ca vicintesi anuggaho: |
Laṅkâdîpe imaṃ kâlaṃ yakkhabhûtâ ca rakkhasâ
sabbe buddhapaṭikuṭṭhâ, sakkâ uddharituṃ balaṃ. |

---

6. âsabhaṇ ṭhânaṃ pallaṅkaṃ? Dasabalasutta: dasabalasamannâgato bhikkhave tathâgato catûhi vesârajjehi samannâgato âsabhaṇ ṭhânaṃ paṭijânâti parisâsu sîhanâdaṃ nadati. — daḷhaṃ X, duṭṭhaṃ Y. — caturo aṅge X. Compare Abhidhânapp. 157. — 7. sahasenam âgataṃ Z, [sahasena]vâ[gataṃ] N, sahasenavâhanaṃ ABFG. The reading of Z may be correct. — 12. anusâsi Ns, anuñâsi F, anussâbhi (corrected into anussâsi) G1, anussâhi ABG2, anussari Z. — 16. pañca cakkhuṃ s.

nîharitvâ yakkhagaṇe pisâce avaruddhake
khemaṃ katvâna taṃ dîpaṃ vasâpessâmi mânuse. |
tiṭṭhantesu ca ime pâpe yâvatâyuṃ asesato,
sâsanantaraṃ bhavissati Laṅkâdîpavare tahiṃ. |
uddharitvân' ahaṃ satte pasâdetvâ bahû jane
âcikkhitvâna taṃ maggaṃ añjasaṃ ariyâpathaṃ |
anupâdâ parinibbâyi suriyo atthaṃgato yathâ.
parinibbute catumâse hessati paṭhamasaṃgaho, |
tato paraṃ vassasate vassân' aṭṭhârasâni ca
tatiyo saṃgaho hoti pavattatthâya sâsanaṃ. |
imasmiṃ Jambudîpamhi bhavissati mahîpati
mahâpuñño tejavanto Asokadhammo 'ti vissuto. |
tassa rañño Asokassa putto hessati paṇḍito
Mahindo sutasampanno Laṅkâdîpaṃ pasâdayaṃ. |
buddho ñatvâ imaṃ hetuṃ bahuṃ atthûpasaṃhitaṃ
kâlâkâlaṃ imaṃ dîpaṃ ârakkhaṃ sugato kari. |
pallaṅkaṃ animisañ ca caṅkamaṃ ratanâgharaṃ
ajapâlamucalindo khîrapâlena sattamaṃ. |
sattasattâhakaraṇîyaṃ katvâna vividhañ jino
Bârâṇasiṃ gato vîro dhammacakkaṃ pavattituṃ. |
dhammacakkaṃ pavattento pakâsento dhammam uttamaṃ
aṭṭhârasannaṃ koṭînaṃ dhammâbhisamayo ahû. |
Koṇḍañño Bhaddiyo Vappo Mahânâmo ca Assaji
ete pañca mahâtherâ vimuttâ anattalakkhaṇe. |
Yasasahâyâ cattâri, puna paññâsa dârake
Bârâṇasi Isipatane vasanto uddharî jino. |

---

22. tiṭṭhantohaṃ ime pâpe XG1 s, tiṭṭhantesucaṃ ime pâpe Z, tiṭṭhantesu ca pâpesu ABG2. I think that at least one line is wanting. We may fill up the gap thus:

„pisâce pavesessâmi Giridîpaṃ manoramaṃ,
tiṭṭhantu ca ime pâpâ yâvatâyuṃ asesato."

24. parinibbâyi G1XZ, parinibbeyaṃ ABG2. parinibbeyyaṃ? — 25. vassasate vassânaṭṭh° XZG1, dve vassasatânaṭṭh° A2BG2, vassasatânaṭṭh° A1. I think that the reading of XZG1 is correct, and that a Çloka which contained a mention of the second Council has been omitted in our MSS. — 27. pasâdaye Y (°yuṃ G1), °yaṃ Xs. — 31. pavattento all the MSS.; pavattente? — pakâsente AB. — 33. Yasasahâye cattâro? — Bârâṇasi may be a locative; compare the note on dhâtu 1, 1, and the expression „jâti vijjante" in the Buddhavaṃsa (Jât. vol. I, p. 4). But perhaps we should write Bârâṇasiṃ, comp. v. 34 and the comment on Kaccâyana's Grammar, 2, 18.

Bârâṇasiṃ vasitvâna vutthavasso tathâgato
Kappâsike vanasaṇḍe uddhari Bhaddavaggiye. |
anupubbañ caramâno Uruvelam avasari,
35 addasa virajo satthâ Uruvelakassapañ jaṭiṃ. |
agyâgâre ahinâgaṃ damesi purisuttamo.
disvâ acchariyaṃ sabbe nimantiṃsu tathâgataṃ: |
hemantañ câtumâsamhi idha vihara Gotama,
mayaṃ taṃ niccabhattena sadâ upaṭṭhahâmase. |
Uruvelâyaṃ hemante vasamâno tathâgato
jaṭile sapârisajje vinesi purisâsabho. |
mahâyaññaṃ pakappiṃsu Aṅgâ ca Magadhâ ubho,
disvâ yaññe mahâlâbhaṃ vicintesi ayoniso: |
mahiddhiko mahâsamaṇo ânubhâvañ ca taṃ mahâ,
40 sace mahâjanakâye vikubbeyya katheyya vâ, |
parihâyissati me lâbho Gotamassa bhavissati,
aho nûna mahâsamaṇo nâgaccheyya samâgamaṃ. |
caritaṃ adhimuttiñ ca âsayañ ca anûsayaṃ
cittassa soḷasâkâre vijânâti tathâgato. |
jaṭilassa cintitaṃ ñatvâ paracittavidû muni
piṇḍapâtaṃ Kurudîpe gantvâna mahâiddhiyâ |
Anotattadahe buddho paribhuñjitvâna bhojanaṃ
tattha jhânasamâpattiṃ samâpajji bahuṃ hitaṃ. |
buddhacakkhûhi lokaggo sabbalokaṃ vilokayi,
45 addasa virajo satthâ Laṅkâdîpavaruttamaṃ. |
mahâvanaṃ mahâbhîmaṃ âhu Laṅkâtalaṃ tadâ.
nânâyakkhâ mahâghorâ luddâ lohitabhakkhasâ |
caṇḍâ ruddâ ca pisâcâ nânârûpavihesikâ
nânâdhimuttikâ sabbe sannipâte samâgatâ. |
tattha gantvâna taṃmajjhe vimaṃsetvâna rakkhase
nîharitvâ pisâcânaṃ manussâ hontu issarâ. |
imaṃ atthaṃ mahâvîro cintayitvâ bahuṃ hitaṃ

37. catumâsamhi? — 40. ca („ca" is wanting in BG) mahâ sace mahâjanakâye ABG, ca taṃ mahâ s° m° Xs, ca mahâ sace mahante janakâye ca Z. If we take the reading of X as correct, ânubhâvaṃ instead of ânubhâvo is well in keeping with the style of the Dîpavaṃsa, and perhaps we may even accept mahâ (or mahaṃ?) as a neuter nominative. — 46. ahû? — 47. nânârûpâ vihesakâ? — 48. gantvâna taṃmajjhe FG1, gantvânabhaṃ majjhe N, gantvân' ahaṃ majjhe s, gantvâna te majjhe Y. — 48. vibhiṃsetvâna (vîbh° G2) ABcG2, vîmaṃsetvâna (vim° X) XG1Z. viddhaṃsetvâna?

nabhaṃ abbhuggamitvâna Jambudîpâ idhâgato. |
yakkhasamâgamamajjhe upari siramatthake
nisîdanaṃ gahetvâna dissamâno nabhe ṭhito. |
ṭhitaṃ passanti sambuddhaṃ yakkhasenâ samâgatâ
buddho 'ti taṃ na maññanti yakkho aññataro iti. |
gañgâtîre Mahiyâsu pokkhalesu patiṭṭhite thûpaṭṭhâne Subhañgaṇe
tasmiṃ padesasmi ṭhito naruttamo samappito jhânasamâdhim uttamaṃ. |
jhânaṃ lahuṃ khippanisantikâro muni samâpajjati cittakkhaṇe,
sahasâ tam uṭṭhâti jhânakhaṇiyâ samâpayi sucittehi pâramîgato. |
ṭhito naro iddhi vikubbamâno yakkho va mahiddhi mahânubhâvo,
khaṇiyaṃ ghanâ meghasahassadhârâ pavassati sîtalavâtaduddini. |
ahaṃ karomi te uṇhaṃ, mama detha nisîdituṃ,
atthi tejabalaṃ mayhaṃ parissayavinodanaṃ. |
sace vinodituṃ sakkâ nisîdâhi yathicchitaṃ,

---

52. Gañgâtîre — Subhañgaṇe is wanting in BG2Z. — Mahiyâpu AG1, Mahissâsu X. I have written Mahiyâsu, this being the site of the Mahiyañgaṇathûpa, as is said in the Mahâvaṃsa (p. 3), or of the „Mahi nâma uyyânaṃ" (Mahâv. Ṭîkâ). — Sutaṃkhaṇe AG1, Subhañgane N, Sutañgaṇe F (which may be correct). — 53. khippanisantikaro NG1, °kâro BG2, °kâ A, khippanippantikaro F, khippati santikâro Z. In several passages of the Añguttara-Nikâya, a man who is endowed with promptitude of attention, is called „khippanisanti kusalesu dhammesu". — cittakkhaṇe F, cittakhaṇe N, cintane A, cittaṇe G1, cintaṇe BG2. Z has the following reading: muni samâpajji sacintaṇe tadâ. There is in the Kathâvatthu (Phayre MS. fol. yâḥ) a chapter called „khaṇikakathâ", in which the proposition is discussed: „ekacittakkhaṇikâ sabbe dhammâ 'ti." This means, I believe: „all qualities may be considered in a moment by one thought". Perhaps we may compare also Lal. Vist. p. 447: „sarvaṃ tad ekacittekshaṇasamâyuktaṃ". I feel inclined, therefore, to correct: muni samâpajjat' ekacittakkhaṇe, and to translate: „he entered upon meditation (by revolving) in a moment by one thought (the whole system of Dhamma's)." — The following hemistich may be corrected thus: sahasâ tamh' uṭṭhâti, jhânaṃ khaṇe viya samâpayi sucittapâramîgato. — 54. naro AG1X, nabhe Z, which may be correct. — iddhi AG1FZ, iddhiṃ N. — khaṇiyam ghanâ meghasahassadhârâ X (khaṇiyaṃkhaṇâ° F), khanayamahâmeghasahassadhâro (khaṇ° G1) AG1, khaṇâya m° dhâro Z. ghaṭayaṃ (ganthayaṃ?) gh° m°? — sîtalavâtaduddini AFG, °dundubhi ZN. Compare Mahâvagga I, 3, 2. — 55. karomi vo uṇhaṃ?

sabbehi samanuññâtam, tava tejabalam kara. |
unham yâcatha mam sabbe, bhiyyo tejam mahâtapam
khippam karoma accunham tumhebi abhipatthitam. |
thite majjhantike kâle gimhânam suriyo yathâ
evam yakkhânam âtâpo kâye thapita dârunam. |
yathâ kappaparivatte catusuriyaâtapo
evam nisîdane satthu tejo hoti tatuttari. |
yathâ suriyam udentam na sakkâ âvaritum nabhe
60 evam nisîdanañ cammam n' atthi âvaranam nabhe. |
nisîdanam kappajâlam va tejam suriyam va pathavî
mahâtapam vikirati aggijâlam v' anappakam. |
angârarâsijalitâtapam tahim nisîdanam abbhasamam pa-
dissati
pakkam va ayomayapabbatûpamam. |
dîpesu unham nidasseti dussaham, yakkhâsu patisaranam
gavesayum
puratthimam pacchimadakkhinuttaram uddham adho dasa
disâ imâyo. |
katham gamissâma sukhî arogâ kadâ pamuñcâma imam
subheravam. |
sace ayam yakkho mahânubhâvo tejo samâpajjati pajjalâyati
sabbeva yakkhâ vilayâ bhavissare bhusam va mutthi ra-
65 jam vâtakhittam. |
buddho ca kho isinisabho sukhâvaho disvâna yakkhe du-
kkhite bhayattite
anukampako kârûniko mahesi vicintayi attasukham amânuse. |

---

56. tava tejabalam phara? Comp. Buddhavamsa (Jât. I, p. 24, v. 168). — 58. bhavittha dârunam, s; thapito d°? — 59. tathuttari (°rî B) AB, taduttari FZ, tatuttari N. tat' uttarim? — 60. naro Y, nabhe X (at the two places). — 61. A1G1F omit va. — pathavî X, patthapi ABG, patthari Z. Mahâvamsa Tîkâ (fol. kho): te pathavisuriyatejacammakhandâbhibhûtâya (sic) yakkhaganâ. — 62. pattam va N, sakkam va F, pakkâ va Y. — 63. dîpisu XG1, dîpesu Y (dîpetu B1). — nidasseti N, nidasoti F, nidayeti Y. I do not think that nidasseti is correct, but I do not know how to correct it. — patissaranam N, saranam F, maranam Y. — gavesayum N, gavesisum F, bhavepisu G1, bhavesupi ABG2, bhayatajjitesu Z. — 64. kaham gamissâma? — 66. nisabha = rishabha or vrishabha? I have found this word at the following passages: in the Samyuttaka-Nikâya (Phayre MS. part I, fol. ko) Buddha is compared with a nâga, a sîha, an âjâniya, a nisabha, a dhorayha. In the Majjhima-Nikâya (Turnour's MS., fol. ñâm) it is said of Buddha „nisabhassa appameyyassa". Sutta-Nipâta (Phayre MS., fol. gau): „gantvâna disvâ isinisabham pasanno". Buddhavamsa (Phayre MS., fol. jî):

ath' aññadîpaṃ paṭirûpakaṃ imaṃ ninnaṃ thalaṃ sabbathânekasâdisaṃ
nadîpabbatatalâkasunimmalaṃ dîpaṃ Giriṃ Laṅkâtalasamûpamaṃ |
sunibbhayaṃ gopitasâgarantakaṃ pahûtabhakkhaṃ bahudhaññamâkulaṃ
utusamatthaṃ harisaddalaṃ mahiṃ varaṃ Giridîpam imassa uttariṃ |
rammaṃ manuññaṃ haritaṃ susîtalaṃ ârâmavanarâmaṇeyyakaṃ varaṃ,
santîdha phullaphaladhârino dumâ, suññaṃ vivittaṃ, na ca koci issaro, |
mahaṇṇave sâgaravârimajjhe sugambhîre ûmi sadâ pabhijjare,
suduggame pabbatajâlamussite sudukkaraṃ attha aniṭṭhamantaraṃ. | 70
paravânarosâ parapiṭṭhimaṃsikâ akâruṇikâ paraheṭhane ratâ
caṇḍâ ca ruddhâ rabhasâ ca niddayâ vidappanikâ sapathe idha ime. |
atha rakkhasâ yakkhagaṇâ ca duṭṭhâ dîpaṃ imaṃ Laṅkâciranivâsitaṃ
dadâmi sabbaṃ Giridîpaporâṇaṃ, vasantu sabbe supajâ anîghâ. |
imañ ca Laṅkâtalaṃ mânusânaṃ porâṇakappaṭṭhitavutthavâsaṃ,
vasantu Laṅkâtale mânusâ bahû pubbe va Ojâvaramaṇḍasâdisaṃ. |
etehi aññehi guṇeh' upeto manussavâso anekabhaddako
dîpesu dîpissati sâsan' âgate supuṇṇacando va nabhe uposathe. |

---

tato padakkhiṇaṃ katvâ bodhimaṇḍaṃ naruttamo aparâjitanisabhaṭṭhâne bodhipallaṅkamuttame pallaṅkena nisiditvâ bujjhissati mahâyaso.

68. gopitas° N, gopikas° F, sobhitas° Y, gobhitas° G1. *gopitam s°?* — uttari XG1. *uttaraṃ?* — 71. ca ruddâ (comp. v. 47) AB, va ruddâ BG2, ca ruddhâ Zn, varuddhâ F. I cannot correct the last words. — 72. °nivâsitaṃ XG1, °nivâsinaṃ Y. — v. 73 is quoted in the Mahâvaṃsa Ṭikâ, fol. khau („tenâhu porâṇâ"). Laṅkâthalamânusânaṃ, °ṭṭhitaṃ, vasanti Laṅkâthalamânusâ, Ojamaṇḍavaradîpe Mahâv. Ṭ. °maṇḍapâdîpaṃ F. *Ojavaramaṇḍadîpe?* — 74. anek° AFG1, va anek° N, api nek° BG2Z. — dîpesu dîpissati sâsanâgate ABG2, dîpassa dîpâ sadisâ anâgate Z, dîpissati (dississati F) sâsanâgate FG1, dîpissati sâsanam etthânâgate N.

dîpaṃ ubho mânusâ rakkhasâ ca ubho ubhinnaṃ tulayaṃ sukhaṃ muni
bhiyyo sukhaṃ lokavidû ubhinnaṃ parivattayi goṇayugaṃ va phâsukaṃ. |
saṃkaḍḍhayi Gotamo dîpam iddhiyâ bandhaṃ va goṇaṃ daḷharajjukaḍḍhitaṃ,
dîpena dîpaṃ upanâmayî muni yugaṃ va nâvaṃ daḷhadhammaveditaṃ. |
dîpena dîpaṃ yugalaṃ tathâgato katvân' uḷâraṃ viparî ca rakkhase,
vasantu sabbe Giridîpa rakkhasâ sapakkamâsâ vasanaṃ va vatthitaṃ. |
gaṅgaṃ gimhamhi yathâ pipâsitâ dhâvanti yakkhâ Giridîpam atthikâ,
paviṭṭhâ sabbe anivattane puna, pamuñca dîpaṃ yathâbhûmiyaṃ muni. |
yakkhâ sutuṭṭhâ supahaṭṭharakkhasâ laddhâ sudîpaṃ manasâbhipatthitaṃ
abhâyiṃsu sabbe atippamoditâ, otariṃsu sabbe chaṇe nakkhattamahaṃ. |
ñatvâna buddho sukhite amânuse katvâna mettaṃ parittaṃ bhaṇi jino.
katvâna dîpaṃ tividhaṃ padakkhiṇaṃ sadâ rakkhaṃ yakkhagaṇavinodanaṃ, |
santappayitvâ pisâce amânuse rakkhañ ca katvâ daḷhaṃ mettâbhâvanaṃ
upaddavaṃ dîpe vinodetvâ gato Uruvelaṃ puna tathâgato 'ti. |

bhâṇavâraṃ paṭhamaṃ. yakkhadamanaṃ niṭṭhitaṃ.

---

75. mânuse rakkhase ca? — 76. daḷhadâmaveṭhitaṃ? — 77. viparîva ANG1, °rîca BMG2, °rica CRF. — Giridîpe? — sapakkamâsâ vasanaṃ va vatthitaṃ Y, sapakkâsâ capanaṃ pavattititaṃ F, disaṃ pakkamânâ manasâ va vatthiṭaṃ N. I do not try any correction. — 78. Gañgañ ca gimh°? — Giridîpavattikâ N, Gîripavattitâ F. — pamuñci AB G2. — 79. Compare Mahâv. Ṭîkâ fol. khau': „atha te (rakkhasâ) ambâkaṃ icchitaṃ patthitaṃ nippannan ti mahâhasitan nâma hasitvâ nakkhattachanakilaṃ kiliṃsu. I propose to read, therefore: ahasiṃsu sabbe; chaṇaṃ nakkh°. — 81. [daḷ]ha[mettabhâva]naṃ N. — Z, apparently for the sake of metrical correctness, reads thus: „up° dîpa vinodayitvâ gatoruvelaṃ puna pi tath°."

II.

Arahaṃ pana sambuddho Kosalânaṃ puruttamaṃ
upanissâya vihâsi Sudattârâme sirîghano. |
tasmiñ Jetavane buddho dhammarâjâ pabhaṃkaro
sabbalokam avekkhanto Tambapaṇṇivar' addasa. |
atikkante pañcavassamhi Tambapaṇṇitalaṃ agâ,
avaruddhake vinodetvâ suññaṃ dîpaṃ akâ sayaṃ. |
uragâ ajja dîpamhi pabbateyyâ samuṭṭhitâ
ubhoviyûḷhasaṃgâmaṃ yuddhaṃ kariṃsu dâruṇaṃ. |
sabbe mahiddhikâ nâgâ sabbe ghoravisâ ahû
sabbeva kibbisâ caṇḍâ madamânâ avassitâ. |
khippakâpi mahâtejâ paduṭṭhâ kakkhalâ kharâ
ujjhânasaññî sukopâ uragâ vilaratthikâ. |
Mahodaro mahâtejo Cûḷodaro ca tejaso
ubho pi balasampannâ ubho pi vaṇṇâtisayâ. |
na passati koci samaṃ samuttari, Mahodaro mânamattena tejasâ
dîpaṃ vinâsesi saselakânanaṃ: ghâtemi sabbe paṭipakkhapannage. |
Cûḷodaro gajjati mânanissito: âgacchantu nâgasahassakoṭiyo,
hanâmi sabbe raṇamajjham âgate, thalaṃ karomi satayojanaṃ dîpaṃ. |
padûsayanti visavegadussahâ sampajjalanti uragâ mahiddhikâ
rosadhammâ bhujagindamucchitâ ussahanti raṇasatthu madditum. |
disvâna buddho uragindakuppanaṃ dîpaṃ vinassanti nivattahetukaṃ

II, 2. samuṭṭhitâ G1XZ, samuddikâ ABG2, comp. Mahâvaṃsa, p. 5, ll. 1. 2. — 4. ubhatoviyûḷhas°? Mah. Ṭîkâ fol. gû: saṃgâman ti ubhatobyulhasaṃgâmaṃ. — 5. avassutâ? — 6. viralattikâ Z, viralatthikâ N, pilarathikâ F, vilarattikâ ABG. vilayatthikâ? bilaraṭṭhikâ? — 8. samuttari AFG1nZ, °riṃ BcG2. samuttaraṃ (instead of samuttâraṃ)? — 10. padhûpâyanti? comp. Mahâvagga I, 15, 4. — °sattu ABG2, °satthu G1Zn, °pattuṃ F. — pararosadhammâ (comp. I, 71) bhujagindâ mucchitâ ussâhayanti raṇasattû madditum? — 11. °kuppanaṃ F, °kubbanaṃ N, °dubbalaṃ Y. — vinâsanti F, vinâsenti N, vinassanti G1Z, vinâsassa ABG2. uragiṅdakuppanaṃ d° vinassantaṃ nivattihetukaṃ?

lokassa cârî sugato bahuṃ hitaṃ vicintayi aggasukhaṃ sadevake. |
sace na gaccheyyaṃ na pannagâ sukhî, dîpaṃ vinâsaṃ na ca sâdhu 'nâgate, |
nâge anukampamâno sukhatthiko gacchâm' ahaṃ dîpasukhaṃ samicchituṃ. |
Laṅkâdîpe guṇaṃ disvâ pubbe yakkhavinoditaṃ
mama sâdhukataṃ dîpaṃ mâ vinâsentu pannagâ. |
idaṃ vatvâna sambuddho uṭṭhahitvâna âsanâ
gandhakuṭito nikkhamma dvâre aṭṭhâsi cakkhumâ. |
yâvatâ Jetavane ca ârâme vanadevatâ
sabbe 'va upaṭṭhahiṃsu mayaṃ gacchâma cakkhuma. |
alaṃ sabbe pi tiṭṭhantu Samiddhi yeko 'vagacchatu,
avagaccha saharukkho dhârayitvâna piṭṭhito. |
buddhassa vacanaṃ sutvâ Samiddhi sumano ahû
samûlaṃ rukkham âdâya saha gacchi tathâgataṃ. |
naruttaman taṃ sambuddhaṃ devarâjâ mahiddhiko
châyaṃ katvâna dhâresi buddhaseṭṭhassa piṭṭhito. |
yattha nâgânaṃ saṃgâmaṃ tattha gantvâ naruttamo
ubhonâgavaramajjhe ṭhito satthânukampako. |
nabhe gantvâna sambuddho ubhonâgânam upari
tibbandhakâratamamaṃ ghoraṃ akâsi lokanâyako. |
andhaṃ tamaṃ tadâ hoti kesaramayaïddhiyâ,
andhakârena onaddho sihitâ yarukkho ahû. |
aññamaññaṃ na passanti tasitâ nâgâ bhayaṭṭitâ
jitam pi na passanti kuto saṃgâma kârituṃ. |
sabbe saṃgâmaṃ bhinditvâ pamuñcitvâna âvudhaṃ
namassamânâ sambuddhaṃ sabbe ṭhitâ katañjalî. |
salomahaṭṭhe ñatvâna disvâ nâge bhayaṭṭite
mettacittena pharitvâna uṇharaṃsiṃ pamuñcayi. |

---

11. attasukhaṃ? comp. 1, 66. In the Mahâv. Ṭîkâ (fol. khau) a stanza of the Porâṇâ is quoted which contains the words „so cintayi attasukhaṃ acintamassa (sic).“ — 13. disapamukham icchituṃ ABG, dîpavuddhiṃ samicchituṃ Z, dîpasamukhaṃ icchituṃ F, dîpasukhaṃ samijjhituṃ N. samicchituṃ = sk. sam-îrta? dîpasukhaṃ samijjhatu? — 17. avagaccha FG1N, âgaccha ABcG2, agaccha Z. avagacchi? — 20. sattânukampako? comp. v. 47. — 22. kesarimahâiddhiyâ? — onaddhâ A1X, °ddho A2BGZ. — sahitâ Y, patitâ F, sihitâ N. — yarukkho ahu Y, yarukkho ahosi F, yadukhâ ahuṃ N. on° pihito sarukkho ahû? — 23. jitam pi BG, jinam pi A, jiyam pi te Z, jîvitaṃ pi F, jvitam pi N. jinam pi te?

âloko 'va mahâ âsi abbhuto lomahaṃsano
sabbe passanti sambuddhaṃ nabhe candaṃ va nimmalaṃ. |
chabi vaṇṇehi upeto jalanto nabhakantare
dasa disâ virocanto ṭhito nâge abhâsatha: |
kimatthiyaṃ mahârâja nâgânaṃ vivâdo ahû?
tumheva anukampâya javâgacchiṃ tato ahaṃ. |
ayañ Cûḷodaro nâgo ayan nâgo Mahodaro
mâtulo bhâgineyyo ca vivadanto dhanatthiko. |
anudayañ caṇḍanâgânaṃ sambuddho ajjhabhâsatha:
appo hutvâ mahâ hoti kodho bâlassa âgamo. |
kim udisvâ bahû nâgâ mahâdukkhaṃ nigacchatha,
imaṃ parittaṃ pallañkaṃ mâ tumhe nâsayissatha,
aññamaññaṃ vinâsetha akataṃ jîvitakkhayaṃ. |
saṃvejesi tadâ nâge nirayadukkhena cakkhumâ.
manussayoniṃ dibbañ ca nibbânañ ca pakittayi. |
pakâsayantaṃ saddhammaṃ sambuddhaṃ dipaduttamaṃ
sabbe nâgâ nipatitvâ khamâpesuṃ tathâgataṃ. |
sabbe nâgâ samâgantvâ samaggâ hutvâna pannagâ
upesuṃ saraṇaṃ sabbe asîti pâṇakoṭiyo. |
sabbe nâgâ vinassâma imaṃ pallañkahetukaṃ. |
âdâya pallañkavaraṃ ubho nâgâ samatthikâ:
paṭigaṇhatha pallañkaṃ anukampâya cakkhuma. |
adhivâsesi sambuddho tuṇhibhâvena cakkhumâ,
adhivâsanaṃ viditvâna tuṭṭhâ mahoragâ ubho: |
nisîdatu 'maṃ sugato pallañkaṃ veḷuriyamayaṃ
pabhassarañ jâtivantaṃ nâgânaṃ abhipatthitaṃ. |
patiṭṭhapiṃsu pallañkaṃ nâgâ dîpânam antare,
nisîdi tattha pallañke dhammarâjâ pabhaṃkaro. |
pasâdetvâna sambuddhaṃ asîti nâgakoṭiyo
tattha nâgâ parivisuṃ annapânañ ca bhojanaṃ. |
onîtapattapâṇin taṃ asîti nâgakoṭiyo
parivâretvâ nisîdiṃsu buddhaseṭṭhassa santike. |
Kalyâṇike gañgâmukhe nâgo ahû saputtako
mahânâgaparivâro nâmenâpi Maṇiakkhiko, |

27. jalante Y, which may be correct. — virocento F. — 28. kimatthâya? comp. 13, 2. — 31. kim udisvâ ABG2, kiṃ d° Z, kimad° G1, kamaṃ d° F, kimaṃ d° N. kim uddissa? — 36. samatthikâ ABG, samaggikâ Z, sapattikâ N, papattikâ F. — 42. nâmenâsi AZ, °âpi BGX.

saddho saraṇasampanno sammâdiṭṭhi ca sîlavâ.
nâgasamâgamam gantvâ bhiyyo abhipasîdati. |
disvâ buddhabalaṃ nâgo anukampaṃ phaṇimayaṃ
abhivâdetvâ nisîdi âyâcesi tathâgataṃ: |
imaṃ dîpânukampâya paṭhamaṃ yakkhavinoditaṃ,
idaṃ nâgânaṃ 'nuggahaṃ dutiyaṃ dîpânukampanaṃ, |
puna pi bhagavâ imaṃ anukampaṃ mahâmuni,
ahañ c' upaṭṭhahissâmi veyyâvaccaṃ karom' ahaṃ. |
nâgassa bhâsitaṃ sutvâ buddho sattânukampako
Laṅkâdîpahitatthâya adhivâsesi sugato. |
paribhuñjitvâ pallaṅkaṃ vuṭṭhahitvâ pabhaṃkaro
divâvihâraṃ akâsi tattha dîpantare muni. |
dîpantare dîpân' aggo divasaṃ vîtinâmayi
samâpatti samâpajji brahmavihârena cakkhumâ. |
sâyaṇhakâlasamaye nâge âmantayî jino:
idh' eva hotu pallaṅko, khîrapâlo idhâgacchatu,
nâgâ sabbe imaṃ rukkhaṃ pallaṅkañ ca namassatha. |
idaṃ vatvâna sambuddho anusâsetvâna pannage
paribhogacetiyaṃ datvâ puna Jetavanaṃ gato. |

nâgadamanaṃ niṭṭhitaṃ.

Aparam pi aṭṭhame vasse nâgarâjâ Maṇikkhiko
nimantayi mahâvîraṃ pañcabhikkhusate saha. |
parivâretvâna sambuddhaṃ vasibhûtâ mahiddhikâ,
uppatitvâ Jetavane kamamâno nabhe muni
Laṅkâdîpaṃ anuppatto gaṅgaṃ Kalyâṇisammukhaṃ. |
sabbe ratanamaṇḍapaṃ uragâ katvâ mahâtale
nânâraṅgehi vatthehi dibbadussehi châdayuṃ. |
nânâratanalaṃkârâ nânâphullavicittakâ
nânâraṅgadhajâ nekâ maṇḍapaṃ nânâlaṃkataṃ. |
sabbasanthataṃ santharitvâ paññâpetvâna âsanaṃ
buddhapamukhasaṃghassa pavesetvâ nisîdiṃsu. |

---

44. phaṇimayaṃ ACG2R, paṇim° G1, phanim° BM, manimayaṃ X. phaṇibhayaṃ? — 46. imaṃ AB2G1X, maṃ B1G2, ambaṃ Z. — anukampa A, °paṃ BGX, °pâya Z. — 49. samâpattiṃ N. samâpattî? — 50. idha gacchatu XG1, idhâg° ABcG2, idhacchatu Z. — 53. gaṅgak° ABFG, gaṅgaṃ k° N, gaṅgâk° Z. gaṅgaṃ Kalyâṇikaṃ mukhaṃ? comp. v. 42. — 54. sabbaratanam°? — mahîtale? — 56. nisîdasuṃ A, °disuṃ BG, °dayuṃ Z, °diṃsu F, °disu N. nisîdayuṃ appears to be the correct reading.

nisîditvâna sambuddho pañcabhikkhusate saha
samâpatti samâpajji mettaṃ sabbadisaṃ phari. |
sattakkhattuṃ samâpajji buddho jhânaṃ sasâvako
tasmiṃ ṭhâne mahâthûpo patiṭṭhâsi cetiyam uttamaṃ. |
mahâdânaṃ pavattesi nâgarâjâ Maṇikkhiko,
paṭiggahetvâ sambuddho nâgadânaṃ sasâvako
bhutvâna anumoditvâ nabh' uggacchi sasâvako. |
orohitvâ nabhe buddho ṭhâne Dîghavâpicetiye
samâpajji samâpattiṃ jhânaṃ lokânukampako. | 60
vuṭṭhahitvâ samâpatti tamhi ṭhâne pabhaṃkaro
vehâyasaṃ kamamâno dhammarâjâ sasâvako
Mahâmeghavane tattha bodhiṭṭhânaṃ upâgami. |
purimâ tîṇi mahâbodhi patiṭṭhiṃsu mahîtale
taṃ thânaṃ upagantvâna tattha jhânaṃ samâpayi. |
tisso bodhi imaṃ ṭhâne tayo buddhâna sâsane,
mamañ ca bodhi idh' eva patiṭṭhissat' anâgate. |
sasâvako samâpatti vuṭṭhahitvâ naruttamo
yattha Meghavanârammaṃ agamâsi narâsabho. |
tatthâpi so samâpattiṃ samâpajji sasâvako.
vuṭṭhahitvâ samâpatti byâkarosi pabhaṃkaro: | 65
imaṃ padesaṃ paṭhamaṃ Kakusandho lokanâyako
imaṃ pallaṅkaṭhânamhi nisîditvâ paṭiggahi. |
imaṃ padesaṃ dutiyaṃ Konâgamano narâsabho
imaṃ pallaṅkaṭhânamhi nisîditvâ paṭiggahi. |
imaṃ padesaṃ tatiyaṃ Kassapo lokanâyako
imaṃ pallaṅkaṭhânamhi nisîditvâ paṭiggahi. |
ahaṃ Gotamasambuddho Sakyaputto narâsabho
imaṃ pallaṅkaṭhânamhi nisîditvâ samappito 'ti. |

bhâṇavâraṃ dutiyaṃ.

III.

Atîtakappe râjâno ṭhapetvâna bhavâbhave
imamhi kappe râjâno pakâsissâmi sabbaso, |

---

57. samâpattiṃ N. samâpatti? — 60. nabhe X, nate G1, nage AB G2, nabhaṃ Z. nabhâ? — 62. mahâbodhî? — 63. tisso bodhî? — 64. °vane ramme G1N, °vane rame F, °vanârâmaṃ ABcG2, °vanârammaṃ Z. °vanaṃ rammaṃ?

jâtiñ ca nâmagottañ ca âyuñ ca anupâlanaṃ
sabban taṃ kittayissâmi, taṃ suṇâtha yathâkathaṃ. |
paṭhamâbhisitto râjâ bhûmipâlo jutindharo
Mahâsammato nâma nâmena rajjaṃ kâresi khattiyo. |
tassa putto Rojo nâma, Vararojo nâma khattiyo,
Kalyâṇavarakalyâṇâ, Uposatho mahissaro, |
Mandhâtâ sattamo tesañ catudîpamhi issaro,
5 Caro, Upacaro râjâ, Cetiyo ca mahissaro, |
Mucalo, Mahâmucalo, Mucalindo, Sâgaro pi ca,
Sâgaradevo, Bharato ca, Añgîso nâma khattiyo, |
Ruci, Mahâruci nâma, Patâpo, Mahâpatâpo pi ca,
Panâdo, Mahâpanâdo ca, Sudassano nâma khattiyo, |
Mahâsudassano nâma, duve Nerû ca, Accimâ,
aṭṭhavîsati râjâno, âyu tesaṃ asaṃkhayâ. |
Kusâvatî, Râjagahe, Mithilâyaṃ puruttame
rajjaṃ kâriṃsu râjâno, tesaṃ âyu asaṃkhayâ. |
dasa dasa satañ c' eva, sataṃ dasa sahassiyo,
sahassaṃ dasa dasasahassañ ca, dasa dasasahassaṃ satasa-
10 hassiyo, |
dasa satasahassañ ca koṭi, dasakoṭi, koṭippakoṭiyo,
nahutañ ca, ninnahutañ ca, abbudo ca, nirabbudo, |
ababaṃ, aṭaṭañ c' eva, ahahaṃ, kumudâni ca,
sogandhikaṃ, uppalako, puṇḍarîkapadumako, |
ettakâ gaṇitâ saṃkhepâ gaṇanâgaṇikâ tahiṃ,
tato uparimabhûmi asaṃkheyyâ 'ti vuccati. |
ekasatañ ca râjâno Accimassâpi atrajâ
mahârajjaṃ akâresuṃ nagare Pakulasavhaye. |
tesaṃ pacchimako râjâ Arindamo nâma khattiyo,
puttâ paputtakâ tassa chapaññâsañ ca khattiyâ
15 mahârajjaṃ akâresuṃ Ayujjhanagare pure. |
tesaṃ pacchimako râjâ Duppasaho mahissaro,

III, 2. yathâtathaṃ? — 6. Bhagîraso nâma? — 8. 9. asaṃkhiyâ ABcG2. — 9. kâresuṃ? — 11. dasa satasahassañ ca koṭi, pakoṭi, koṭippakoṭiyo? compare Burnouf, Lotus, p. 854; Sp. Hardy, Manual, p. 6. — 12. kumudena ca? — 13. gaṇanâgaṇikâ ABGX, °tâ Z. ettakâ gaṇitâ saṃkheyyâ gaṇanâgaṇiyâ tahiṃ? — uparimâ XG1Z, °maṃ ABcG2. — bhûmi XC1G1R, °miṃ ABcG2M. — 14. Sakulasavhaye ABG, Bakulasavhaye N, Pagulavhaye F, Kapilavhaye Z. Sâgalasavhaye?

puttâ paputtakâ tassa saṭṭhi te bhûmipâlakâ
mahârajjaṃ akâresuṃ Bârâṇasipuruttame. |
tesaṃ pacchimako râjâ Abhitatto nâma khattiyo,
caturâsîti sahassâni tassa puttapaputtakâ
mahârajjaṃ akâresuṃ Kapilanagare pure. |
tesaṃ pacchimako râjâ Brahmadatto mahissaro,
puttâ paputtakâ tassa chattiṃsâpi ca khattiyâ
mahârajjaṃ akâresuṃ Hatthipuravaruttame. |
tesaṃ pacchimako râjâ Kambalavasabho ahû,
puttâ paputtakâ tassa battiṃsâpi ca khattiyâ
nagare Ekacakkhumhi rajjaṃ kâresuṃ te idha. |
tesaṃ pacchimako râjâ Purindado Devapûjito
puttâ paputtakâ tassa aṭṭhavîsati khattiyâ
mahârajjaṃ akâresuṃ Vajirâyaṃ puruttame. |
tesaṃ pacchimako râjâ Sâdhino nâma khattiyo,
puttâ paputtakâ tassa dvâvîsa râjakhattiyâ
mahârajjaṃ akâresuṃ Madhurâyaṃ puruttame. |
tesaṃ pacchimako râjâ Dhammagutto mahabbalo,
puttâ paputtakâ tassa aṭṭhârasa ca khattiyâ
nagare Ariṭṭhapure rajjaṃ kâresuṃ te idha. |
tesaṃ pacchimako râjâ narindo Siṭṭhinâmako,
puttâ paputtakâ tassa sattarasa ca khattiyâ
nagare Indapattamhi rajjaṃ kâresuṃ te idha. |
tesaṃ pacchimako râjâ Brahmadevo mahîpati,
puttâ paputtakâ tassa pannarasa ca khattiyâ
nagare Ekacakkhumhi rajjaṃ kâresuṃ te idha. |
tesaṃ pacchimako râjâ Baladatto mahîpati,
puttâ paputtakâ tassa cuddasa râjakhattiyâ
mahârajjaṃ akâresuṃ Kosambimhi nagare pure. |
tesaṃ pacchimako râjâ Bhaddadevo 'ti vissuto,
puttâ paputtakâ tassa nava râjâ ca khattiyâ
nagare Kaṇṇagocchamhi rajjaṃ kâresuṃ te idha. |
tesaṃ pacchimako râjâ Naradevo 'ti vissuto,
puttâ paputtakâ tassa satta ca râjakhattiyâ

---

17. Ajitajano (instead of Abhitatto) A2. — 21. Sâdino Z. Mahâvaṃsa Ṭîkâ: Sâdhano. — 23. Mahâv. Ṭîkâ: Brahmasivi. — 24. 25. Mahâv. Ṭîkâ: Brahmadatta, Baladeva. — 26. Mahâv. Ṭîkâ: Hatthideva.

mahârajjaṃ akâresuṃ Rojânanagare pure. |
tesaṃ pacchimako râjâ Mahindo nâma khattiyo,
puttâ paputtakâ tassa dvâdasa râjakhattiyâ
mahârajjaṃ akâresuṃ Campâkanagare pure. |
tesaṃ pacchimako râjâ Nâgadevo mahîpati,
puttâ paputtakâ tassa pañcavîsa ca khattiyâ
mahârajjaṃ kârayiṃsu Mithilânagare pure. |
tesaṃ pacchimako râjâ Buddhadatto mahabbalo,
puttâ paputtakâ tassa pañcavîsa ca khattiyâ
30 mahârajjam kârayiṃsu Râjagahapuruttame. |
tesaṃ pacchimako râjâ Dîpaṃkaro nâma khattiyo,
puttâ paputtakâ tassa dvâdasa râjakhattiyâ
mahârajjaṃ kârayiṃsu Takkasilâpuruttame. |
tesaṃ pacchimako râjâ Tâlissaro nâma khattiyo,
puttâ paputtakâ tassa dvâdasa râjakhattiyâ
mahârajjaṃ kârayiṃsu Kusinârâpuruttame. |
tesaṃ pacchimako râjâ Purindo nâma khattiyo,
puttâ paputtakâ tassa nava râjâ ca khattiyâ
mahârajjaṃ kârayiṃsu nagare Malitthiyake. |
tesaṃ pacchimako râjâ Sâgaradevo mahissaro,
tassa putto Makhâdevo mahâdânapati ahû. |
caturâsîti sahassâni tassa puttapaputtakâ
35 mahârajjaṃ kârayiṃsu Mithilânagare pure. |
tesaṃ pacchimako râjâ Nemiyo Devapûjito
balacakkavatti râjâ sâgarantamahîpati. |
Nemiyaputto Kalârajanako, tassa putto Samaṃkaro,
Asoko nâma so râjâ muddhâvasittakhattiyo. |
caturâsîti sahassâni tassa puttapaputtakâ
mahârajjaṃ kârayiṃsu Bârâṇasipuruttame. |
tesaṃ pacchimako râjâ Vijayo nâma mahissaro,
tassa putto Vijitaseno abhijâtajutindharo. |
Dhammaseno, Nâgaseno, Samatho nâma, Disampati,
40 Reṇu, Kuso, Mahâkuso, Navaratho, Dasaratho pi ca, |

---

27. Rocanagare N. Mahâv. Ṭikâ: Rojanâmamhî nagare. — 30. Mahâv. Ṭikâ: Samuddadatto. — 32. Tâlissaro ABG2X, Tâliyaro G1, Tâlisajo Z. Mah. Ṭikâ: Kâlissaro. — 33. Purindo ABG, [Puri]ndo N, Purindado Z, Sudinno F, Mahâv. Ṭikâ. — Mahâv. Ṭikâ: Tâmalittiyanâmamhi nagare. — 37. Samañkuro ABcG2, Mah. Ṭikâ.

Râmo, Biḷâratho nâma, Cittadassî, Atthadassî,
Sujâto, Okkâko c' eva, Okkâmukho ca, Nipuro, |
Candimâ, Candamukho ca, Sivi râjâ ca, Sañjayo,
Vessantaro janapati, Jâlî ca, Sîhavâhano,
Sîhassaro ca yo dhîro paveṇipâlo ca khattiyo, |
dveasîti sahassâni tassa puttapaputtakâ
rajjaṃ kâresuṃ râjâno nagare Kapilasavhaye. |
tesaṃ pacchimako râjâ Jayaseno mahîpati,
tassa putto Sîhahanu abhijâtajutindharo. |
Sîhahanussa ye puttâ yassa te pañca bhâtaro
Suddhodano ca Dhoto ca Sakkodano ca khattiyo | 45
Sukkodano ca so râjâ râjâ ca Amitodano,
ete pañca pi râjâno sabbe Odananâmakâ. |
Suddhodanassâyaṃ putto Siddhattho lokanâyako
janetvâ Râhulabhaddaṃ bodhâya abhinikkhami. |
sabbe te satasahassâni cattâri nahutâni ca
apare tîṇi satarâjâno mahesakkhâ siyâyaca. |
ettakâ paṭhavîpâlâ bodhisattakule vuttâ. |
aniccâ vata saṃkhârâ uppâdavayadhammino,
uppajjitvâ nirujjhanti, tesaṃ vûpasamo sukho 'ti. | 50

Mahârâjavaṃso niṭṭhito.

Suddhodano nâma râjâ nagare Kapilasavhaye
Sîhahanussâyaṃ putto rajjaṃ kâresi khattiyo. |
pañcannaṃ pabbatamajjhe Râjagahe puruttame
Bodhiso nâma so râjâ rajjaṃ kâresi khattiyo. |
sahâyâ aññamaññâ te Suddhodano ca Bhâtiyo.
[imamhi paṭhame kappe paveṇipâ janâdhipâ.]
jâtiyâ aṭṭhavassamhi uppannâ pañca âsayâ: |

41. Bilâratho AZ, Biḷâratho BG, Pi[ḷâratho] N, Piḷâratho F. Vilâratho Mah. Ṭ. — Mah. Ṭ.: Cittarasî Ambarasî. — ca Nipuno N, va Nisuro F, ca Nipuro A, va Nimukho BGC, va Timukho R, va Tîmukho M. Mah. Ṭ.: Nipuro; Lokadîpasâra (India Off. MS., fol. khâ): Nipuno. — 42. yo dhîro Y (ye dhîrâ A2), bodhiro N, rodhiro F. — 45. tassa te? — 48. apare A2N, aparo A1BGZF. — mahâyakaṇiyâya ca G1N, mahâyananiyâya ca F, mahesakkhâ (°sakkâ Z) siyâya (siyâpi A) ca Y. mahesakkhâ vinâyakâ, or something like that? — 49. vuttâ X, putâ G1, jâtâ Y. — 52. pabbatamajjhe Y, °tâmajjhe F, °tâna m° N. — Bodhiso XG1, Bodhi Z, Bhâtiyo ABG2. — 53. Bhâtiyo AZ, Bhâtiso B, Bhâti G2, Bodhiso G1N, Bodhiyo F. — imamhi — janâdhipâ appears to be the second hemistich of v. 49. One or two lines containing a mention of Bimbisâra, are wanting here.

pitâ maṃ anusâseyya attho rajjena khattiyo,
yo mayhaṃ vijite buddho uppajjeyya narâsabho, |
dassanaṃ paṭhamaṃ mayhaṃ upasaṃkame tathâgato,
deseyya amataṃ dhammaṃ, paṭivijjheyyam uttamaṃ. |
uppannâ Bimbisârassa pañca âsayakâ ime.
jâtiyâ pannarase vasse 'bhisitto pitu accaye, |
so tassa vijite ramme uppanno lokanâyako,
dassanaṃ paṭhamaṃ tassa upasaṃkami tathâgato,
desitaṃ amataṃ dhammam abbhaññâsi mahîpati. |
jâtivassaṃ mahâvîraṃ pañcatiṃsa anûnakaṃ,
Bimbisâra samâ tiṃsâ jâtavasso mahîpati.
viseso pañcahi vassehi Bimbisârassa Gotamo. |
paññâsañ ca dve vassâni rajjaṃ kâresi khattiyo,
sattatiṃsam pi vassâni saha buddhehi kârayi. |
Ajâtasattu battiṃsa rajjaṃ kâresi khattiyo,
aṭṭhavassâbhisittassa sambuddho parinibbuto. |
parinibbute ca sambuddhe lokajeṭṭhe narâsabhe
catuvîsativassâni rajjaṃ kâresi khattiyo. |

bhâṇavâraṃ tatiyaṃ.

IV.

Satt' eva satasahassâni bhikkhusaṃghâ samâgatâ
arahâ khîṇâsavâ suddhâ sabbe guṇaggataṃ gatâ. |
te sabbe vicinitvâna uccinitvâ varaṃ varaṃ
pañcasatânaṃ therânaṃ akaṃsu saṃghasammataṃ. |
dhutavâdânaṃ aggo so Kassapo jinasâsane,
bahussutânaṃ Ânando, vinaye Upâlipaṇḍito, |
dibbacakkhumhi Anuruddho, Vaṅgîso paṭibhânavâ,
Puṇṇo ca dhammakathikânaṃ, vicitrakathî Kumârakassapo, |
vibhajjanamhi Kaccâno, Koṭṭhito paṭisambhidâ.
aññe p' atthi mahâtherâ agganikkhittakâ bahû. |

---

54. atthe râjûna(ṃ)? Comp. Mahâvagga V, 1, 8. — so mayhaṃ vijite? — 58. mahâvîra A1FG, °raṃ N, °vîro A2. „mahâvîraṃ" is correct, comp. „Upâlipaṇḍitaṃ" 4, 28 (5, 76). — samâ hisâ A1GF, samâ hissa N, samatiṃsâ A2. Bimbisâro samâ tiṃsa (or: samatiṃsa) jâtivasso m°. — 59. buddhena ABcG2.

IV, 5. Koṭṭhito Yn, Koṭṭhiko G, Koṭipakoṭi F.

tehi c' aññehi therehi katakiccehi sâdhuhi
pañcasatehi therehi dhammavinayasaṃgaho
therehi katasaṃgaho theravâdo 'ti vuccati. |
Upâliṃ vinayaṃ pucchitvâ dhammam Ânandasavhayaṃ
akaṃsu dhammasaṃgahaṃ vinayañ câpi bhikkhavo. |
Mahâkassapathero ca Anuruddho mahâgaṇî
Upâlithero satimâ Ânando ca bahussuto |
aññe bahuabhiññâtâ sâvakâ satthuvaṇṇitâ
pattapaṭisambhidâ dhîrâ chaḷabhiññâ mahiddhikâ
samâdhijhânam anuciṇṇâ saddhamme pâramîgatâ, |
sabbe pañcasatâ therâ navañgaṃ jinasâsanaṃ
uggahetvâna dhâresuṃ buddhaseṭṭhassa santike. | 10
bhagavato sammukhâ sutâ paṭiggahitâ ca sammukhâ
dhammañ ca vinayañ câpi kevalaṃ buddhadesitaṃ, |
dhammadharâ vinayadharâ sabbe pi âgatâgamâ
asaṃhîrâ asaṃkuppâ satthukappâ sadâ garû, |
aggasantike gahetvâ aggadhammâ tathâgatâ
agganikkhittakâ therâ aggaṃ akaṃsu saṃgahaṃ.
sabbo pi so theravâdo aggavâdo 'ti vuccati. |
Sattapaṇṇaguhe ramme therâ pañcasatâ gaṇî
nisinnâ pavibhajjiṃsu navañgaṃ satthusâsanaṃ. |
suttaṃ geyyaṃ veyyâkaraṇaṃ gâthudânitivuttakaṃ
jâtakabbhutavedallaṃ navañgaṃ satthusâsanaṃ. | 15
pavibhattâ imaṃ therâ saddhammaṃ avinâsanaṃ
vaggapaññâsakan nâma saṃyuttañ ca nipâtakaṃ
âgamapiṭakaṃ nâma akaṃsu suttasammataṃ. |
yâva tiṭṭhanti saddhammâ saṃgahaṃ na vinassati
tâvatâ sâsan' addhânaṃ ciraṃ tiṭṭhati satthuno. |
katadhammañ ca vinayaṃ saṃgahaṃ sâsanârahaṃ
asaṃkampi acalaṃ bhûmi daḷham appaṭivattiyaṃ. |
yo koci samaṇo vâpi brahmaṇo ca bahussuto
parappavâdakusalo vâlavedhi samâgato
na sakkâ paṭivattetuṃ, Sineru va suppatiṭṭhito. |

---

6. pañcasatehi saṃgîto (or a similar word) dhammav°? comp. 5, 10. — 9. bahû abhiññâtâ, d'Alwis (Catal., p. 133). — 13. aggadhammaṃ tathâgataṃ? comp. 5, 14. — 14. pavibhajiṃsu? — 18. kataṃ dhammaṃ ca A. — saṃkampi BG2. — ubbî ABG2, bhûmi M2n, bhumi F; this word is wanting in Z.

devo Mâro vâ Brahmâ ca ye keci paṭhaviṭṭhitâ
na passanti anumattaṃ kiñci dubbhâsitaṃ padaṃ. |
evaṃ sabbaṅgasampannaṃ dhammavinayasaṃgahaṃ
suvibhattaṃ supaṭicchannaṃ satthu sabbaññutâya ca |
Mahâkassapapâmokkhâ thera pañcasatâ ca te
kataṃ dhammañ ca vinayasaṃgahaṃ avinâsanaṃ |
sammâsambuddhasadisaṃ dhammakâyasabhâvanaṃ
ñatvâ janassa sandehaṃ akaṃsu dhammasaṃgahaṃ. |
anaññavâdo sârattho saddhammamanurakkhano
ṭhiti sâsanaaddhânaṃ theravâdo sahetuko. |
yâvatâ ariyâ atthi sâsane buddhasâvakâ
sabbe pi samanuññanti paṭhamaṃ dhammasaṃgahaṃ. |
mûlanidânaṃ paṭhamaṃ âdipubbaṃgamaṃ dhuraṃ
therâ pañcasatâ katâ aggâ âjâniyâ kulan ti. |

Mahâkassapasaṃgahaṃ niṭṭhitaṃ.

Nibbute lokanâthasmiṃ vassâni soḷasaṃ tadâ,
Ajâtasattu catuvîsaṃ, Vijayassa soḷasaṃ ahû, |
samasaṭṭhi tadâ hoti vassaṃ Upâlipaṇḍitaṃ,
Dâsako upasampanno Upâlitherasantike. |
yavatâ buddhaseṭṭhassa dhammappatti pakâsitâ
sabbaṃ Upâli vâcesi navaṅgaṃ jinabhâsitaṃ. |
paripuṇṇaṃ kevalaṃ sabbaṃ navaṅgaṃ suttamâgataṃ
uggahetvâna vâcesi Upâli buddhasantike. |
saṃghamajjhe viyâkâsi buddho Upâlipaṇḍitaṃ:
aggo vinayapâmokkho Upâli mayha sâsane. |
evaṃ upanîto santo saṃghamajjhe mahâgaṇî
sahassaṃ Dâsakapâmokkhaṃ vâcesi piṭake tayo. |
khîṇâsavânaṃ vimalânaṃ santânaṃ atthavâdinaṃ
therânaṃ pañcasatânaṃ Upâli vâcesi Dâsakaṃ. |
parinibbutamhi sambuddhe Upâlithero mahâgaṇî
vinayaṃ tâva vâcesi tiṃsa vassaṃ anûnakaṃ. |

---

21. suparich° N. — 22. katâ Y, kataṃ N, kata F; comp. v. 18. — vinayaṃ saṃgahaṃ Z. — 23. °kâyasabhâvanaṃ AFG1Z, °kâyassa bh° BNG2, °kâyaṃ sabhâvato, d'Alwis. — 24. °rakkhaṇo? — ṭhitiyâ sâsanaddhânaṃ, d'Alwis. ṭhâti sâsanaaddhânam („it will last as long as the Doctrine")? — 26. I do not know how to correct kulaṃ. — 29. dhammapâli? — 33. atthav° ABc, athav° GZ, tathav° N, tatthâvâdînaṃ F. — Upâli vâcesi sâsanaṃ?

caturâsîti sahassâni navaṅgaṃ satthusâsanaṃ
vâcesi Upâli sabbaṃ Dâsakaṃ nâma paṇḍitaṃ. | 35
Dâsako piṭakaṃ sabbaṃ Upâlitherasantike
uggahetvâna vâcesi upajjhâyo va sâsane. |
saddhivihârikaṃ theraṃ Dâsakaṃ nâma paṇḍitaṃ
vinayaṃ sabbaṃ ṭhapetvâna nibbuto so mahâgaṇî. |
Udayo soḷasa vassâni rajjaṃ kâresi khattiyo,
chabbasse Udayabhaddamhi Upâlithero sa nibbuto. |
Sonako mânasampanno vâṇijo Kâsim âgato
Giribbaje Veḷuvane pabbaji satthusâsane. |
Dâsako gaṇapâmokkho Magadhânaṃ Giribbaje
vihâsi sattatiṃsamhi pabbâjesi ca Sonakaṃ. | 40
pañcatâlîsavasso so Dâsako nâma paṇḍito,
Nâgadâsadasavassaṃ, Paṇḍurâjassa vîsati,
upasampanno Sonako thero Dâsakasantike. |
vâcesi Dâsako thero navaṅgaṃ Sonakassa pi,
uggahetvâna vâcesi upajjhâyassa santike. |
Dâsako Sonakaṃ theraṃ saddhivihâri anupubbakaṃ
katvâ vinayapâmokkhaṃ catusaṭṭhimhi nibbuto. |
cattârîs' eva vasso so thero Sonakasavhayo,
Kâlâsokassa dasavasse aḍḍhamâsañ ca sesake, |
sattarasannaṃ vassânaṃ thero âsi paguṇako,
atikkantekâdasavassaṃ chamâsañ câvasesake, | 45
tasmiñ ca samaye thero Sonako gaṇapuṃgavo
Siggavaṃ Candavajjiñ ca akâsi upasampadaṃ. |
tena kho pana samayena vassasatamhi nibbute bhagavati Vesâlikâ Vajjiputtakâ Vesâliyaṃ dasa vatthûni dîpenti: kappati siṅgiloṇakappo, kappati dvaṅgulakappo, kappati gâmantarakappo, kappati âvâsakappo, kappati anumatikappo, kappati âciṇṇakappo, kappati amathitakappo, kappati jalogiṃ pâtuṃ, kappati adasakaṃ nisîdanaṃ, kappati jâtarûparajatan ti. |

37. vinayaṭṭhâne ṭhapetvâna? — 39. Kâsiyâgato A2, comp. Mahâvaṃsa, p. 29, l. 9. — 41. Dâsakatherasantike ABC2G2. Probably we ought to adopt this reading and to expunge „thero". — 43. saddhivihârinupubbakaṃ N. saddhivihâriṃ anuppadaṃ? comp. 5, 91. 104. — 44. aṭṭhamâsañ F. — 45. satt° vass° coro âsi Pakuṇḍako? comp. 11, 2. — 46. Instead of Candavajjî, °vajjiṃ, the MSS. often have Candavajjo, °vajjaṃ.

dasadasakavassamhi sambuddhe parinibbute
Vesâliyaṃ Vajjiputtâ dîpenti dasa vatthuke. |
tathâgatena paṭikkhittaṃ sabbaṃ dîpenti akappiyaṃ.
Sabbakâmî ca Sâḷho ca Revato Khujjasobhito |
Yaso ca Sâṇasambhûto ete saddhivihârikâ
50 therâ Ânandatherassa diṭṭhapubbâ tathâgataṃ, |
Sumano Vâsabhagâmi ca seyyâ saddhivihârikâ
dve ime Anuruddhassa diṭṭhapubbâ tathâgataṃ, |
ete sattasatâ bhikkhû Vesâliyaṃ samâgatâ
vinayaṃ paṭigaṇhanti ṭhapitaṃ buddhasâsane. |
sabbe pi visuddhacakkhû samâpattimhi kovidâ
pannabhârâ visaṃyuttâ sannipâte samâgatâ. |

dutiyasaṃgahaṃ niṭṭhitaṃ. bhâṇavâraṃ catutthaṃ.

V.

Parinibbânasamaye Kusinârâyaṃ naruttame
satta satasahassâni jinaputtâ samâgatâ. |
etasmiṃ sannipâtamhi thero Kassapasavhayo
satthukappo mahânâgo, paṭhavyâ n' atthi îdiso, |
arahantânaṃ pañcasataṃ uccinitvâna Kassapo
varaṃ varaṃ gahetvâna akâsi dhammasaṃgahaṃ. |
pâṇînaṃ anukampâya sâsanaṃ dîghakâlikaṃ
akâsi dhammasaṃgahaṃ tiṇṇaṃ mâsânam accaye
sampatte catutthe mâse dutiye vassupanâyike. |
Sattapaṇṇaguhadvâre Mâgadhânaṃ Giribbaje
5 sattamâsehi niṭṭhâsi paṭhamo saṃgaho ayaṃ. |
etasmiṃ saṃgahe bhikkhû agganikkhittakâ bahû
sabbe pi pâramippattâ lokanâthassa sâsane. |
dhutavâdânam aggo so Kassapo jinasâsane,
bahussutânam Ânando, vinaye Upâlisavhayo, |
dibbacakkhumhi Anuruddho, Vaṅgîso paṭibhânavâ,
Puṇṇo ca dhammakathikânaṃ, vicitrakathî Kumârakassapo, |
vibhajjanamhi Kaccâno, Koṭṭhiko paṭisambhidâ,

---

48. °vassambhi Y, °vassâni FGl, °vassânaṃ N. — 51. The Samantapâsâdikâ, in which this stanza is quoted, has ñeyyâ instead of seyyâ.

V, 1. puruttame Z. — 4: comp. 7, 57. — 5. Magadhânaṃ! —

aññe p' atthi mahâtherâ agganikkhittakâ bahû. |
tehi c' aññehi therehi katakiccehi sâdhuhi
pañcasatehi therehi dhammavinayo ca saṃgîto.
therehi katasaṃgaho theravâdo 'ti vuccati. | 10
Upâliṃ vinayaṃ pucchitvâ dhammaṃ Ânandapaṇḍitaṃ
akaṃsu dhammasaṃgahaṃ vinayañ câpi kevalaṃ. |
jinassa santike gahitâ dhammavinayâ ca te ubho
Upâlithero ca Ânando saddhamme pâramîgato |
pariyâyadesitañ câpi atho nippariyâyadesitaṃ
nîtatthañ c' eva neyyatthaṃ dîpiṃsu suttakovidâ. |
aggassa santike aggaṃ gahetvâ vâkyaṃ tathâgataṃ
agganikkhittakâ therâ aggaṃ akaṃsu saṃgahaṃ,
tasmâ hi so theravâdo aggavâdo 'ti vuccati. |
visuddho apagatadoso theravâdânam uttamo
pavattittha cirakâlaṃ vassânaṃ dasadhâ dasâ 'ti. | 15

Nikkhante paṭhame vassasate sampatte dutiye sate
mahâbhedo ajâyittha theravâdanam uttamo. |
Vesâlivajjiputtakâ dvâdasa sahassâ samâgatâ
dasa vatthûni dîpesuṃ Vesâliyaṃ puruttame. |
siṅgiloṇadvaṅgulakappaṃ gâmantarârâmavâsanaṃ
numatiâciṇṇamathitajalogiñ câpi rûpiyaṃ
nisîdanaṃ adasakaṃ dîpiṃsu buddhasâsane. |
uddhammaṃ ubbinayañ ca apagataṃ satthusâsane
atthaṃ dhammañ ca bhinditvâ vilomâni dîpayiṃsu te. |
tesaṃ niggahanatthâya bahû buddhassa sâvakâ
dvâdasa satasahassâni jinaputtâ samâgatâ. | 20
etasmiṃ sannipâtasmiṃ pâmokkhâ aṭṭha bhikkhavo
satthukappâ mahânâgâ durâsadâ mahâgaṇî: |
Sabbakâmî ca Sâḷho ca Revato Khujjasobhito
Vâsabhagâmi Sumano ca Sâṇavâsi ca Sambhuto |
Yaso Kâkaṇḍakaputto jinena thomito isi,
pâpânaṃ niggahatthâya Vesâliyaṃ samâgatâ. |

---

10. The words „pañcasatehi therehi" are wanting in all the MSS. except N. Comp. 4, 6. — 12. dhammavinayaṃ Z. — 15. vassâni? — 16. theravâdânaṃ AF. — anumati° Z. — 19 et seq. Compare d'Alwis, Introd. to Kaccâyana, p. 54 et seq., Catalogue, p. 142 et seq. — 19. apagataṃ satthusâsanâ? apagatasatthusâsanaṃ? Cullavagga: iti p' idaṃ vatthuṃ uddhammaṃ ubbinayaṃ apagatasatthusâsanaṃ. — vilomâyi ABG, °mâsi F, °mâni N, °maṃ Z.

Vâsabhagâmi ca Sumano Anuruddhassânuvattakâ,
avasesâ therânandassa diṭṭhapubbâ tathâgataṃ. |
Susunâgassa putto Asoko tadâ âsi mahîpati,
25 Pâṭaliputte nagaramhi rajjaṃ kâresi khattiyo. |
tañ ca pakkhaṃ labhitvâna aṭṭha therâ mahiddhikâ
dasa vatthûni bhinditvâ pâpe niddhamayiṃsu te. |
niddhametvâ pâpabhikkhû madditvâ vâdapâpakaṃ
sakavâdasodhanatthâya aṭṭha therâ mahiddhikâ |
arahantânaṃ sattasataṃ uccinitvâna bhikkhavo
varaṃ varaṃ gahetvâna akaṃsu dhammasaṃgahaṃ. |
Kûṭâgârasâlây' eva Vesâliyaṃ puruttame
aṭṭhamâsehi niṭṭhâsi dutiyo saṃgaho ayan ti. |
Nikkaḍḍhitvâ pâpabhikkhû therehi Vajjiputtakâ
30 aññaṃ pakkhaṃ labhitvâna adhammavâdî bahû janâ |
dasa sahassi samâgantvâ akaṃsu dhammasaṃgahaṃ,
tasmâyaṃ dhammasaṃgîti Mahâsaṃgîti vuccati. |
Mahâsaṃgîtikâ bhikkhû vilomaṃ akaṃsu sâsanaṃ,
bhinditvâ mûlasaṃgahaṃ aññaṃ akaṃsu saṃgahaṃ. |
aññattha saṃgahitaṃ suttaṃ aññattha akariṃsu te,
atthaṃ dhammañ ca bhindiṃsu ye nikâyesu pañcasu. |
pariyâyadesitañ câpi atho nippariyâyadesitaṃ
nîtatthañ c' eva neyyatthaṃ ajânitvâna bhikkhavo |
aññaṃ sandhâya bhaṇitaṃ aññatthaṃ ṭhapayiṃsu te,
35 byañjanacchâyâya te bhikkhû bahu atthaṃ vinâsayuṃ. |
chaḍḍetvâ ekadesañ ca suttaṃ vinayañ ca gambhîraṃ
paṭirûpaṃ suttavinayaṃ tañ ca aññaṃ kariṃsu te. |
parivâraṃ atthuddhâraṃ abhidhammappakaraṇaṃ
paṭisambhidañ ca niddesaṃ ekadesañ ca jâtakaṃ
ettakaṃ vissajjetvâna aññâni akariṃsu te. |
nâmaṃ liṅgaṃ parikkhâraṃ âkappakaraṇâni ca
pakatibhâvaṃ vijahetvâ tañ ca aññaṃ akaṃsu te. |

30—38. These stanzas are quoted in the Kathâvatthu-Aṭṭhakathâ (MS. of the Paris National Library, fonds Pâli, 229); I designate the readings of this MS. by K. — 30. nikkaḍḍhitâ K, d'Alwis. — 31. sahassâ K, d'Alwis. — mahâsaṃgîti vuccati NK, d'Alwis, vuccati (omitting mahâsaṃgîti) FG1, sattasatikâ ti v° Z, saṃgîtiti pavuccati ABG2. mahâsaṃgîtiti vuccati? — 33. bh° nikâyesu ca pañcasu, d'Alwis; bh° vinaye nikâyesu ca pañcasu K. — 35. bahuṃ K, d'Alwis. — 36. vinayagambhîraṃ ZK, d'Alwis. — abhidhammaṃ chappakaraṇaṃ K, d'Alwis. — 38. vijahitvâ AK.

pubbaṃgamâ bhinnavâdâ Mahâsaṃgîtikârakâ,
tesañ ca anukâreṇa bhinnavâdâ bahû ahû. |
tato aparakâlamhi tasmiṃ bhedo ajâyatha:
Gokulikâ Ekabyohârâ duvidhâ bhijjittha bhikkhavo. | 40
Gokulikânaṃ dve bhedâ aparakâlamhi jâyatha:
Bahussutakâ ca Paññatti duvidhâ bhijjittha bhikkhavo. |
Cetiyâ ca punavâdi Mahâsaṃgîtibhedakâ.
pañca vâdâ ime sabbe Mahâsaṃgîtimûlakâ |
atthaṃ dhammañ ca bhindiṃsu ekadesañ ca saṃgahaṃ
ganṭhiñ ca ekadesamhi chaḍḍetvâ aññaṃ akaṃsu te. |
nâmaṃ liṅgaṃ parikkhâraṃ âkappakaraṇâni ca
pakatibhâvaṃ vijahetvâ tañ ca aññaṃ akaṃsu te. |
visuddhatheravâdamhi puna bhedo ajâyatha:
Mahiṃsâsakâ Vajjiputtakâ duvidhâ bhijjittha bhikkhavo. | 45
Vajjiputtakavâdamhi catudhâ bhedo ajâyatha:
Dhammuttarikâ Bhaddayânikâ Chandagârikâ ca Sammiti. |
Mahiṃsâsakânaṃ dve bhedâ aparakâlamhi jâyatha:
Sabbatthavâdâ Dhammaguttâ duvidhâ bhijjittha bhikkhavo. |
Sabbatthavâdâ Kassapikâ Kassapikâ Saṃkantikâ,
Suttavâdâ tato aññâ anupubbena bhijjatha. |
ime ekâdasa vâdâ pabhinnâ theravâdato
atthaṃ dhammañ ca bhindiṃsu ekadesañ ca saṃgahaṃ
ganṭhiñ ca ekadesamhi chaḍḍetvâna akaṃsu te. |
nâmaṃ liṅgaṃ parikkhâraṃ âkappakaraṇâni ca
pakatibhâvaṃ vijahetvâ tañ ca aññaṃ akaṃsu te. | 50
sattarasa bhinnavâdâ eko vâdo abhinnako,
sabbev' aṭṭhârasa honti 'bhinnavâdena te saha. |
nigrodho va mahârukkho theravâdânam uttamo
anûnam anadhikañ c' eva kevalaṃ jinasâsanaṃ,
kaṇṭakâ viya rukkhamhi nibbattâ vâdasesakâ. |
paṭhame vassasate n' atthi, dutiye vassasatantare
bhinnâ sattarasa vâdâ uppannâ jinasâsane. |

---

39. ahuṃ N. — 41. Bahussutikâ K, d'Alwis; Bâhulikâ ABG2. — Paññattî. — 42. punavâdî. — 44. vijahitvâ AK. — 46. Channagarikâ ca Sammitî? — 47. 48. Sabbatthivâdâ, d'Alwis. — 48. aññe? K: Sakantikânaṃ Suttavâdi anupubbena bhijjatha. — 49. chaḍḍetvâ aññaṃ akaṃsu te K. — 50. vijahitvâ AK.

Hemavatikâ Râjagirikâ Siddhatthâ Pubbâparaselikâ
aparo Râjagiriko chaṭṭhâ uppannâ aparâparâ. |

âcariyavâdaṃ niṭṭhitaṃ.

Anâgate vassasate vassân' aṭṭhârasâni ca
55 uppajjissati so bhikkhu samaṇo paṭirûpako, |
brahmalokâ cavitvâna uppajjissati mânuse
jacco brâhmaṇagottena sabbamantâna pâragu, |
Tisso 'ti nâma nâmena Putto Moggalisavhayo.
Siggavo Candavajjo ca pabbâjessanti dârakaṃ. |
pabbajito tadâ Tisso pariyattiñ ca pâpuṇi
bhinditvâ titthiyavâdaṃ patiṭṭhapessati sâsanaṃ. |
Pâṭaliputte tadâ râjâ Asoko nâma nâyako
anusâsati so rajjaṃ dhammiko raṭṭhavaḍḍhano. |
sabbe sattasatâ bhikkhû anusâsetvâna sâsanaṃ
60 dasa vatthûni bhinditvâ therâ te parinibbutâ. |
brahmalokâ cavitvâna uppanno mânuse bhave,
jâtiyâ soḷasavasso sabbamantâna pâragu. |
pucchâmi samaṇaṃ pañhaṃ ime pañhe viyâkara,
iruvedaṃ yajuvedaṃ sâmavedam pi nighaṇḍuṃ itihâsañ ca pañcamaṃ. |
therena ca katokâso pañhaṃ pucchi anantaro.
paripakkañâṇaṃ mâṇavaṃ Siggavo etad abravi: |
aham pi mâṇava pañhaṃ pucchâmi buddhadesitaṃ,
yadi pi kusalo pañhaṃ byâkarohi yathâtathaṃ. |
bhâsitena saha pañhe: na me diṭṭhaṃ na me sutaṃ,
65 pariyâpuṇâmi taṃ mantaṃ, pabbajjâ mama ruccati. |
sambâdhâya gharâvâsâ nikkhamitvâna mâṇavo
anagâriyaṃ santibhâvaṃ pabbaji jinasâsane. |
sikkhâkâmaṃ garucittaṃ Candavajjo bahussuto
anusâsittha sâmaṇeraṃ navaṅgaṃ satthusâsanaṃ, |
Siggavo nîharitvâna pabbajâpesi dârakaṃ,
susikkhitaṃ mantadharaṃ Candavajjo bahussuto
navaṅgaṃ anusâsetvâ therâ te parinibbutâ 'ti. |

---

54. Apararâjagirikâ? — chadhâ N. — 57. The MSS. almost constantly read Candavajjo instead of Candavajji. — 60. anusâsitvâna? — 62. samaṇa? comp. v. 65: mâṇava. — 63. anantaraṃ A1, °ro A2G1N, °râ BG2F, °re Z. anuttaraṃ? comp. 6, 28. — 65. bhâsitena saha pañhena? — 66. sambâdhasmâ?

Candaguttassa dvevasse catusaṭṭhi ca Siggavo tadâ,
aṭṭhapaññâsa vassâni Pakuṇḍakassa râjino,
upasampanno Moggaliputto Siggavatherasantike. |
Tisso Moggaliputto ca Candavajjassa santike
vinayaṃ uggahetvâna vimutto upadhisaṃkhaye. | 70
Siggavo Candavajjo ca Moggaliputtaṃ mahâjutiṃ
vâcesuṃ piṭakaṃ sabbaṃ ubhatosaṃgahapuṇṇakaṃ. |
Siggavo ñâṇasampanno Moggaliputtaṃ mahâjutiṃ
katvâ vinayapâmokkhaṃ nibbuto so chasattati. |
Candagutto rajjaṃ kâresi vassâni catuvîsati,
tasmiñ cuddasavassamhi Siggavo parinibbuto |
âraññako dhutavâdo appiccho kânane rato
sabbaso so rato danto saddhamme pâramîgato |
pantasenâsane ramme ogâhetvâ mahâvanaṃ
eko adutiyo sûro sîho va girigabbhare. | 75
nibbute lokanâthassa vassâni soḷasaṃ ahû,
samasaṭṭhi tadâ hoti vassaṃ Upâlipaṇḍitaṃ, |
Ajâtasattu catuvîsaṃ, Vijayassa soḷasaṃ ahû,
Dâsako upasampanno Upâlitherasantike. |
cattâlîs' eva vassâni Dâsako nâma paṇḍito,
Nâgadâse dasavasse, Pakuṇḍakassa vîsati, |
upasampanno Sonako thero Dâsakasantike.
cattâlîsavasso dhîro thero Sonakasavhayo, |
Kâlâsokassa dasavasse, Tambapaṇṇiantarâvâse vassaṃ ekâdasaṃ bhave,
Siggavo upasampanno Sonakatherasantike. | 80
Candaguttassa dvevasse, catusaṭṭhi Siggavo tadâ,
aṭṭhapaññâsa vassâni Pakuṇḍakassa râjino,
upasampanno Moggaliputto Siggavatherasantike. |
Asokadhammassa chavasse chasaṭṭhi Moggaliputto ahû,
aṭṭhacattârîsa [vassâni] Muṭasîvassa râjino,
Mahindo upasampanno Moggaliputtassa santike. |
uggahesi vinayañ ca Upâli buddhasantike,

---

71. ubhosaṃgahasuttakaṃ? Comp. 7, 28. — 76. lokanâthasmiṃ? comp. 4, 27. — 78. Paṇḍuṇâjassa vîsati? comp. 4, 41. — 82. Instead of chasaṭṭhi it ought to be saṭṭhi. — aṭṭhacattâlîsaṃ Muṭasîvassa râjino N, aṭṭhacattârîsaṃ (°sa A) ABG, omitting the following words; aṭhavattâdîpaṃ F. Z: aṭṭhacattârisavassamhi Mahindo nâma yatissaro upasampanno suvisuddho Mogg° s°.

Dâsako vinayaṃ sabbaṃ Upâlitherasantike
uggahetvâna vâcesi upajjhâyo va sâsane. |
vâcesi Dâsako thero vinayaṃ Sonakassa pi,
pariyâpuṇitvâ vâcesi upajjhâyassa santike. |
Sonako buddhisampanno dhammavinayakovido
85 vâcesi vinayaṃ sabbaṃ Siggavassa anuppadaṃ. |
Siggavo Candavajjo ca Sonakasaddhivihârikâ,
vâcesi vinayaṃ thero ubho saddhivihârike. |
Tisso Moggaliputto ca Candavajjassa santike
vinayaṃ uggahetvâna vimutto upadhisaṃkhaye. |
Moggaliputto upajjhâyo Mahindaṃ saddhivihârikaṃ
vâcesi vinayaṃ sabbaṃ theravâdaṃ anûnakaṃ. |
parinibbute sambuddhe Upâlithero mahâjuti
vinayaṃ tâva vâcesi tiṃsa vassaṃ anûnakaṃ. |
saddhivihârikaṃ theraṃ Dâsakaṃ nâma paṇḍitaṃ
90 vinayaṭṭhâne ṭhapetvâna nibbuto so mahâmati. |
Dâsako Sonakaṃ theraṃ saddhivihâriṃ anuppadaṃ
katvâ vinayapâmokkhaṃ catusaṭṭhimhi nibbuto. |
Sonako chaḷabhiññâṇo Siggavaṃ ariyatrajaṃ
vinayaṭṭhâne ṭhapetvâna chasaṭṭhimhi ca nibbuto. |
Siggavo ñâṇasampanno Moggaliputtañ ca dârakaṃ
katvâ vinayapâmokkhaṃ nibbuto so chasattati. |
Tisso Moggaliputto ca Mahindaṃ saddhivihârikaṃ
katvâ vinayapâmokkhaṃ châsîtivassamhi nibbuto. |
catusattati Upâli ca, catusaṭṭhi ca Dâsako,
chasaṭṭhi Sonako thero, Siggavo tu chasattati,
95 asîti Moggaliputto, sabbesaṃ upasampadâ. |
sabbakâlamhi pâmokkho vinaye Upâlipaṇḍito,
paññâsaṃ Dâsako thero, catucattârîsañ ca Sonako,
pañcapaññâsavassaṃ Siggavassa, aṭṭhasaṭṭhi Moggaliputta-
savhayo. |
Udayo soḷasa vassâni rajjaṃ kâresi khattiyo,
chavasse Udayabhaddamhi Upâlithero nibbuto. |
Susunâgo dasavassaṃ rajjaṃ kâresi issaro,
aṭṭhavasse Susunâgamhi Dâsako parinibbuto. |

---

85. dhammavinayiko muni N, °yako muni F, °sokâ muni G1. — 94. châsîtivassamhi N, aṭṭhatiṃsamhi Y, aṭṭhatisâmbi F. The correct number would be eighty.

Susunâgass' accayena honti te dasa bhâtaro,
sabbe bâvîsati vassaṃ rajjaṃ kâresu vaṃsato.
imesaṃ chaṭṭhe vassânaṃ Sonako parinibbuto. |
Candagutto rajjaṃ kâresi vassâni catuvîsati,
tasmiñ cuddasavassamhi Siggavo parinibbuto. | 100
Bindusârassa yo putto Asokadhammo mahâyaso
vassâni sattatiṃsam pi rajjaṃ kâresi khattiyo. |
Asokassa chavîsativasse Moggaliputtasavhayo
sâsanaṃ jotayitvâna nibbuto âyusaṃkhaye. |
catusattativassamhi thero Upâlipaṇḍito
saddhivihârikaṃ theraṃ Dâsakaṃ nâma paṇḍitaṃ
vinayaṭṭhâne ṭhapetvâna nibbuto so mahâgaṇî. |
Dâsako Sonakaṃ theraṃ saddhivihârikaṃ anuppadaṃ
katvà vinayapâmokkhaṃ catusaṭṭhimhi nibbuto. |
Sonako chaḷabhiññâṇo Siggavaṃ ariyatrajaṃ
vinayaṭṭhâne ṭhapetvâna chasaṭṭhimhi parinibbuto. | 105
Siggavo ñâṇasampanno Moggaliputtañ ca dârakaṃ
katvâ vinayapâmokkhaṃ nibbuto so chasattati. |
Tisso Moggaliputto so Mahindaṃ saddhivihârikaṃ
katvâ vinayapâmokkhaṃ asîtivassamhi nibbuto. |
bhâṇavâraṃ pañcamaṃ niṭṭhitaṃ.

VI.

Dve satâni ca vassâni aṭṭhârasa vassâni ca
sambuddhe parinibbute abhisitto Piyadassano. |
âgatâ râjaiddhiyo abhisitte Piyadassane,
pharati puññatejañ ca uddhaṃ adho ca yojanaṃ,
Jambudîpe mahârajje balacakke pavattati. |
vaso Anotatto daho Himavâpabbatamuddhani,
sabbosadhena saṃyuttâ soḷasam pi kumbhiyo
tadâ devasikaṃ niccaṃ devâ abhiharanti te. |

---

99. Kâlâsokass' accayena? — vissuto AZ, vissutâ BG2, vaṃsato X. — 107. châsiti N; asîti, the other MSS.

VI, 2. mahârajje ABG2, °jja CG1R, °jjaṃ MnF. — balacakkaṃ? — 3. vasso Anotatto yo A, vasso Anodatto dayo G, vaso Anotatte dahe N, vahe Anodattadahe F, Anodattodakaṃ yeva Z. In B these words are wanting. yo so An°.daho? tassa Anotatte dahe? Samantapâs.: „devasikam eva tassa devatâ ... âharanti.“ — soḷasamhi k° A1, °sam pi A2, °saṃ pi BG,

nâgalatâdantakaṭṭhaṃ sugandhaṃ pabbateyyakaṃ
muḍusiniddhaṃ madhuraṃ rasavantaṃ manoramaṃ
taḍâ ḍevasikaṃ niccaṃ devatâbhiharanti te. |
âmalakaṃ osadhañ ca sugandhaṃ pabbateyyakaṃ
mudusiniddhaṃ rasavantaṃ mahâbhûteh' upaṭṭhitaṃ
5 tadâ ḍevasikaṃ niccaṃ devatâbhiharanti te. |
dibbapânaṃ ambapakkañ ca rasavantaṃ sugandhakaṃ
taḍâ devasikaṃ niccaṃ devatâbhiharanti te. |
Chandadahato vaṇ pañcavaṇṇaṃ pâpuraṇanivâsanaṃ
tadâ ḍevasikaṃ niccaṃ devatâbhiharanti te. |
sîsanhânagandhacuṇṇaṃ tathâ cânuvilepanaṃ
mudukaṃ pârupattâya sumanadussam asuttakaṃ |
mahâraham añjanañ ca sabban taṃ nâgalokato
tadâ devasikaṃ niccaṃ nâgarâjâharanti te. |
ucchuyaṭṭhipûgamattaṃ pîtakaṃ hatthapuñchanaṃ
10 tadâ devasikaṃ niccaṃ devatâbhiharanti te. |
nava vâhasahassâni suvâharanti sâliyo undurehi visodhitâ,
makkhikâ madhukaṃ karuṃ, acchâ kûṭamhi koṭayuṃ, |
sakuṇâ suvaggajâtâ karavikâ madhurassarâ
Asokapuññatejena sadâ sâventi mânuse. |
kappâyuko mahânâgo catubuddhaparicârako
suvaṇṇasaṃkhalikâbaddho puññatejena âgato, |
pûjesi rattamâlehi Piyadassi mahâyaso.
vipâko piṇḍapâtassa paṭiladdho sudassano. |
Candaguttassâyaṃ nattâ Bindusârassa atrajo
râjaputto tadâ âsi Ujjenikaramolino,
15 anupubbena gacchanto Vedissanagaraṃ gato. |
tatrâpi ca seṭṭhidhîtâ Devî nâmâ 'ti vissutâ
tassa saṃvâsam anvâya ajâyi puttam uttamaṃ. |
Mahindo Saṃghamittâ ca pabbajjaṃ samarocayuṃ,

°saṃ ca Z, °sam pi ca N, °sa pi caca F. soḷasa ambukumbhiyo? soḷ° pânîyakumbhiyo? Samantapâs.: „Anotattadahato ... soḷasa pânîyaghaṭe ... devatâ âharanti."

5. °hupaṭṭhito A, °hûpaṭṭhitaṃ B, °hupaṭṭhitaṃ G, °su paṭṭhitaṃ Z, °hi patthitaṃ N, °hi patiṭṭhitaṃ F, mahâbhûpehi patthitaṃ? — vv. 6—10 are wanting in all the Sinhalese MSS., vv. 6—9 in F also. — 7. Chaddantato pañc°? — pârupanatthâya? Samantapâs.: pârupanatthâya asuttamayikaṃ sumanapupphapaṭaṃ." — 11. kûṭehi koṭṭayuṃ? — 15. [Ujjeni]-nagara[moli]no N, Ujjenikaramolino (°yo Z) Y, Uccenikaramolino F. — 16. tassâ Y. — uttamo YF.

ubho pi pabbajitvâna bhindiṃsu bhavabandhanaṃ. |
Asoko rajjaṃ kâresi Pâṭaliputte puruttame,
abhisitto tîṇi vassâni pasanno buddhasâsane. |
yadâ ca parinibbâyi sambuddho Upavattane
yadâ ca Mahindo jâto Moriyakulasambhavo
etthantare yaṃ gaṇitaṃ vassaṃ bhavati kittakaṃ? |
dve vassasatâni honti catuvassaṃ pan' uttari
samantarambhi so jâto Mahindo Asokatrajo. | 20
Mahindadasavassamhi pitâ bhâte aghâtayi,
Jambudîpaṃ 'nusâsento catuvassaṃ atikkami, |
hantvâ ekasate bhâte vaṃsaṃ katvâna ekato
Mahindacuddasame vasse Asokaṃ abbisiñcayuṃ. |
Asokadhammo 'bhisitto paṭiladdhâ ca iddhiyo,
mahâtejo puññavanto dîpe cakkapavattako. |
paripuṇṇavîsavassamhi Piyadass' âbhisiñcayuṃ.
pâsaṇḍaṃ pariganhanto tîṇi vassaṃ atikkami. |
dvasaṭṭhidiṭṭhigatikâ pâsaṇḍâ channavutikâ,
sassataucchedamûlâ sabbe dvîhi patiṭṭhitâ, | 25
nigaṇṭhâcelakâ c' eva itarâ paribbâjakâ
itarâ brâhmaṇâ 'ti ca aññe ca puthuladdhikâ. |
niyantisassatucchede sammûḷhe hînadiṭṭhike
itobahiddhâpâsaṇḍe titthiye nânâdiṭṭhike
sârâsâraṃ gavesanto puthuladdhî nimantayi. |
titthigaṇe nimantitvâ pavesetvâ nivesanaṃ
mahâdânaṃ padatvâna pañhaṃ pucchi anuttaraṃ. |
pañhaṃ puṭṭhâ na sakkonti vissajjetuṃ sakâ balâ,
ambaṃ puṭṭhaṃ labujaṃ vâ byâkariṃsu apaññakâ. |
anumattam pi sabbesaṃ alan te puna desanaṃ.
bhinditvâ sabbapâsaṇḍaṃ haritvâ puthuladdhike | 30

---

22. Mahindacuddasavasse Z, °dacuddasame vasso (°sse A) ABG, °dacuddasamavasse F, °de cuddasame vasse N. — 24. pâsaṇḍe A. Comp. v. 30. — 26. itarâ brâhmaṇâ N; itarâ is wanting in the other MSS. — brâhmaṇâpi ca? — 27. niyatisass°? nigaṇṭhasass°? — 28. nimantetvâ A. — nivesane YF. — 29b. puṭṭho AZ, °ṭṭhaṃ BGN, suṭṭhaṃ F. ambaṃ puṭṭho (puṭṭhâ?) labujaṃ va? — 30. The king, as is related in the Samantapâsâdikâ, invited the ascetics to sit down on what seats they judged due to themselves. They placed themselves on different kinds of low seats, whereas Nigrodha took his seat on the royal throne. I therefore propose to correct this line thus: anumattam pi sabbesaṃ alan tesaṃ nisîdanaṃ.

iti râjâ vincintesi: aññe pi ke labhâmase
ye loke arahanto ca arahattamaggañ ca passanti? |
saṃvijjanti ime loke, na yimaṃ lokaṃ asuññataṃ,
kadâhaṃ sappurisânaṃ dassanaṃ upasaṃkame?
tassa subhâsitaṃ sutvâ rajjaṃ demi savîjitaṃ. |
iti râjâ vicintento dakkhiṇeyye na passati,
niccaṃ gavesati râjâ sîlavante supesale. |
caṅkaman tamhi pâsâde pekkhamâno bahû jane
rathiyâ piṇḍâya carantaṃ Nigrodhaṃ samaṇaṃ addasa. |
pâsâdikaṃ abhikkantaṃ paṭikkantaṃ vilokitaṃ
ukkhittacakkhusampannaṃ arahantaṃ santamânasaṃ |
uttamadamathappattaṃ dantaṃ guttaṃ surakkhitaṃ
kulagaṇe asaṃsaṭṭhaṃ nabhe candaṃ va nimmalaṃ, |
kesarî va asantâsaṃ, aggikkhandhaṃ va tejitaṃ,
garuṃ durâsadaṃ dhîraṃ santacittaṃ samâhitaṃ, |
khîṇâsavaṃ sabbaklesasodhitaṃ purisuttamaṃ
câravihârasampannaṃ sampassaṃ samaṇuttamaṃ |
sabbaguṇagataṃ Nigrodhaṃ pubbasahâyaṃ vicintayi
pubbe suciṇṇakusalaṃ ariyamaggaphale ṭhitaṃ, |
rathiyâ piṇḍâya carantaṃ muniṃ moneyyavussati. |
jigiṃsamâno sa dhîro cintayi: |
buddho ca loke arahâ sâvako lokuttaramaggaphale ṭhito
mokkhañ ca nibbânagato asaṃsayaṃ aññataro esa thero gurûnaṃ. |
so pañcapîtipasâdaṃ paṭilabhi uḷâraṃ pâmojjamanappasâdito,
nidhiṃ va laddhâ adhano pamodito iddho manoicchitaṃ va Sakkopamo. |

---

32. apaññakaṃ N. suññataṃ? Comp. the following stanza of the Buddhavaṃsa: evaṃ nirâkulaṃ âsi suññataṃ titthiyehi taṃ, vicittaṃ arahantehi vasibhûtehi tâdihi. — sajîvitaṃ A, savijitaṃ BG, yaṃ jitaṃ Z, savîjitaṃ N, saṃvâjitaṃ F. — 35. okkhittac° A. Comp. Mahâvagga I, 23, 2. — 36. kulaṅgaṇe A. — 38. sampassaṃ X, °ssa G1, °ssi Y. — 39. pubbasamayaṃ? — 40. piṇḍâya is wanting in all the MSS., except in N. — 40. 41. sunimonavayitaṃ jigiṃsamâno virâcintayi AG1, sunimonavassitaṃ jigisamâno sa viro cintayi F, muniṃ moneyyavussati jigisamâno sa dhîro cintayi N, passitvâ so vicintayi Z. These words are wanting in BG2. muniṃ moneyyavusitaṃ ... jigiṃsamâno sa dhîro vicintayi? — 42. buddho va? — sasâvako A. — After „ṭhito“ we ought to insert „muni“ or a similar expression. — 43. pâmojjaṃ manappasâdito?

âmantayî aññatarekamaccaṃ: handa bhikkhan taṃ taramânarûpo
nayehi pâsâdikaṃ santavuttiṃ nâgo va yantaṃ rathiyâ kumârakaṃ |
asantâsaṃ santaguṇâdhivâsitaṃ. |
râjâ pasâdavipulaṃ paṭilabhi udaggahaṭṭho manasâbhicintayi:
nissaṃsayaṃ uttamadhammapatto adiṭṭhapubbo ayaṃ purisuttamo. |
vîmaṃsamâno punad evam abravî: supaññattaṃ âsanaṃ ... patthataṃ,
nisîdayî pabbajitattham âsane, mayâ anuññâtaṃ tassâbhipatthitaṃ. |
âdâya rañño vacanaṃ padakkhiṇaṃ ... gahetvâ abhirûhi âsane,
nisîdi pallaṅkavare asantâso Sakko va devarâjâ Paṇḍukambale. |
vicintayî râjâ: ayaṃ aggadârako niccalo asantayî .. atthi nu taṃ .... |
disvâ râjâ taṃ taruṇaṃ kumârakaṃ ariyavattaparihârakaṃ varaṃ
susikkhitaṃ dhammavinayakovidaṃ disvâ râjâ taruṇaṃ kumârakaṃ pasannacitto punad evam abravi: |
desehi dhammaṃ tava sikkhitaṃ mama, tvam eva satthâ, anusâsitaṃ tayâ
karomi tuyhaṃ vacanaṃ mahâmuni, anusâsa maṃ ... suṇoma desanaṃ. |
sutvâna rañño vacanaṃ sutejitaṃ navaṅgasatthe paṭisambhidaṭṭhito

---

44. bhikkhantaṃ Y, °nto G1N, °nte F. bhikkhun taṃ? — 45. nayeha? — santaguṇavâsitaṃ (°kaṃ F) YF, santaguṇâdhivâsitaṃ N. santaguṇâdhivasitaṃ? — 46. pasâdaṃ v°? — uttamadamathapatto N. — 47. nisîdâhi pabbajitagghamâsane (Mahâvaṃsa, p. 25, l. 6: „anurûpe âsane") mayâ anuññâtaṃ tayâbhipatthitaṃ? — 48. ca dakkhiṇaṃ AB. sa dakkhiṇaṃ karaṃ (see Mahâvaṃsa, p. 25, l. 8) gahetvâ? — 49. asantâpiti (°piti BG2) taṃ ABG2, asantapi akatthinu taṃ G1, asantapi (°yî N) atthi nu taṃ X, santapiti atthi Z. asantâso ...? — 50. varaṃ N, cari F, dhari Y. — The repetition of „disvâ — kumârakaṃ" ought to be expunged. — 51. sutopadesanaṃ (sun° G1) ABG, which may be correct. In Z, v. 52 and the last Pâda of v. 51 are wanting.

viloḷayî tepiṭakaṃ mahârahaṃ, tam addasa appamâdasudesanaṃ: |
appamâdo amatapadaṃ, pamâdo maccuno padaṃ,
appamattâ na mîyanti, ye pamattâ yathâ matâ. |
Nigrodhadhîraṃ anumodayantaṃ râjâ vijâniya tam aggahetuṃ,
ye keci sabbaññubuddhadesitâ sabbesaṃ dhammânam imassa mûlakâ. |
ajj' eva tumhe saraṇam upemi buddhañ ca dhammaṃ saraṇañ ca saṃghaṃ,
55 saputtadâro sahaññâtakajjano upâsakattaṃ paṭivedayâmi taṃ. |
saputtadâro saraṇe patiṭṭhito Nigrodhakalyâṇamittassa âgamâ:
pûjemi caturo satasahassarûpiyaṃ aṭṭhaṭṭhakaṃ niccabhattañ ca theraṃ. |
tevijjâ iddhippattâ ca cetopariyâyakovidâ
khîṇâsavâ arahanto bahû buddhassa sâvakâ. |
theraṃ avoca punad eva râjâ: icchâmi saṃgharatanassa dassanaṃ,
samâgamaṃ sannipatanti yâvatâ abhivâdayâmi suṇâmi dhammaṃ. |
samâgatâ saṭṭhisahassabhikkhû, dûtâ ca rañño paṭivedayiṃsu:
saṃgho mahâsannipâto sutuṭṭho, gacchasi tvaṃ icchasi saṃghadassanaṃ. |
dûtassa vacanaṃ sutvâ Asokadhammo mahîpati
60 âmantayi ñatisaṃghamittâmacce ca bandhave: |
dakkhiṇadânaṃ dassâma mahâsaṃghasamâgame,
karoma veyyâvatikaṃ yathâsattiṃ yathâbalaṃ. |
maṇḍapaṃ âsanaṃ udakaṃ upaṭṭhânam dânabhojanaṃ
paṭiyâdentu me khippaṃ dânârahaṃ anucchavaṃ. |

---

54. vijâniya taṃ aggahetuṃ ABG2, vijâniṃsu taṃ aggahetuṃ Z, vijâni (°nî N) bahuni (°hûni N) gahetuṃ (ggahetuṃ G1) XG1. — °buddhena desitâ ABG2. — imassa mûlakâ XG1, imaṃ mûlakaṃ ti (°kan ti A, °kâ ti B) ABG2, imassa mulakâ Z. im(aṃ) assu mûlakaṃ? — 58. sannipatanti ABG, santi patanti Z, sannipatantu X. — 59. sannipatiṃsu tuṭṭhâ (sant° A; kuṭṭhâ Z) Y, sannipâtâ sutuṭṭhâ G1, sannipâto sutuṭṭho N, sannipâdâtâ suduṭṭhâ F. — gacchâhi Z. — icchâmi F. gacchâhi tvaṃ icchitaṃ s°? — 61. dakkhinadhammaṃ (°dammaṃ N) XG1. dakkhiṇâdânaṃ? — 62. pânabhojanaṃ? — anucchaviṃ ABG2.

supeyyabhattakârâ ca suciyâgususaṃkhatâ
paṭiyâdentu me khippaṃ manuññaṃ bhojanaṃ suciṃ. |
mahâdânañ ca dassâmi bhikkhusaṃghe gaṇuttame,
nagaramhi bheriyo vajjantu, vîthi sammajjantu te,
vikirantu vâlukaṃ setaṃ pupphañ ca pañcavaṇṇakaṃ, |
mâlagghiyaṃ toraṇañ ca kadalî puṇṇaghaṭaṃ subhaṃ
utukkamaparaṃ thûpaṃ ṭhapayantu tahiṃ-tahiṃ. | 65
vatthehi ca dhajaṃ katvâ bandhayantu tahiṃ-tahiṃ,
mâlâdâmasamâyuttâ sobhayantu imaṃ puraṃ. |
khattiyâ brâhmaṇâ vessâ suddâ aññakulâsu ca
vatthaṃ âbharaṇaṃ pupphaṃ nânâlaṃkârabhûsitâ
âdâya dîpañ jalamânaṃ gacchantu saṃghadassanaṃ. |
sabbañ ca tâlâvacaraṃ gandhabbâ nânâkulâ sikkhitâ
vajjantu vaggusavanîyâ sussarâ, gacchantu aggavaraṃ saṃghadassanaṃ. |
laṃkârakâmadâ c' eva sotthiyanaṭanâṭakâ
sabbe saṃgham upayantu hâsayantu samâgataṃ. |
pupphañ ca anekavidhaṃ puṇṇakañ ca anekadhâ vividhaṃ
vaṇṇakañ c' eva karontu pûjaṃ anekarâsiyo. | 70
nagarassa paṭihâram antare
dânaṃ sabbaṃ paṭiyantu patthitaṃ. |
pûjaṃ samâdaya sabbaṃ divasaṃ raṭṭhavâsikâ
rattiñ ca sabbaṃ niyâme asesato karontu saṃghâdhikârassa ârabhi. |
taṃ rattiyâ accayena bhattaṃ sakanivesane
paṇîtarasasampannaṃ paṭiyâdetvâna khattiyo |
sâmacce saparivâre âṇâpesi mahâyaso:

---

63. suciyâgû susaṃkhatâ? — 64. vîthiyaṃ Z. vîthiyo? — 65. utukkamaparaṃ (°paraṃ ce F) XG1, upakkamma paraṃ ABG2, ussâpitadhajaṃ Z. — tupuṃ G1. — ṭhapayantu N, paṭhayanta F, upayantu G1, ussâpentu ABG2, ussâpetuṃ Z. I prefer no to try any conjecture. — 67. °kulâni BG2, °kulâsu AZ, °kulesu XG1. aññakulâpi ca? — 68. vâdentu? — 69. laṅkârapamadâ ABG2. Comp. 21, 27. — 70. puṇṇakaṃ G1X, puṇṇaghaṭaṃ Z, cuṇṇakaṃ ABG2. — puñjaṃ? — 71. paṭiyantu N, °ntaṃ FZ, °nta BG1, °tta AG2. — patthitaṃ N, paṭṭhitaṃ YF. — 72. samâdaya N, °yi FG1M, °yî ARC, °yuṃ BG2. — rattiṃ ... ârabhi taṃ is wanting in BG2Z. — niyâme asesato F, niyamenasesato N, niyâme aseto AG1. — saṃghâdh° N, saṃgha adh° AFG1.

... dânaṃ sabbaṃ asesato paṭiyâdentu patthitaṃ. |
pûjaṃ samâdâya sabbaṃ divasaṃ raṭṭhavâsikâ
rattiñ ca sabbaṃ tiyâmaṃ karontu saṃghâbhiratâ. | ??

gandhamâlâpupphakûṭaṃ pupphachattadhajaṃ bahuṃ |
divâ dîpañ jalamânaṃ abhiharantu mahâjanâ.
75 yâvatâ mayâ âṇattâ tâvatâ abhiharantu te. |
imamhi nagare sabbe negamâ ca catuddisâ
sabbeva râjaparisâ sayoggabalavâhanâ
sabbe maṃ anugacchantu bhikkhusaṃghassa dassanaṃ. |
mahatâ râjânubhâvena nîyâsi râjakuñjaro
Sakko va Nandavanuyyânaṃ evaṃ sobhi mahîpati. |
gatvâna râjâ taramânarûpo bhikkhusaṃghassa santike
abhivâdetvâna sammodi vedajâto katañjali. |
ârocayi bhikkhusaṃghaṃ: mam' atthaṃ anukampatu.
yâva bhikkhu anuppatte sabbe antonivesane, |
saṃghassa pitaraṃ theraṃ pattaṃ âdâya khattiyo
80 pûjamâno bahupupphehi pâvisi nagaraṃ puraṃ. |
nivesanaṃ pavesetvâ nisîdâpetvâna âsane
yâguṃ nânâvidhaṃ khajjaṃ bhojanañ ca mahârahaṃ
adâsi payatapâṇi yâvadatthaṃ yadicchakaṃ. |
bhuttâvi bhikkhusaṃghassa onîtapattapâṇino
ekamekassa bhikkhuno adâsi yugasâṭakaṃ. |
pâdasambhañjanaṃ telaṃ chattañ câpi upâhanaṃ
sabbaṃ samaṇaparikkhâraṃ adâsi phâṇitam madhuṃ. |
parivâretvâna nisîdi Asokadhammo mahîpati,
nisajja râjâ pavâresi bhikkhusaṃghassa paccayaṃ: |
85 yâvatâ bhikkhû icchanti tâva demi yadicchakaṃ. |
santappetvâ parikkhârena sampavâretvâna paccaye
tato pucchiṃsu gambhîraṃ dhammakkhandhaṃ sudesitaṃ: |
atthi bhante paricchedo desit' âdiccabandhunâ
nâmaṃ liṅgaṃ vibhattiñ ca koṭṭhâsañ câpi saṃkhataṃ
ettakaṃ 'va dhammakkhandhaṃ gaṇanaṃ atthi pavediya? |
atthi râja gaṇitvâna desit' âdiccabandhunâ
suvibhattaṃ supaññattaṃ suniddiṭṭhaṃ sudesitaṃ |

---

76. The words „sabbeva râjaparisâ" are wanting in the Sinhalese MSS. sabbe ca râjapurisâ? — 77. Nandanuyyânaṃ Z. — 78. The metre is correct if we expunge „râjâ". — 79. The second hemistich seems to be out of its place here; we should insert it perhaps before v. 84. — yâva bhikkhû anuppattâ? — 83. pâdukaṃ añjanaṃ? Comp. the Apadâna (Phayre MS., fol. ñe): „pâduke .. datvâ ... osadhaṃ añjanaṃ datvâ". — 84. pavâretvâna? — 86. pucchi sugambhîraṃ BCG2R.

sahetuṃ atthasampannaṃ khalitaṃ n' atthi subhâsitaṃ,
satipaṭṭhânaṃ sammappadhânaṃ iddhipâdañ ca indriyaṃ |
balaṃ bojjhañgaṃ maggañgaṃ suvibhattaṃ sudesitaṃ,
evaṃ sattappabhedañ ca bodhipakkhiyam uttamaṃ, | 90
lokuttaraṃ dhammavaraṃ navañgaṃ satthusâsanaṃ
vitthâritaṃ suvibhattaṃ desesi dipaduttamo; |
caturâsîtisahassâni dhammakkhandhaṃ anûnakaṃ
pâṇânaṃ anukampâya desit' âdiccabandhunâ. |
amatuttamaṃ varadhammaṃ saṃsâraparimocanaṃ
sabbadukkhakkhayaṃ maggaṃ desesi amatosadhaṃ. |
sutvâna vacanaṃ râjâ bhikkhusaṃghassa bhâsitaṃ
pâmojjahâsabahulo devajâto narâsabho
sarâjikâparisâya imaṃ vâkyaṃ udâhari: |
caturâsîtisahassâni paripuṇṇaṃ anûnakaṃ
desitaṃ buddhaseṭṭhassa dhammakkhandhaṃ mahârahaṃ, | 95
caturâsîtisahassâni ârâmaṃ kârayâm' ahaṃ
ekekadhammakkhandhassa ekekârâmaṃ pûjayaṃ. |
channavutikoṭidhanaṃ vissajjetvâna khattiyo
tam eva divasaṃ râjâ âṇâpesi ca tâvade. |
tasmiṃ samaye Jambudîpe nagarañ caturâsîtiyo
ekekanagaraṭṭhâne paccekârâmaṃ kârayi. |
anto tîṇi ca vassâni vihâraṃ katvâna khattiyo
pariniṭṭhitamhi ârâme pûjaṃ sattâha kârayi. |

bhâṇavârañ chaṭṭhaṃ.

VII.

Mahâsamâgamo hoti Jambudîpasamantato,
bhikkhû asîti koṭiyo bhikkhunî channavuti sahassiyo,
bhikkhû ca bhikkhuniyo ca chaḷabhiññâ bahûtarâ. |
bhikkhû iddhânubhâvena samaṃ katvâ mahîtalaṃ
lokavivaraṇaṃ katvâ dassesuṃ pûjiye mahe. |
Asokârâme ṭhito râjâ Jambudîpaṃ avekkhati,
bhikkhuiddhânubhâvena Asoko sabbattha passati. |

---

90. In Y the words „evaṃ satt. ca" are wanting. — 92. pâṇînaṃ? — 94. vedajâto? — sarâjikâya par° Z. — 97. ca tâvade N, ca kovide ABG, mahâjane Z. — 98. caturâsîti sahassiyo? With regard to the metre comp. 7, 1.

addasa vihâraṃ sabbaṃ sabbattha mahiyaṃ kataṃ
dhajaṃ ubhopiyaṃ pupphaṃ toraṇañ ca mâlagghiyaṃ |
kadalî puṇṇaghaṭañ c' eva nânâpupphasamohitaṃ,
5 addasa dîpamaṇḍalaṃ vibhûsan taṃ catuddisaṃ. |
pamodito haṭṭhamano pekkhanto vattate mahe
samâgate bhikkhusaṃghe bhikkhunî ca samâgate |
mahâdânañ ca paññattaṃ dîyamâne vanibbake
caturâsîtisahassâni vihâre disvâna pûjite |
Asoko 'pi attamano bhikkhusaṃghaṃ pavedayi:
ahañ ca bhante dâyâdo satthu buddhassa sâsane. |
bahu mayhaṃ pariccâgo sâsane sâravâdino; |
channavutikoṭiyo ca vissajjetvâ mahâdhanaṃ
10 caturâsîtisahassâni ârâmâ kâritâ mayâ |
pûjâya dhammakkhandhassa buddhaseṭṭhassa desite;
cattâri satasahassâni devasikaṃ pavattayi, |
ekañ ca cetiyaṃ pûjaṃ ekaṃ Nigrodhasavhayaṃ
ekañ ca dhammakathikânaṃ ekaṃ gilânapaccayaṃ;
dîyati devasikaṃ niccaṃ Mahâgaṅgâ va odanaṃ. |
añño koci pariccâgo bhiyyo mayhaṃ na vijjati, .
saddhâ mayhaṃ daḷhatarâ, tasmâ dâyâdo sâsane. |
sutvâna vacanaṃ rañño Asokadhammassa bhâsitaṃ
paṇḍito sutasampanno nipuṇatthavinicchayo |
saṃghassa tesu vihâraṃ anuggahatthâya sâsanaṃ
15 anâgate ca addhâne pavattiṃ sutvâ vicakkhaṇo |
byâkâsi Moggaliputto Asokadhammapucchitaṃ:
paccayadâyako nâma sâsane paṭibâhiro, |
yassa puttaṃ vâ dhîtaraṃ vâ urasmiñ jâtam anvayaṃ
pabbâjesi cajetvâna so ve dâyâdo sâsane. |

VII, 4. sabbattha mahiyâ kataṃ A, s° mahiyaṃ k° B, s° mahi[ya]laṃgataṃ G (ya is crossed), s° mahilaṃkataṃ N, sabbatthâpi mahitalaṃ Z. — dhajaṃ ussâpitaṃ? — 5. °samâhitaṃ A. — 6. ca samâgatâ? — 9. sâravâdino ABG2, ravâdino G1, gârav° Z, varav° N. gâravâ dino (= dinno)? — 11. pavattayiṃ. — 12. cetiyapûjaṃ ABG2. — 15. saṃghassa thero suvihâro A B G2, saṃghassa theraṃ tasuvihâraṃ G1, [saṃghassa] tesu [vihâraṃ] N, saṃghassa tâni vihâraṃ Z. saṃghassa phâsuvihâraṃ? As to the construction, comp. vv. 55. 57. — Instead of „sutvâ" I should prefer „ñatvâ", which looks very similar in Burmese characters. — 17. pabbâjeti Z. — dâyâdasâsane NG1. — yo saputtaṃ vâ ... pabbâjesi cajitvâna? As to the preterite tense „pabbâjesi", comp. Mahâvaṃsa, p. 36, l. 7, and the Thûpavaṃsa: „paccayadâyako nâma tvaṃ mahârâja, yo pana attano puttañ ca dhîtarañ ca pabbâjesi ayaṃ sâsanassa dâyâdo nâmâ 'ti."

sutvâna vacanaṃ râjâ Asokadhammo mahîpati
Mahindakumâraṃ puttaṃ Saṃghamittañ ca dhîtaraṃ |
ubho amantayi râjâ: dâyâdo homi sâsane.
sutvâna pituno vâkyaṃ ubho puttâdhivâsayuṃ: |
suṭṭhu deva sampaṭicchâma karoma vacanaṃ tava,
pabbâjehi ca no khippaṃ, dâyâdo hohi sâsane. |
paripuṇṇavîsativasso Mahindo Asokatrajo
Saṃghamittâ ca jâtiyâ vassaṃ aṭṭhârasaṃ bhave. |
chavassamhi Asokassa ubho pabbajitâ pajâ,
tath' eva upasampanno Mahindo dîpajotako, |
Saṃghamittâ tadâ yeva sikkhâyo 'va samâdiyi.
ahû Moggaliputto va theravâdo mahâgaṇî. |
catupaññâsavassamhi Asokadhammo abhisitto,
Asokassâbhisittato chasaṭṭhi Moggalisavhayo,
tato Mahindo pabbajito Moggaliputtassa santike. |
pabbâjesi Mahâdevo, Majjhanto upasampade.
ime te nâyakâ tîṇi Mahindassânukampakâ. |
Moggaliputto upajjhâyo Mahindaṃ dîpajotakaṃ
vâcesi piṭakaṃ sabbaṃ atthaṃ dhammañ ca kevalaṃ. |
Asokassa dasavassamhi Mahindo catuvassiko
sabbaṃ sutapariyattiṃ gaṇipâcariyo ahû. |
sudesitaṃ suvibhattaṃ ubhosaṃgahasuttakaṃ
Mahindo theravâdakaṃ uggahetvâna dhârayi. |
vinîto Moggaliputto Mahindaṃ Asokaatrajaṃ
tisso vijjâ chalabhiñña caturo paṭisambhidâ. |
Tisso Moggaliputto ca Mahindaṃ saddhivihârikaṃ
âgamapiṭakaṃ sabbaṃ sikkhâpesi nirantaraṃ. |
tîṇi vassamhi Nigrodho, catuvassamhi bhâtaro,
chavassamhi pabbajito Mahindo Asokatrajo. |
Kontiputtâ ubho therâ Tisso câpi Sumittako
aṭṭhavassamhi 'sokassa parinibbiṃsu mahiddhikâ. |
ime kumârâ pabbajitâ ubho therâ ca nibbutâ. |

---

20. paṭicchâma Y. — 23. theravâde B. — 24. Asokâbhisitte chavasse saṭṭhi M°? — 25. upasampado Z. — 27. sutapariyattiṃ AG1, suttapariyattiṃ Z, sutapariyatti BG2N. — gaṇi° BG, gaṇî° A, gani° CR, ganî° M, gaṇhi N. gaṇî âcariyo? „pâcariya“ does not mean „a pupil“, as Childers says, but „the teacher's teacher“. — 28. chalabhiñña M2n; the other MSS. omit these words. chaḷ abhiññâ. — catasso? — 32. Comp. Mahâvaṃsa, p. 38.

upâsakattaṃ desiṃsu khattiyâ brâhmaṇâ bahû,
mahâlâbho ca sakkâro uppajji buddhasâsane, |
pahînalâbhasakkârâ titthiyâ puthuladdhikâ.
35 paṇḍaraṅgâ jaṭilâ ca nigaṇṭhâcelakâdikâ |
aṭṭhaṃsu satta vassâni, ahosi vagguposatho.
ariyâ pesalâ lajjî na pavisanti uposathaṃ. |
sampatte ca vassasate vassañ chattiṃsa satâni ca
saṭṭhi bhikkhusahassâni Asokârâme vasiṃsu te. |
âjîvakâ aññaladdhikâ nânâ dûsenti sâsanaṃ,
sabbe kâsâyavasanâ dûsenti jinasâsanaṃ. |
bhikkhusahassaparivuto chaḷabhiñño mahiddhiko
Moggaliputto gaṇapâmokkho akâsi dhammasaṃgahaṃ. |
Moggaliputto mahâpañño paravâdappamaddano
40 theravâdaṃ daḷhaṃ katvâ saṃgahaṃ tatiyaṃ kato. |
madditvâ nânâvâdâni nîharitvâ alajjino bahû
sâsanaṃ jotayitvâna kathâvatthuṃ pakâsayi. |
tassa Moggaliputtassa Mahindo saddhivihâriko
upajjhâyassa santike saddhammaṃ pariyâpuṇi. |
nikâye pañca vâcesi satta c' eva pakaraṇe,
ubhatovibhaṅgaṃ vinayaṃ parivârañ ca khandhakaṃ
uggahi vîro nipuṇo upajjhâyassa santike 'ti. |
Nikkhante dutiye vassasate vassâni chattiṃsati
puna bhedo ajâyatha theravâdânam uttamo. |
Pâṭaliputtanagaramhi rajjaṃ kâresi khattiyo
45 Dhammâsoko mahârâjâ pasanno buddhasâsane. |
mahâdânaṃ pavattesi saṃghe gaṇavaruttame,
cattâri satasahassâni ekâhen' eva nissaji. |
cetiyassa yajâ ekaṃ dhammassa savanassa ca
gilânânañ ca paccayaṃ ekaṃ saṃghassa nissaji. |
titthiyâ lâbhaṃ disvâna sakkârañ ca mahârahaṃ
saṭṭhimattasahassâni theyyasaṃvâsakâ ahû. |
Asokârâmavihâramhi pâtimokkho paricchiji,
kârâpento pâtimokkhaṃ amacco ariyânaṃ aghâtayi. |

---

34. desayiṃsu Z. — 37. ca vassasate G1NZ, dve vassasate ABG2. — vassa N, vassaṃ Y. — chattiṃsatâni ABG2, chattiṃsa satâni G1NZ. — 43. dhîro N, vîro Y. — 44. vassâni ca chattiṃsati? — 47. yajâ ekaṃ N, yajâjakaṃ G1, ca ekaṃ ABG2, ca ekassa Z. pûjaṃ ekaṃ? — savanassa ca N, cassa ca G1, ca tatheva ca AZ, ca tatheva kâ BG2. — 48. ahuṃ N. — 49. paricchajî A, °ccaji BZ, °cchijji N, °cchiji G1.

titthiye niggahatthâya bahû buddhassa sâvakâ
saṭṭhimattasahassâni jinaputtâ samâgatâ. | 50
ekasmiṃ sannipâtamhi thero Moggaliatrajo
satthukappo mahânâgo paṭhavyâ n' atthi îdiso. |
ariyânaṃ ghâtitaṃ kammaṃ râjâ theraṃ apucchatha,
pâṭihîraṃ karitvâna rañño kaṅkhaṃ vinodayi. |
therassa santike râjâ uggahetvâna sâsanaṃ
theyyasaṃvâsabhikkhuno nâseti liṅganâsanaṃ. |
titthiyâ sakavâdena pabbajitvâ anâdarâ
buddhavacanaṃ bhindiṃsu visuddhakañcanaṃ iva. |
sabbe pi te bhinnavâdâ vilomâ theravâdato,
tesañ ca niggahatthâya, sakavâdavirocanaṃ, | 55
desesi thero abhidhammaṃ kathâvatthuppakaraṇaṃ.
niggaho îdiso n' atthi paravâdappamaddanaṃ. |
desetvâ thero abhidhammaṃ kathâvatthuppakaraṇaṃ
sakavâdasodhanatthâya, sâsanaṃ dîghakâlikaṃ, |
arahantânaṃ sahassaṃ uccinitvâna nâyako
varaṃ varaṃ gahetvâna akâsi dhammasaṃgahaṃ. |
Asokârâmavihâramhi Dhammarâjena kârite
navamâsehi niṭṭhâsi tatiyo saṃgaho ayan ti. |

saddhammasaṃgahaṃ navamâsaṃ niṭṭhitaṃ.
bhâṇavâraṃ sattamaṃ.

VIII.

Moggaliputto dîghadassî sâsanassa anâgate
paccantamhi patiṭṭhânaṃ disvâ dibbena cakkhunâ |
Majjhantikâdayo there pâhesi attapañcame:
sâsanassa patiṭṭhâya paccante sattabuddhiyâ |
paccantakânaṃ desânaṃ anukampâya pâṇinaṃ
pabhâtukâ balappattâ desetha dhammam uttamaṃ. |
gantvâ Gandhâravisayaṃ Majjhantiko mahâ isi
kupitaṃ nâgaṃ pasâdetvâ mocesi bandhanâ bahu. |
gantvâna raṭṭhaṃ Mahisaṃ Mahâdevo mahiddhiko
coditvâ nirayadukkhena mocesi bandhanâ bahu. | 5

---

51. etasmiṃ ABG2. — 53. °bhikkhunaṃ G2, °bhikkhûnaṃ B. — nâsesi ABG2. — 54. °kañcanaṃ riva N, °kañcanâm iva Y.
VIII, 3. pabhâtakâ N. sabhâtukâ? (comp. 15, 18). — 4. bahuṃ AB. bahû? — 5. codetvâ? — bahuṃ ABG2. bahû?

athâparo pi Rakkhito vikubbanesu kovido
vehâsaṃ abbhuggantvâna desesi anamataggiyaṃ. |
Yonakadhammarakkhitathero nâma mahâmati
aggikkhandhopamasuttakathâya Aparantakaṃ pasâdayi. |
Mahâdhammarakkhitathero Mahâraṭṭhaṃ pasâdayi
Nâradakassapajâtakakathâya ca mahiddhiko. |
Mahârakkhitathero pi Yonakalokaṃ pasâdayi
kâlakârâmasuttantakathâya ca mahiddhiko. |
Kassapagotto ca yo thero Majjhimo Durabhisaro
10 Sahadevo Mûlakadevo Himavante yakkhagaṇaṃ pasâdayuṃ, |
kathesuṃ tattha suttantaṃ dhammacakkappavattanaṃ. |
Suvaṇṇabhûmiṃ gantvâna Sonuttarâ mahiddhikâ
niddhametvâ pisâcagaṇe mocesi bandhanâ bahu. |
Laṅkâdîpavaraṃ gantvâ Mahindo attapañcamo
sâsanaṃ thâvaraṃ katvâ mocesi bandhanâ bahu. |

bhâṇavâraṃ aṭṭhamaṃ.

IX.

Laṅkâdîpo ayaṃ ahû sîhena Sîhalâ iti.
dîpuppattiṃ imaṃ vaṃsaṃ suṇâtha vacanaṃ mama. |
Vaṅgarâjassâyaṃ dhîtâ araññe vanagocaraṃ
sîhasaṃvâsam anvâya bhâtaro janayî duve. |
Sîhabâhu ca Sîvalî kumârâ cârudassanâ
mâtâ ca Susimâ nâma pitâ ca Sîhasavhayo. |
atikkante soḷasavasse nikkhamitvâ guhantarâ
mâpesi nagaraṃ tattha Sîhapuraṃ varuttamaṃ. |
Lâḷaraṭṭhe tahiṃ râjâ Sîhaputto mahabbalo
5 anusâsi mahârajjaṃ Sîhapuravaruttame. |

---

6. The country which was converted by Rakkhita, is not named; and even in a work so full of the greatest blunders, as the Dîpavaṃsa, we should scarcely be justified in changing „athâparo“ into „Vanavâse“. I rather conjecture: atha thero pi R°. — 10. Dundubhissaro ABG2, Durabhisaro G1, Durabhiyâparo N, durâsado Z. The Mahâv. Ṭîkâ has Dundhabhinnassarathero; the Sam. Pâsâdikâ, Dundubhissara (Paris MS.) and Duddabhiya (MS. of the British Museum); the Inscription given by Cunningham (the Bhilsa Topes, p. 316), Dadabhisâra. — 12. mocesuṃ A2. — 12. 13. bahû?

IX, 1. Sîhalaṃ ABG2, Sîhalâ G1Zn. — dîpuppattiṃ N, dîpuppatti Y, which may be the correct reading; comp. the note on „dhâtu“ 1, 1. — 2. sîhaṃ s° N, which possibly is correct. — 4. rahantare Y, guhantarâ N.

battiṃsa bhâtaro honti Sîhaputtassa atrajâ,
Vijayo ca Sumitto ca subhajeṭṭhabhâtarâ ahuṃ. |
Vijayo nâma so kumâro pagabbho âsi asikkhito
karoti vilopakammaṃ atikiccaṃ sudâruṇaṃ. |
samâgatâ jânapadâ negamâ ca samâgatâ
upasaṃkamma râjânaṃ Vijayadosaṃ pakâsayuṃ. |
tesaṃ vacanaṃ sutvâna râjâ kupitamânaso
âṇâpesi amaccânaṃ: kumâraṃ nîharatha imaṃ, |
paricârikâ ime sabbe puttadârâ ca bandhavâ
dâsîdâsakammakare nîharantu janappadâ. |
tato taṃ nîharitvâna visuṃ katvâna bandhave
âropetvâna te nâvaṃ vuyhittha aṇṇave tadâ. |
pakkamantu yathâkâmaṃ honti sabbe adassanaṃ
raṭṭhe janapade vâsaṃ mâ puna âgamicchati. |
kumârânaṃ ârûḷhanâvâ gatâ dîpaṃ avassakaṃ,
nâmadheyyaṃ tadâ âsi Naggadîpan ti vuccati. |
mahilânaṃ ârûḷhanâvâ gatâ dîpaṃ avassakaṃ,
nâmadheyyaṃ tadâ âsi Mahilâraṭṭhan ti vuccati. |
purisânaṃ ârûḷhanâvâ apilavantâ va sâgaraṃ
vippanaṭṭhâ disâmûḷhâ gatâ Suppârapaṭṭanaṃ. |
orohetvâna Suppâraṃ sattasatañ ca te tadâ
vipulaṃ sakkârasammânaṃ akaṃsu te Suppârakâ. |
tesu sakkariyamânesu Vijayo ca sahâyakâ
sabbe luddâni kammâni kurumânâ nabujjhakâ, |
pânaṃ adinnaṃ paradâraṃ musâvâdañ ca pesuṇaṃ
anâcârañ ca dussîlaṃ âcaranti sudâruṇaṃ. |
kakkhalaṃ pharusaṃ ghoraṃ kammaṃ katvâ sudâruṇaṃ
ujjhâyetvâna mantiṃsu: khippaṃ ghâtema dhuttake. |
Ojadîpo Varadîpo Maṇḍadîpo 'ti vâ ahû
Laṅkâdîpo ca paṇṇatti Tambapaṇṇîti ñâyati. |

---

6. subhajeṭṭhabhâtarâ ABG, subhajeṭṭhamâtarâ Z, sutajeṭṭhabhâtarâ N. — 9. nihatha N. — 10. paricârake? — bandhave? — 11. vuyhaṭṭhuṃ ABG2, vuyhatthe G1, vuyhittha N, uyihâpetuṃ Z. — 12. yantu sabbe adassanaṃ? — adassanâ N. — raṭṭhe N, vuṭṭhâ Y. — vasaṃ G1N. — âgamicchati N, âgamicchatu G1, âgacchantu ABG2, âgamantu yaṃ Z. âgamissati? — 15. apilavantâva N, apilavanto G1, uplavantâ A, upallavantâ BG2, upalavanto ca Z. pilavantâ 'va? comp. v. 27. — 16. sambhâraṃ Y, Suppâraṃ N. — 17. nabujjhakâ N, na bujjhati G1, caranti te Y. nabujjhaka = na-budhya-ka? — 19. katâ sudâruṇaṃ ujjhâyitvâna? — 20. ti vâ N, ca ABG, ca tadâ Z, d'Alwis (Attanag., p. 7).

parinibbânasamaye sambuddhe dîpaduttame
Sîhabâhussâyaṃ putto Vijayo nâma khattiyo |
Lañkâdîpaṃ anuppatto jahetvâ Jambudîpavhayaṃ.
byâkâsi buddhaseṭṭho: so râjâ hessati khattiyo. |
tato âmantayi satthâ Sakkaṃ devânam issaraṃ:
Lañkâdîpassa ussukkaṃ mâ pamajjatha Kosiya. |
sambuddhassa vaco sutvâ devarâjâ Sujampati
Uppalavaṇṇassa âcikkhi dîpaṃ ârakkhakâraṇaṃ. |
Sakkassa vacanaṃ sutvâ devaputto mahiddhiko
25 Lañkâdîpassa ârakkhaṃ sapariso paccupaṭṭhâti. |
tayo mâse vasitvâna Vijayo Bhârukacchake
ujjhâyetvâ janakâyaṃ tam eva nâvam âruhi. |
ârohitvâ sakaṃ navaṃ pilavantâ 'va sâgaraṃ
ukkhittavâtavegena nadîmûḷhâ mahâjanâ |
Lañkâdîpam upâgamma orohitvâ thale ṭhitâ,
patiṭṭhitâ dharaṇîtale atijighacchitâ have
pipâsitâ kilantâ ca, padasâgamanaṃ jâyati. |
ubhopâṇîhi jannûhi yogaṃ katvâ puthuviyaṃ
majjhe vuṭṭhâya ṭhatvâna pâṇî passanti sobhaṇâ. |
surattaṃ paṃsu bhûmibhâge hatthapâṇimhi makkhite,
30 nâmadheyyaṃ tadâ âsi Tambapaṇṇîti taṃ ahû. |
paṭhamaṃ nagaraṃ Tambapaṇṇi Lañkâdîpavaruttame,
Vijayo tahiṃ vasanto issariyaṃ anusâsi so. |
Vijayo Vijito ca so nâvaṃ anurakkhena ca
Accutagâmi Upatisso paṭhaman to idh' âgato. |
âkiṇṇâ naranârîhi bahû sabbe samâgatâ
tahiṃ tahiṃ disâbhâge nagaraṃ mâpesi khattiyo. |

---

22. jahitvâ Z. — 25. sapariso (sapârûso G1) paccupaṭṭhâti A G1, sahadayo paccubandhati N, ṭhapesi Vâsudevako Z; the whole stanza is wanting in B G2. sapuriso paccupaṭṭhâti? — 26. ujjhâyatâni kâyaṃ taṃ (kâyânaṃ A, kâyaṃ naṃ G2) A B G2, ujjhâyatâni kânaṃyaṃ Z, ujjhâyetvâ kâyaṃ G1, ujjhâyetvâ janakâyaṃ N. — 27. ukkhittâ vât°? — disâmûḷhâ A B G2, d'Alwis (Attanag. 8); nadîmûḷhâ G1 n Z. Comp. v. 15. — 28. have A Z, bhave B G, vade N. — padasâgamanaṃ jâyati N, °gamanena jâyati G1 Z, °gamanaṃ na jâtayuṃ (jânayuṃ A) A B G2; padasâgamanena ca, d'Alwis. Dr. Bühler proposes to read: padasâgamanaṃ jhâyati. — 29. yogaṃ N, viyâgaṃ Y, viyâtan d'Alwis. — majjhe G1 Z n, d'Alwis, pacchâ A B G2. — nahipassanti Y, d'Alwis. — 30. surattapaṃsu A. — makkhittaṃ A B G, makkhitaṃ Z, d'Alwis, makkhite N. makkhito? — v. 32 is wanting in B G2 Z. — nâvaṃ anurakkhana ca A G, °kkhena ca N. Anurâdhanakkhattena ca? comp. v. 35. — paṭhamanto idhâgato G N, °nte idhâgato A. paṭhaman te idhâgatâ? — 33. bahû sattâ? comp. 12, 27; 13, 10.

Tambapaṇṇi dakkhiṇato nadîtîre varuttame
Vijayena mâpitaṃ nagaraṃ samantâpuṭabhedanaṃ. |
Vijito Vijitaṃ mâpesi, so Uruvelaṃ mâpayi,
Nakkhattanâmako 'macco mâpesi Anurâdhapuraṃ. | 35
Accutagâmi yo nâma Ujjeniṃ tattha mâpayi,
Upatisso Upatissaṃ nagaraṃ suvibhattantarâpaṇaṃ
iddhaṃ phîtaṃ suvitthâraṃ ramaṇîyaṃ manoramaṃ. |
Laṅkâdîpavhaye ramme Tambapaṇṇimhi issaro
Vijayo nâma nâmena paṭhamaṃ rajjaṃ akârayi. |
âgate sattavassamhi âkiṇṇo janapado ahû.
aṭṭhatiṃsati vassâni rajjaṃ kâresi khattiyo. |
sambuddhe navame mâse yakkhasenaṃ vidhamitaṃ,
sambuddhe pañcame vasse nâgânaṃ damayî jino,
sambuddhe aṭṭhame vasse samâpatti samâpayi. |
imâni tîṇi ṭhânâni idhâgami tathâgato.
sambuddhe pacchime vasse Vijayo idham âgato. | 40
manussâvâsaṃ akârayi sambuddho dipaduttamo.
anupâdisesâya sambuddho nibbuto upadhisaṃkhaye. |
parinibbutamhi sambuddhe dhammarâje pabhaṃkare
aṭṭhatiṃsati vassâni rajjaṃ kâresi khattiyo. |
dûtaṃ pâhesi Sîhapuraṃ Sumittavhassa santike,
lahuṃ âgacchatu 'mheko Laṅkâdîpavaruttamaṃ. |
n' atthi koci mam' accaye imaṃ rajjânusâsako,
niyyâdemi imaṃ dîpaṃ mamaṃ kataparakkamaṃ. |

bhâṇavâraṃ navamaṃ.

X.

Paṇḍusakkassâyaṃ dhîtâ Kaccânâ nâma khattiyâ
kulavaṃsânurakkhanatthâya Jambudîpâ idhâgatâ. |
abhisittâ khattiyâbhisekena Paṇḍuvâsamahesiyâ,
tassâ saṃvâsam anvâya jâyiṃsu ekâdasa atrajâ, |
Abhayo Tisso ca Utti ca Tisso Aselapañcamo

---

35. Vijito N, Vijayo Y. — so BGN, yo AZ. — Nakkhattanâmako N, Nakkhattarâdhanâma so (°nâmo so ABG2) Y. — 39. vidhamitaṃ G1N, vidhaṃsitaṃ ABG2, vimadditaṃ Z. — samâpatti? — 43. °tumeko BG2. — 44. mamaṃ N, mama G1, mayâ ABG2Z.

X, 2. mahesiyâ ZG1n, mahesi sâ A, mahesi BG2.

Vibhâto Râmo ca Sivo ca Matto Mattakalena ca,
tesaṃ kaniṭṭhadhîtâ tu Cittâ nâmâ 'ti vissutâ,
rañjayati jane diṭṭhe Ummâdacittâ 'ti vuccati. |
saṅkâbhisekavassena âgami Upatissagâmake.
paripuṇṇatiṃsavassâni rajjaṃ kâresi khattiyo. |
Amitodanassa nattâ te ahesuṃ satta Sâkiyâ,
Râmo Tisso Anurâdho ca Mahâli Dîghâvu Rohinî
Gâmanî sattamo tesaṃ lokanâthassa vaṃsajâ. |
Paṇḍuvâsassa atrajo Abhayo nâma khattiyo
vîsati c' eva vassâni rajjaṃ kâresi tâvade. |
Dîghâvuss' atrajo dhîro Gâmanîpaṇḍito ca yo
Paṇḍuvâsaṃ upaṭṭhanto Cittakaññâya saṃvasi. |
tassa saṃvâsam anvâya ajâyi Paṇḍukasavhayo,
attânaṃ anurakkhanto avasi Dovârikamaṇḍale. |

bhâṇavâraṃ dasamaṃ.

XI.

Abhayassa vîsativasse Pakuṇḍassa vîsati ahû,
sattatiṃsavasso jâtiyâ abhisitto Pakuṇḍako. |
Abhayassa vîsativasse coro âsi Pakuṇḍako.
sattarasamhi vassamhi hantvâna satta mâtule
abhisitto râjâbhisekena nagare Anurâdhapure. |
atikkante dasavassamhi saṭṭhivassam anâgate
ṭhapesi gâmasîmâyo abhayâni gâḷhaṃ kârayi. |
ubhato paribhuñjitvâ yakkhamânusakâni ca
anûnâni sattati vassâni Pakuṇḍo rajjaṃ akârayi. |
Pakuṇḍassa ca atrajo Muṭasîvo nâma khattiyo
issaro Tambapaṇṇimhi saṭṭhi vassaṃ akârayi. |
Muṭasîvassa atrajâ ath' aññe dasa bhâtukâ,
Abhayo Tisso Nâgo ca Utti Mattâbhayena ca |

---

4. rañjayanti AZ, °yati NG1, °yaṃti BG2. rañjayantî jane diṭṭhâ? — 5. saṅkâbh° BGZ, Laṅkâbh° N, sakâbhisekavassena A. — 6. te is wanting in NG1. nattâro ahesuṃ? — Rohano A, Rohinî BCR, Rohini GMn. Comp. Mahâvaṃsa, p. 57, l. 1. — 7. vîsatiṃ Z. — 8. upaṭṭhahanto A. — 9. tassa N, vassa G1, va asso B, assâ AG2Z.

XI, 1. Pakuṇḍassa N, Paṇḍukassa (Paṇḍakassa G1) Y. — sattatiṃsavasso ABG2, sattatiṃsativassehi Z, sattatiṃsavassa G1, sattatiṃsâya N. — 3. °sîmâni N, °simâni G1. °sîmâni may be correct; comp. 14, 34. 37. 74; 13, 6; 22, 1. — gâḷha N, kulaṃ Y.

Mitto Sivo Aselo ca Tisso Kirena te dasa,
Anulâdevî Sîvalâ ca Muṭasîvassa dhîtaro. |
Ajâtasattu aṭṭhame vasse Vijayo idham âgato,
Udayassa cuddasavassamhi Vijayo kâlaṃkato tadâ.
Udayassa soḷase vasse Paṇḍuvâsaṃ abhisiñcayi. |
Vijayassa Paṇḍuvâsassa ubhorâjânam antare
saṃvaccharaṃ tadâ âsi Tambapaṇṇi aparâjikâ. |
ekavîsaṃ Nâgadâso Paṇḍuvâso tadâ gato,
Abhayam pi Nâgadâsassa ekâbhisekaṃ siñcayuṃ. |
... sattaras' eva vassâni catuvîsati. |
Candagutte cuddase ca vasse gato Pakuṇḍakasavhayo,
Candaguttassa cuddasavasse Muṭasîvaṃ abhisiñcayi. |
Asokassâbhisittato sattarasavasso ahû Muṭasîvo tadâ gato. |
tamhi sattarase vasse chamâse ca anâgate
hemante dutiye mâse âsâḷhînakkhattamuttame
abhisitto Devânampiyo Tambapaṇṇimhi issaro. |
Châtapabbatapâdamhi veḷuyaṭṭhi tayo ahû:
setâ rajatayaṭṭhi ca latâ kañcanasannibhâ, |
nîlaṃ pîtaṃ lohitakaṃ odâtañ ca pabhassaraṃ
kâlakaṃ hoti sassirîkaṃ pupphasaṇṭhanatâdisaṃ, |
tathâpi pupphayaṭṭhi sâ, dijayaṭṭhi tathete,
dijâ yattha yathâvaṇṇe evaṃ tattha catuppade. |

---

7. Khîrena N. — Sîvalâ A, Sivalâ BG, Silâ N, Sivalî Z. Comp. 17, 76. — 8. Paṇḍuvâso abhisiñcayî A, °saṃ abhisiñcayi BG, °saṃ bhisiñcayi N, Vaṇḍuvâsaṃ abhisiñcayi Z. Comp. vv. 12. 39. It seems to me rather doubtful if we are to read „abhisiñcayuṃ" in all these passages. — 9. saṃvaccharaṃ Y, sabbabhûri N, sabbabhari G1. — hoti G1N, âsi Y. — arâjikâ A. — 10. Nâgadâse? — ekâbhisekam abhis° N; ekavîse 'bhisiñcayuṃ A2. — vv. 11—14 [anâgate] are wanting in BG2Z. — 11. sattarase vassâni Y. — 12. Muṭasîvo abhisiñcayi (°sivâtis° G1, °sivâbhis° G2) Y, Muṭasîvaṃ abhisiñcayi N. Comp. v. 8. — 14. asâḷhânakkh°. — 15. veḷuyaṭṭhî? — vv. 16 [kâlakaṃ] ... 17 [tath' eva te] are wanting in BG2. — 17. °[ya]ṭṭhî sâ N, yaṭṭhalatâ CM, °yaṭṭhilatâ R, °laṭṭhitâ AG1. — tath' eva te AG1, tathete N, tatheteti Z. — [dijâ ya]ttha yathâ[vaṇṇe evaṃ] tattha cat[uppade] N, dijâyaṭṭhi (°laṭṭhi BG1) latâvaṇṇa (°ṇṇo Z, °ṇṇe G1M2) evaṃ yaṭṭhi (laṭṭhi G1) catuppade Y. — The Samantapâsâdikâ contains the following quotation: vuttaṃ pi c' etaṃ Dîpavaṃse:

> Châtapabbatapâdamhi veṇuyaṭṭhi tayo ahu,
> setâ rajatayaṭṭhi ca latâ kañcanasannibhâ,
> nîlâdiyâdisaṃ pupphaṃ pupphayaṭṭhimhi tâdisaṃ,
> sakuṇâ sakuṇayaṭṭhimhi sarûpen' eva saṇṭhitâ 'ti.

We may try to correct vv. 15—17 in some such manner:

> setâ rajatayaṭṭhi ca, latâ kañcanasannibhâ;
> tathâpi pupphayaṭṭhi sâ, [tattha atimanoramaṃ] |

hayagajarathâ pattâ âmalakavalayamuddikâ
kakudhasadisâ nâma ete aṭṭha tadâ muttâ. |
uppanne Devânampiye tassâbhisekatejasâ
tayo maṇî âhariṃsu Malayâ ca janappadâ,
tayo yaṭṭhî Châtapâdâ, aṭṭha muttâ samuddakâ. |
maṇiyo Malayâ jâtâ râjârahâ mahâjanâ
20 Devânampiyapuññena anto sattâham âharuṃ. |
disvâna râjâ ratanaṃ mahagghañ ca mahârahaṃ
asamaṃ atulaṃ ratanaṃ acchariyam pi dullabhaṃ |
pasannacitto giram abbhudîrayi: ahaṃ sujâto kulino naraggo,
suciṇṇakammassa me îdisaṃ phalaṃ, ratanaṃ bahusatasahassajâtikaṃ |
laddhaṃ mama puññakammasambhavaṃ.
ko me arahati ratanânaṃ abhihâraṃ sampaṭicchituṃ, |
mâtâ pitâ ca bhâtâ vâ ñâtimittâ sakhâ ca me?
iti râjâ vicintento Asokaṃ khattiyaṃ sari. |
Devânampiyatisso ca Dhammâsoko narâbhibhû
25 adiṭṭhasahâyâ ubho kalyâṇâ daḷhabhattikâ. |
atthi me piyasahâyo Jambudîpassa issaro
Asokadhammo mahapuñño sakhâ pâṇasamo mama, |
so me arahati ratanânaṃ abhihâraṃ sampaṭicchituṃ,
aham pi dâtum arahâmi aggaṃ sâsanaṃ dhanaṃ. |
uṭṭhehi kattâra taramâno âdâya ratanaṃ imaṃ
Jambudîpavhayaṃ gantvâ nagaraṃ Pupphanâmakaṃ
aggaratanaṃ payacchehi Asokaṃ mama sahâyakaṃ. |

---

nîlaṃ pîtaṃ lohitakaṃ odâtañ ca pabhassaraṃ
kâḷakaṃ hoti sassirîkaṃ pupphasaṇṭhânasâdisaṃ; |
dijayaṭṭhi tath' eva sâ, [sajîvâ viya dissare]
dijâ yattha yathâvaṇṇâ evaṃ tattha catuppadâ. |

Comp. Mahâvaṃsa, p. 68.

18. kakudhâyavisâ Z, kakudhasadisâ N, kakudhâsavisâ ABG. kakudhapâkatikâ? — etâ aṭṭha? — Between vv. 18 and 19 probably a description was given of the three kinds of maṇi (see Mahâvaṃsa, p. 69, l. 2). Possibly the words „maṇiyo Malayâ jâtâ“ (v. 20) belonged to this lost passage. — 22. balaṃ Y, phalaṃ N. — bahuanekasah° N, bahuchakenasah° G1. — 23. In the collation of N, in the first hemistich the word „passatha“ is given, without any indication of the word it is intended to replace. laddhaṃ mama passatha puññasambhavaṃ? — 26. Jambudîpassa Y, Jambumaṇḍassa G1N. — 27. sâsanaṃ dhanaṃ ABG2, sâsanakaṃ dhanaṃ Z, sâsanaodanaṃ N, sâsanaṃ odakaṃ G1. pasâdhanaṃ dhanaṃ? — 28. uṭṭhehi kattâra N, uṭṭh° sattâ G1, aṭṭhehi muttehi Y. uṭṭhehi tâta? — payacchehi G1N, payacchehi Y. paṭicchehi? — mama sahâyakaṃ N, sahâyaṃ mama Y.

Mahâariṭṭho Sâlo ca brâhmaṇo Parantapabbato Putto Tisso ca gaṇako
... ime caturo dûte pâhesi Devânampiyo. |
pabhassaramaṇî tayo aṭṭha muttâvarâni ca
patodayaṭṭhittayañ c' etaṃ sañkharatanam uttamaṃ
bahuratanaṃ parivârena pâhesi Devânampiyo. |
amaccaṃ senâpatiṃ Ariṭṭhaṃ Sâlañ ca Paraṃcapabbataṃ
Puttaṃ Tissagaṇakañ ca batthe pâhesi khattiyo. |
chattañ câmarasañkhañ ca veṭhanaṃ kannabhûsanaṃ
Gañgodakañ ca bhiñkâraṃ sañkhañ ca sivikena ca |
nandiyâvaṭṭaṃ vaḍḍhamânaṃ râjâbhiseke pesitâ
adhovimaṃ vatthayugaṃ aggañ ca hatthapuñchanaṃ |
haricandanaṃ mahâagghaṃ aruṇavaṇṇamattikaṃ
harîtakaṃ âmalakaṃ imaṃ sâsanam pi pesayi: |
buddho dakkhiṇeyyân' aggo, dhammo aggo virâginaṃ,
saṃgho ca puññakkhettaggo, tîṇi aggâ sadevake. |
imañ câhaṃ namassâmi uttamatthâya khattiyo. |
pañca mâse vasitvâna te dûtâ caturo janâ
âdâya te paṇṇâkâraṃ Asokadhammena pesitaṃ |
visâkhamâse dvâdasapakkhe Jambudîpâ idhâgatâ.
abhisekaṃ saparivâraṃ Asokadhammena pesitaṃ |
dutiyaṃ abhisiñcittha râjânaṃ Devânampiyaṃ.
abhisitto dutiyâbhiseko visâkhamâse uposathe. |
tayo mâse atikkamma jeṭṭhamâse uposathe
Mahindo sattamo hutvâ Jambudîpâ idhâgato. |

râjâbhisekabhaṇḍaṃ niṭṭhitaṃ.
bhâṇavâraṃ ekâdasamaṃ.

---

29. Comp. Mahâvaṃsa Ṭîkâ: dijan ti Hâlipabbataṃ nâma brâhmaṇaṃ, amaccan ti Mallânâmakañ ca amaccaṃ, gaṇakan ti Gaṇakaputtatissaṃ nâma gaṇakañ câ 'ti. — 30. °ttayaṃ cetaṃ ABG2, °ttayaṃ ceva Z, sayaṃ câtaṃ G1, sayañjâta N. — bahuratanapar° A. — 31. Parantapabbataṃ? — haṭṭhe? — 32. chattaṃ ca sârapâmañgañ? comp. 12, 1. 17, 33. — kannasîvakaṃ G1N, kannabhûsanaṃ Y; kaṇṇabhûsanaṃ? — saṃkhaṃ Y, kaññaṃ N. — 33. râjâbhisekapesitâ X. — dussayugaṃ N, dukkavhagaṃ (corr. into dukkavagaṃ) G1, vatthayugaṃ ABG2Z. vatthakoṭiṃ? comp. 12, 2. 17, 34. — aggaṃ B, agghaṃ AG2, anaggaṃ CR, anagghaṃ M, ekaṃ G1N. — 36. uttamattâya ABG. After „khattiyo", one or two lines similar to 12, 6 are wanting. — 38. vesâkhamâse A. — 39. dutiyâbhisekena? comp. 17, 37. — vesâkhamâse! — 40. tato mâsaṃ ABG2.

XII.

Vâlavîjanim uṇhîsam khaggañ chattañ ca pâdukam
veṭhanam sârapâmañgam bhiṅkâram nandivaṭṭakam |
sivikam sañkham Gañgodakam adhovimam vatthakoṭiyam
suvaṇṇapâtikaṭacchum mahaggham hatthapuñchanam |
Anotattodakam kâjam uttamam haricandanam
aruṇavaṇṇamattikam añjanam nâgamâhaṭam |
harîtakam âmalakam mahaggham amatosadham
saṭṭhivâhasatam sâlim sugandham sukamâhaṭam
puññakammâbhinibbattam pâhesi Asokasavhayo. |
aham buddhañ ca dhammañ ca saṃghañ ca saraṇam gato
5 upâsakattam desemi Sakyaputtassa sâsane. |
imesu tîsu vatthusu uttame jinasâsane
tvam pi cittam pasâdehi saraṇam upehi satthuno. |
imam sambhâvanam katvâ Asokadhammo mahâyaso
pâhesi Devânampiyassa; gatadûtena te saha |
Asokârâme pavare bahû therâ mahiddhikâ
Lañkâtalânukampâya Mahindam etad abravum: |
samayo Lañkâdîpamhi patiṭṭhâpetu sâsanam,
gacchatu tvam mahâpuñña pasâda dîpalañjakam. |
paṇḍito sutasampanno Mahindo dîpajotako
10 saṃghassa vacanam sutvâ sampaṭicchi sahaggaṇo |
ekamsañ cîvaram katvâ paggahetvâna añjalim
abhivâdayitvâ sirasâ: gacchâmi dîpalañjakam. |
Mahindo nâma nâmena saṃghathero tadâ ahû,
Iṭṭhiyo Uttiyo thero Bhaddasâlo ca Sambalo |

XII, 1—6. Comp. 17, 83 et seq. These verses are quoted („vuttam pi c' etam Dîpavaṃse") in the Samantapâsâdikâ. — 2. Instead of „Gañgodakam adhovimam" the Samantap. reads „vaṭaṃsañ ca adhovim". — °koṭikam, the Samantap. — 5. upâsakattam vedesim, the Samantap. — 6. saddhâsaraṇam upehisi, the Samantap. — 7. samasamam N, chamagham (corrected into samasamam) G1, sambhâvanam ABG2Z. — gatam dûtena BGZ. — 9. gaccha tuvam A. — pasâda (°dâ BG) dîpalaṃcakam ABG, pasâda dîpalañjakam N, Lañkâdîpam pasâditum Z. pasâdaya dîp°? I cannot give any satisfactory explanation of the last word, which is spelt in N with ñj, in the other MSS. frequently with ñc, sometimes with ñch. In the Apadâna (Phayre MS., fol. khai) it is said of a Buddha wo is going to cross the Gañgâ: âgantvâna ca sambuddho âruhi nâvalañcakam. Prof. E. Kuhn proposes to take °lañjaka as connected with sansc. lañja which the lexicographers give as a synonym of kaccha.

sâmaṇero ca Sumano chaḷabhiñño mahiddhiko,
ime pañca mahâtherâ chaḷabhiññâ mahiddhikâ
Asokârâmamhâ nikkhantâ caramânâ sahaggaṇâ, |
anupubbena caramânâ Vedissagiriyaṃ gatâ.
vihâre Vedissagirimhi vasitvâ yâvadicchakaṃ |
mâtaraṃ anusâsetvâ saraṇe sîle uposathe
patiṭṭhapesi saddhamme sâsane dîpavâsinaṃ. |
sâyaṇhe paṭisallâna Mahindathero mahâgaṇî
samayaṃ vâ asamayaṃ vâ vicintesi rahogato. |
terasaṃkappaṃ aññâya Sakko devânam issaro
pâtur ahû therasammukhe santike ajjhabhâsatha: |
kâlo te hi mahâvîra Laṅkâdîpapasâdanaṃ,
khippaṃ gaccha varadîpaṃ anukampâya pâṇinaṃ. |
Laṅkâdîpavaraṃ gaccha dhammaṃ desehi pâṇinaṃ,
pakâsaya catusaccaṃ satte mocehi bandhanâ. |
sâsanaṃ buddhajeṭṭhassa Laṅkâdîpamhi jotaya.
byâkataṃ c' asi nâgassa bhikkhusaṃgho ca sammato, |
ahaṃ ca veyyâvatikaṃ Laṅkâdîpassa câgame
karomi sabbakiccâni, samayo pakkamituṃ tayâ. |
Sakkassa vacanaṃ sutvâ Mahindo dîpajotako
bhagavatâ subyâkato bhikkhusaṃghena sammato |
Sakko ca maṃ samâyâci, patiṭṭhissâmi sâsanaṃ.
gacchâm' ahaṃ Tambapaṇṇiṃ, nipuṇâ Tambapaṇṇikâ, |
sabbadukkhakkhayaṃ maggaṃ na suṇanti subhâsitaṃ.
tesaṃ pakâsayissâmi, gamissaṃ dîpalañjakaṃ. |
kâlaññû samayaññû ca Mahindo Asokatrajo
gamanaṃ Laṅkâtalaṃ ñatvâ âmantayi sahaggaṇe
Mahindo gaṇapâmokkho samânupajjhâyake catu, |
sâmaṇero ca Sumano Bhaṇḍuko ca upâsako,
channañ ca chaḷabhiññânaṃ pakâsesi mahiddhiko: |

---

14. Vedissagiriyaṃgatâ N, Vediyagirisaṃgatâ G1, Cetiyagirisaṃgatâ Y. Vedissagirikaṃ gatâ? — Cetiyagirimhi ABG, Cetiyagiri Z, Vedissagirimhi N. — 16. paṭisallîno? — 17. terasaṃkappaṃ N, tesaṃ saṃk° Y, therasaṃkappaṃ? — 20. byâkataṃ casi (câsi N) nâgassa G1N, byâkato Sakyasîho ca (°sîho A) ABG2, byâkate Sakyasîhassa Z. byâkato c' asi nâgassa? — 23. patiṭṭhassâmi G1. patiṭṭhapessâmi? — 25. „Laṅkâtalaṃ" may be the correct reading; I should prefer, however, „kâlâkâlaṃ" (the right and the wrong time). — sahaggaṇo N, sahagaṇo BG2, sahâgaṇe AZ, samâgaṇe G1.

âyâma bahulaṃ ajja Laṅkâdîpaṃ varuttamaṃ, pasâdema bahû satte, patiṭṭhâpessâma sâsanaṃ. |

sâdhû 'ti te paṭissutvâ sabbe attamanâ ahû: gacchâma bhante samayo nage Missakanâmake, râjâ ca so nikkhamati katvâna migavaṃ purâ. |

Sakko tuṭṭho vâsavindo Mahindatherassa santike paṭisallânagatassa idaṃ vacanam abravi: |

mârisa tvam pi bhagavatâ subyâkato: anâgatamaddhâne Mahindo bhikkhu dîpaṃ pasâdayissati, vitthârikaṃ karissati jinasâsanaṃ, anupavattissati dhammacakkaṃ, satte mahâdukkhâ uddharitvâ thale patiṭṭhâpessati, bahujanahitâya paṭipajjissati bahujanasukhâya lokânukampâya atthâya hitâya sukhâya devamanussânan ti. |

evañ ca pana bhagavatâ niddiṭṭho idâni etarahi therena ca âṇatto bhikkhûhi ca dîpapasâdanâya. kâlo mahâvîra dîpaṃ pasâdetuṃ, samayo mahâvîra dîpaṃ pasâdetuṃ, tuyh' eso vâro anuppatto, vahassu etaṃ bhâraṃ, pasâdehi Tambapaṇṇiṃ, vitthârikaṃ karohi jinasâsanaṃ. ahaṃ tava sisso pubbuṭṭhâyî paṭṭhacaro veyyâvaccakaro homîti. |

bhagavato satthuno vacanaṃ sampaṭicchitvâ Tambapaṇṇiṃ târessâmi âlokañ ca dassessâmi, jinatejaṃ sammâ vaḍḍhissami. aññânabhavatimirapaṭalapihitapaṭikujjitâ issâmaccheraparetadandhaduddhammavipallâsânuggatâ kummaggapaṭipanna vipathe pakkhantâ tantâ kulakajâtâ gulâguṇṭhikajâtâ muñjababbajabhûtâ aññânabhavatimiraavijjandhakârâ nîvaraṇakilesasakalabhûtâ mahâtimiraavijjandhakârena âvutaophuṭapihitapaṭicchannapariyonaddhâ Tambapaṇṇi. |

---

27. lahuṃ ABG2, balaṃ Z, bahulaṃ G1N. — 28. nagaṃ °makaṃ ABG2. — 30. Mahindo nâma bhikkhu A. Comp. the following passage which occurs identical both in the Samantapâs. and in the Thûpavaṃsa: „sammâsambuddhena ca tumhe byâkatâ anâgate Mahindo nâma bhikkhu Tambapaṇṇidîpaṃ pasâdessatîti". — anuppavattessati? — phale ABG2. — 31. paṭhacaro N. piṭṭhacaro? I owe this conjecture to M. Senart. — homîti N, niddiṭṭhaṃ A, niddiṭṭhiṃ B, niṭṭhiṭṭhiṃ G, niccaṃ Z. — 32. târessâmi AZ, târassâmi BG, tarissâmi N. — sambhâyissâmi N, sammâ vaḍḍhissâmi ABG2, sammâ vayissâmi G1, vaḍḍhissâmi Z. sammâ vaḍḍhessâmi? — °paretâ dandha°? — °paṭipannâ? — Comp. Grimblot, Sept. S., p. 245. — °kilesajâlabb° A, °kilesajalabh° BG2, °kilesasalabh° G1, °kilesasalilabh° Z, kilesasakalabh° N. kilesasakalâbhibhûtâ? — °ophuṭa° N, °omuka° A, °omukka° BG2, °omuta° G1Z.

avijjandhakâraṃ bhinditvâ âlokaṃ dassayissâmi, jotayissâmi kevalaṃ Tambapaṇṇiṃ jinasâsanan ti. evam ussâhito ca pana vâsavindena devarâjena evaṃvâcasiṃkena uṭṭhâya paṭisallânâ viriyapâramippatto apalokayi bhikkhusaṃghan ti. |

gacchâma mayaṃ Tambapaṇṇiṃ, nipuṇâ Tambapaṇṇikâ,
sabbadukkhakkhayaṃ maggaṃ na suṇanti subhâsitaṃ.
tesaṃ santappayissâma gacchâma dîpalañjakan ti. |
Vedissagiriye ramme vasitvâ tiṃsa rattiyo:
kâlañ ca gamanaṃ dâni, gacchâma dîpam uttamaṃ. |
palinâ Jambudîpato haṃsarâjâ va ambare,
evam uppatitâ therâ nipatiṃsu naguttame. |
purato puraseṭṭhassa pabbate meghasannibhe
patiṭṭhahiṃsu Missakakûṭamhi haṃsâ va nagamuddhani. |
Mahindo nâma nâmena saṃghatthero tadâ ahû,
Iṭṭhiyo Uttiyo thero Bhaddasâlo ca Sambalo |
sâmaṇero ca Sumano Bhaṇḍuko ca upâsako,
sabbe mahiddhikâ ete Tambapaṇṇipasâdakâ. |
tattha uppatito thero haṃsarâjâ va ambare
purato puraseṭṭhassa pabbate meghasannibhe |
patiṭṭhito Missakakûṭamhi haṃsâ va nagamuddhani.
tasmiñ ca samaye râjâ Tambapaṇṇimhi issaro |
Devânampiyatisso so Muṭasîvassa atrajo.
Asoko abhisitto ca vassaṃ aṭṭhârasaṃ ahû, |
Tissassa ca abhisitte sattamâse anûnake
Mahindo dvâdasavasso Jambudîpâ idhâgato. |
gimhâne pacchime mâse jeṭṭhamâse uposathe anurâdha-jeṭṭhanakkhatte
Mahindo gaṇapâmokkho Missakagirim âgato. |
migavaṃ nikkhami râjâ, Missakagirim upâgami.
devo gokaṇṇarûpena râjânaṃ abhidassayi. |

33. jotayissâmi is wanting in Y. — âlokaṃ dassayissâmi kevalaṃ Tambapaṇṇiṃ, jotayissâmi jinasâsanan ti? — °vâcayitena A, °vâcayiṃtena BG2. evaṃvâcakena? — 34. tesaṃ pakâsayissâma? (comp. v. 24.) — 35. Cetiyagiriye AZ, Cetiye g° BG, Vedissagîriye N. — Samantap.: kâlo ca gamanassâ 'ti. I believe that we ought to adopt this reading in the Dîpavaṃsa also. — 36. patitâ AG2, patinâ B, paṭinâ G1, palinâ N, Samantap.; idaṃ vatvâ mahâvîro uggaṃchi Z. paḷînâ? — 40. uppatitâ therâ? — 41. patiṭṭhitâ? — 44. gimhânaṃ GN, °na B, °ne AZ. — °girim âgato ABG2, °gîrim uggato N, °giripabbato G1, °giripabbate Z.

disvâna râjâ gokaṇṇaṃ tararûpo 'va pakkami,
piṭṭhito anugacchanto pâvisi pabbatantaraṃ. |
tatth' eva antaradhâyi yakkho therassa sammukhâ,
nisinnaṃ theraṃ adakkhi, bhîto râjâ ahû tadâ. |
mamaṃ yeva passatu râjâ eko ekaṃ, na bhâyati,
samâgate balakâye atho passatu bhikkhunaṃ. |
tatth' addasaṃ khattiyabhûmipâlaṃ paduṭṭharûpaṃ migavañ carantaṃ,
nâmena taṃ âlapi khattiyassa: âgaccha Tissâ 'ti tadâ avoca. |
ko 'yaṃ kâsâvavasano muṇḍo saṃghâṭipâruto
50 eko adutiyo vâcaṃ bhâsati maṃ amânusiṃ? |
samaṇo 'ti maṃ manussalokeyaṃ khattiya pucchasi bhûmipâla.
samaṇâ mayaṃ mahârâja dhammarâjassa sâvakâ
tam eva anukampâya Jambudîpâ idhâgatâ. |
âvudhaṃ nikkhipitvâna ekamantaṃ upâvisi,
nisajja râjâ sammodi bahuṃ atthûpasaṃhitaṃ. |
sutvâ therassa vacanaṃ nikkhipitvâna âvudhaṃ
tato theraṃ upagantvâ sammoditvâ ca pâvisi. |
amaccabalakâyo ca anupubbaṃ samâgatâ
parivâretvâna aṭṭhaṃsu cattârîsa sahassiyo. |
disvâ nisinnatherânaṃ balakâye samâgate:
55 aññe atthi bahû bhikkhû sammâsambuddhasâvakâ? |
tevijjâ iddhipattâ ca cetopariyakovidâ
khîṇâsavâ arahanto bahû buddhassa sâvakâ. |
ambopamena jânitvâ paṇḍit' âyaṃ arindamo
desesi tattha suttantaṃ hatthipadam anuttaraṃ. |
sutvâna taṃ dhammavaraṃ saddhâjâto va buddhimâ
cattârîsasahassâni saraṇaṃ te upâgamuṃ. |
tato attamano râjâ tuṭṭhahaṭṭho pamodito
âmantayi bhikkhusaṃghaṃ: gacchâma nagaraṃ puraṃ. |

---

46. tararûpo N, tadarûpo G1, tathârûpo Y. — 49. addasa A. — duṭṭhar° ABG, paduṭṭhar° Zn. — 51. The first line (samaṇo — bhûmipâla) is given in AG1N only, the second (samaṇâ — sâvakâ) in ABG2Z; in A in which both lines are given *manu prima*, the first is included in brackets. I believe, that both are written by the author of the Dîpavaṃsa; see the Introduction, p. 6. — °lokiyaṃ? — pucchasi N, passasi A, pacchasi G1. — 53. sammoditvâna Y, °tvâ ca N. — c' upâvisi! — 59. 60. Probably we ought to transpose these two verses.

Devânavhayarâjânaṃ subbataṃ sabalavâhanaṃ
paṇḍitaṃ buddhisampannaṃ khippam eva pasâdayi. |
sutvâna rañño vacanaṃ Mahindo etad abravi:
gacchasi tvaṃ mahârâja, vasissâma mayaṃ idha. |
uyyojetvâna râjânaṃ Mahindo dîpajotako
âmantayi bhikkhusaṃghaṃ: pabbâjessâma Bhaṇḍukaṃ. |
therassa vacanaṃ sutvâ sabbe turitamânasâ
gâmasîmaṃ vicinitvâ pabbâjetvâna Bhaṇḍukaṃ,
upasampadañ ca tatth' eva arahattañ ca pâpuṇi. |
girimuddhani ṭhito thero sârathiṃ ajjhabhâsatha:
alaṃ yânaṃ na kappati paṭikkhittaṃ tathâgataṃ. |
uyyojetvâna sârathiṃ thero vasî mahiddhiko
gagane haṃsarâjâ va pakkamiṃsu vehâyasâ,
orohetvâna gaganâ paṭhaviyaṃ patiṭṭhitâ. |
nivâsanaṃ nivâsente pârupite ca cîvaraṃ
disvâna sârathi tuṭṭho râjânañ ca pavedayi. |
pesetvâ sârathiṃ râjâ amacce ajjhabhâsatha:
maṇḍapaṃ paṭiyâdetha antonivesane pure. |
kumârâ kumâriyo ca itthâgârañ ca deviyo
dassanaṃ abhikañkhantâ there passantu âgate. |
sutvâna rañño vacanaṃ amaccâ kulajâtikâ
antonivesanamajjhe akaṃsu dussamaṇḍapaṃ. |
vitânañ châditaṃ vatthaṃ suddhaṃ setaṃ sunimmalaṃ
dhajasañkhaparivâraṃ setavatthehi 'laṃkataṃ, |
vikiṇṇavâlukâ setâ setapupphasusanthatâ
alaṃkatamaṇḍapâ setâ himagabbhasamûpamâ. |
sabbasetehi vatthehi alaṃkâretvâna maṇḍapaṃ
abbhantaraṃ samaṃ katvâ râjânaṃ paṭivedayuṃ: |
pariniṭṭhitaṃ mahârâja maṇḍapaṃ sukataṃ subhaṃ,
âsanaṃ deva jânâhi pabbajitânulomikaṃ. |
taṃkhaṇe sârathi rañño anuppatto paveditum:

60. Devânavhayarâjânaṃ (°vharâj° M) Y, Devânampiyarâjânaṃ N. — 61. gacchâhi? — 64. tathâgate? With regard to the grammatical construction comp. 14, 22. 62. — 65. therâ v° mahiddhikâ? — ârohitvâna Z, ârohetvâna ABG, orohetvâna N. orohitvâna? — 66. [pârupî]te N, pârupîtaṃ Z, °pitaṃ A, phârupitañ B, phârûpîtañ G. pârupante? — 69. kulapubbajâ G1, kulapabbajâ N. — antonivesane majjhe Y. — 71. alaṃkatamaṇḍapâ seems to be corrupted; only one maṇḍapa was constructed (see also Mahâvaṃsa, p. 82, l. 2). °maṇḍapaṃ setaṃ °maṃ? — 72. abhuttaraṃ N, abbhuntara G1. — 74. pavedayi (°yî A, yiṃ B) ABG2.

yânaṃ deva na kappati bhikkhusaṃghassa nisîdituṃ. |
ayaṃ acchariyaṃ deva sabbe therâ mahiddhikâ
75 paṭhamaṃ maṃ uyyojetvâ pacchâ hutvâ pur' âgatâ. |
uccâsayanamahâsayanaṃ bhikkhûnaṃ na ca kappati,
bhummattharaṇañ jânâtha te therâ âgacchanti. |
sârathissa vaco sutvâ râjâpi tuṭṭhamânaso
paccuggantvâna therânaṃ abhivâdetvâ sammodayi. |
pattaṃ gahetvâ therânaṃ saha therehi khattiyo
pûjento gandhamâlehi râjadvâram upâgami. |
rañño antepuraṃ thero pavisetvâna maṇḍapaṃ
addasa santhataṃ bhûmiṃ âsanaṃ dussavâritaṃ. |
nisîdiṃsu yathâpaññatte âsane dussavârite,
80 nisinne udakaṃ datvâ yâguṃ datvâna khajjakaṃ |
paṇîtaṃ bhojanaṃ rañño sahatthâ sampavârayi.
bhuttâvibhojanaṃ theraṃ onîtapattapâṇinaṃ |
âmantayi Anulâdeviṃ saha antoghare jane:
okâsañ jânâtha devi, kâlo te payirupâsituṃ. |
therânaṃ abhivâdetvâ pûjetvâ yâvadicchakaṃ
Anulâ nâma mahesî kaññâpañcasatâvatâ |
upasaṃkamitvâ therânaṃ abhivâdetvâ upâvisi.
tesaṃ dhammaṃ adesesi petavatthuṃ bhayânakaṃ |
vimânaṃ saccasaṃyuttaṃ pakâsesi mahâgaṇî.
85 sutvâna taṃ dhammavaraṃ saddhâjâtâ vibuddhimâ |
Anulâ mahesî sahakaññâpañcasatâ tadâ
sotâpattiphale 'ṭṭhaṃsu, paṭhamâbhisamayo ahû. |

bhâṇavâraṃ dvâdasamaṃ.

---

74. °saṃghena N, °saṃghe G1. — 75. aho acchariyam? — 76. âgacchanti Y (âgacchante G1), agacchante N. — 79. pavisitvâna! — âsane dussacâruke ABG2, âsanaṃ (âsana G1) dussavâritaṃ G1N, âsanaṃ dussalaṃkataṃ Z. âs° dussacchâditaṃ? — 80. yathâbuḍḍhaṃ santhate dussapîṭhake A, yathâpaññatte âsane dussavârite (dussavirite G1, dussasanthate BG2, dussapasârite Z) BGNZ. dussacchâdite? — 81. râjâ sahatthâ? vv. 81. 82 give a fair specimen of the grammatical incorrectness which prevails through the whole Dîpavaṃsa. I do not think that we ought to make any corrections, or that anything is wanting. The passage of the ancient Sinhalese Aṭṭhakathâ of which this is a metrical paraphrase, has been rendered thus in the Samantap.: „râjâ there paṇîtena khâdaniyena bhojaniyena sahatthâ santappetvâ sampavâretvâ Anulâdevîpamukhâni pañca itthisatâni therânaṃ abhivâdanaṃ pûjâsakkârañ ca karontû 'ti pakkosâpetvâ ekamantaṃ nisîdi." — 83. This stanza is wanting in BG2. — °vatâ AG1, ca tâ Zn. — 84. tâsaṃ? — 85. vibuddhimâ N, bhibuddhimâ Y. saddhâjâto va buddhimâ (comp. v. 58)?

XIII.

Adiṭṭhapubbâ gaṇâ sabbe janakâyâ samâgatâ
râjanivesanadvâre mahâsadd' ânusâvayuṃ. |
sutvâ râjâ mahâsaddaṃ upayuttamakampuraṃ:
kimatthâya puthû sabbe mahâsenâ samâgatâ? |
ayaṃ deva mahâsenâ saṃghadassanam âgatâ,
dassanaṃ alabhamânâ mahâsaddaṃ akaṃsu te. |
antepuraṃ susambâdhaṃ janakâyâ patiṭṭhituṃ,
hatthisâlaṃ asambâdhaṃ, theraṃ passantu te janâ. |
bhuttâvi anumodetvâ uṭṭhahitvâna âsanâ
râjagharâ nikkhamitvâ hatthisâlaṃ upâgami. | 5
hatthisâlamhi pallaṅkaṃ paññâpesuṃ mahârahaṃ,
nisîdi pallaṅkavare Mahindo dîpajotako. |
nisinna pallaṅkavare Mahindo gaṇapuṃgavo
kathesi tattha suttantaṃ devadûtaṃ varuttamaṃ. |
sutvâna devadûtan taṃ pubbakammaṃ sudâruṇaṃ
bhîtâ saṃvegaṃ âpâduṃ nirayabhayatajjitâ. |
ñatvâ bhayaṭṭite satte catusaccaṃ pakâsayi.
pariyosâne sahassânaṃ dutiyâbhisamayo ahû. |
hatthisâlamhâ nikkhamma mahâjanapurakkhato
tosayanto bahû satte buddho Râjagahe yathâ. | 10
nagaramhâ dakkhiṇadvâre nikkhamitvâ mahâjanâ
Mahânandavanaṃ nâma uyyânaṃ dakkhiṇâ pure, |
râjuyyânamhi pallaṅkaṃ paññâpesuṃ mahârahaṃ,
tattha thero nisîditvâ kathesi dhammam uttamaṃ. |
kathesi tattha suttantaṃ bâlapaṇḍitam uttamaṃ,
tattha pâṇasahassânaṃ dhammâbhisamayo ahû. |
mahâsamâgamo âsi uyyâne Nandane tadâ,
kulagharaṇî kumârî ca kulasuṇhâ kulaputtiyo |

XIII, 1. gaṇâ N, vanâ G2, te Y. — 2. upasaṃkamma tepitaṃ A, upasaṃkamma taṃ janaṃ Z, upasaṃkamma kâritaṃ B, upayaṃkamma kâritaṃ G2, upayuttam akaṃpuraṃ N, upayuttanakaṃ mayaṃ G1. I refrain from offering any conjecture. — 7. nisinno AB. — 8. bhîtâ saṃvegam âpâduṃ N, bhîtâ saṃtemâpâruṃ G1, bhîtiṃ sattâ (satte Z) pâpuniṃsu Y. — 10. °sâlâya Y, °sâlama G1, °sâlamhâ N. — 11. dakkhinadvâro A1, °râ A2BG2, °re G1Zn. dakkhiṇadvârâ? comp. 14, 11. 55. — Mahânandavanaṃ BGN, °nandanavanaṃ AZ. — dakkhiṇâ pure N, dakkhine pure ABG2, dakkhiṇaṃ puraṃ G1Z. dakkhiṇâ (°ṇaṃ?) purâ?

saṃgharitâ tadâ hutvâ theraṃ dassanam âgatâ.
15 tehi saddhiṃ sammodento sâyaṇhasamayo ahû. |
idh' eva therâ vasantu uyyâne Mahânandane,
atisâyaṃ gamîyantâ ito dûre giribbaje. |
accâsannañ ca gâmantaṃ vippakiṇṇamahâjanaṃ,
rattiṃ saddo mahâ hoti, Sakkasâlûpamaṃ imaṃ
paṭisallânasâruppaṃ alaṃ gacchâma pabbataṃ. |
Mahâmeghavanaṃ nâma uyyânaṃ vivittaṃ mama
gamanâgamanasampannaṃ nâtidûre na santike, |
atthikânaṃ manussânaṃ abhikkamanasukhâgamaṃ,
appakiṇṇaṃ divâ saddena, rattiṃ saddo na jâyati, |
paṭisallânasâruppaṃ pabbajitânulomikaṃ
20 dassanachâyâsampannaṃ pupphaphaladharaṃ subhaṃ |
vatiyâ suparikkhittaṃ dvâraṭṭâlasugopitaṃ,
râjadvâraṃ suvibhattaṃ uyyâne me manorame, |
suvibhattâ pokkharaṇî saṃchannaṃ padumuppaḷaṃ
sîtûdakaṃ supatiṭṭhaṃ sâdupupphabhigandhiyaṃ. |
evaṃ rammaṃ mam' uyyânaṃ sahasaṃghassa phâsukaṃ,
âvasatu tahiṃ thero, mam' atthaṃ anukampatu. |
sutvâna rañño vacanaṃ Mahindo thero sahagaṇo
amaccasaṃghaparibbûḷho agamâ Meghavanaṃ tadâ. |
âyâcito narindena Mahindathero mahâgaṇî
Mahâmeghavanuyyânaṃ pâvisi yuttajâtikaṃ,
25 uyyâne râjavatthumhi avasi thero mahâgaṇî. |
dutiye puna divase râjâ therân' upâgami
abhivâdetvâ sirasâ râjâ therânam abravî: |
kacci te sukhaṃ sayittha, phâsuvâso tuyhaṃ idha?
vivittaṃ utusampannaṃ manussarâhaseyyakaṃ |
paṭisallânasâruppaṃ sappâyañ ca senâsanaṃ.
tato attamano râjâ haṭṭho saṃviggamânaso |
añjaliṃ paggahetvâna idaṃ vacanaṃ abravî,
sovaṇṇabhiṅkâraṃ gahetvâ onojesi mahîpati: |

---

15. saṃgharitâ N, saṃghariva (°rîva M) Y. saṃghaṭitâ? — tâhi saddhiṃ sammodente? — 16. gamiyantâ BG, gamayantâ A, gamîyantâ Zn. Samantap.: „akâlo bhante idâni tattha gantuṃ.“ I conjecture „agamanîyaṃ“. — 19. appâkiṇṇaṃ BG. — 22. sâdupupphabhigandhiyaṃ N, sâdusuppagandhiyaṃ G1, sâdhu- (sâdhuka- Z) suppagandhiyaṃ Y. sâdupupphâbhigandhitaṃ? — 23. âvasatu N, âsevatu BGZ, âsavetu A. — 25. yuttajâtikaṃ (suttaj° G1) Y, suddhajâtikaṃ N. — 26. kacci vo? — 29. We ought to transpose the two hemistichs.

im âhaṃ bhante uyyânaṃ Mahâmeghavanaṃ subhaṃ
câtuddisassa saṃghassa dadâmi, paṭigaṇhatha. | 30
narindavacanaṃ sutvâ Mahindo dîpajotako
paṭiggahesi uyyânaṃ saṃghârâmassa kâraṇâ. |
dadantaṃ paṭigaṇhantassa Mahâmeghavanaṃ tadâ
kampittha paṭhavî tattha nânâgajjitakampanaṃ. |
patiṭṭhapesi saṃghassa narindo Tissasavhayo,
Mahâmeghavanuyyânaṃ Tissârâmaṃ akaṃsu taṃ. |
patiṭṭhapesi saṃghassa paṭhamaṃ Devânampiyo
Mahâmeghavanaṃ nâma ârâmaṃ sâsanârahaṃ. |
tatthâpi paṭhavî kampi abbhutaṃ lomahaṃsanaṃ.
lomahaṭṭhâ janâ sabbe there pucchittha sarâjikâ. | 35
imaṃ paṭhamaṃ vihâraṃ Laṅkâdîpe varuttame,
sâsânarûhanatâya paṭhamaṃ paṭhavikampanaṃ. |
disvâ acchariyaṃ sabbe abbhutaṃ lomahaṃsanaṃ
celukkhepaṃ pavattiṃsu, n' atthi îdisakaṃ pure. |
tato attamano râjâ vedajâto katañjali
upanâmesi bahuṃ pupphaṃ Mahindaṃ dîpajotakaṃ. |
pupphaṃ thero gahetvâna ekokâse pamuñcayi,
tatthâpi paṭhavî kampi dutiyaṃ paṭhavikampanaṃ. |
idam pi acchariyaṃ disvâ râjasenâ saraṭṭhakâ
ukkuṭṭhisaddaṃ pavattiṃsu dutiyaṃ paṭhavikampanaṃ. | 40
bhiyyo cittaṃ pasâdetvâ râjâpi tuṭṭhamânaso:
mama kaṅkhaṃ vitârehi dutiyaṃ paṭhavikampanaṃ. |
saṃghakammaṃ karissanti akuppaṃ sâsanârahaṃ,
idh' okâse mahârâja mâlakan taṃ bhavissati. |
bhiyyo attamano râjâ pupphaṃ theraṃ abhîhari,
thero pupphaṃ gahetvâna aparokâse pamuñcayi.
tatthâpi paṭhavî kampi tatiyaṃ paṭhavikampanaṃ. |
kimatthâya mahâvîra tatiyaṃ paṭhavikampanaṃ?
sabbe kaṅkhâ vihârehi akkhâhi kusalo tuvaṃ. |
jantâgharapokkharaṇî idh' okâse bhavissati,
bhikkhû jantâgharaṃ ettha paripûrissanti sabbadâ. | 45

---

32. paṭigaṇhante (pat° A) ABG2. — 36. sâsanârûhanatâya N, sâsanar° AG, sâsanarûhatâya B, sâsanarûhanâtâya Z. sâsanassârûḷhatâya? — 40. pi is wanting in Y. — 41. vihârehi ABG, vinodehi Z. — 44. AZ omit sabbe-tuvaṃ. — vitârehi? — 45. paripûrissanti N, paripûriyavanti ABG, paripûrayanti Z.

uḷâraṃ pîtipâmojjaṃ janetvâ Devânampiyo
upanâmesi therassa jâtipupphaṃ suphullitaṃ, |
thero ca pupphaṃ âdâya aparokâse pamuñcayi,
tatthâpi paṭhavî kampi catutthaṃ paṭhavikampanaṃ. |
idaṃ acchariyaṃ disvâ mahâjanâ samâgatâ
añjaliṃ paggahetvâna namassanti mahiddhikaṃ. |
tato attamano râjâ tuṭṭho pucchi anantaraṃ:
kimatthâya mahâvîra catutthaṃ paṭhavikampanaṃ? |
Sakyaputto mahâvîro assatthadumasantike
sabbadhammaṃ paṭibujjhi buddho âsi anuttaro,
50 so dumo idham okâse patiṭṭhissaṃ diputtame. |
sutvâ attamano râjâ tuṭṭho saṃviggamânaso
upanâmesi therassa jâtipupphaṃ varuttamaṃ. |
thero ca pupphaṃ âdâya bhûmibhâge pamuñcayi,
tatthâpi paṭhavî kampi pañcamaṃ paṭhavikampanaṃ. |
tam pi acchariyaṃ disvâ râjâsenâ saraṭṭhakâ
ukkuṭṭhisaddaṃ pavattiṃsu, celukkhepaṃ pavattitha. |
kimatthâya mahâpañña pañcamaṃ paṭhavikampanaṃ?
etam atthaṃ pavakkhâhi tava chandavasânugâ. |
anvaddhamâsaṃ pâtimokkhaṃ uddisissanti te tadâ,
55 uposathagharaṃ nâma idh' okâse bhavissati. |
aparam pi ca okâse theraṃ pupphavaraṃ adâ,
thero ca puppham âdâya tamokâse pamuñcayi.
tatthâpi paṭhavî kampi chaṭṭhaṃ paṭhavikampanaṃ. |
idam pi acchariyaṃ disvâ mahâjanâ samâgatâ
aññamaññaṃ pamodanti vihâro hissatî idha. |
bhiyyo cittaṃ pasâdetvâ râjâ therânam abravi:
kimatthâya mahâpañña chaṭṭhaṃ paṭhavikampanaṃ? |
yâvatâ saṃghikâ lâbhaṃ bhikkhusaṃghâ samâgatâ
idh' okâse mahârâja labhissanti anâgate. |

---

50. paṭibujjhi N, paṭicchi G1, paṭivijjhi Y. — idham okâse patiṭṭhissanti (°ssaṃti G2) uttamo ABG2, i° o° patiṭṭhissaṃ diputtame G1N, idha hessati Z. i° o° patiṭṭhissati diputtame (comp. Mah., p. 86, l. 11)? — 53. râjasenâ! — °ukkhepe pavattitha ABG, [°ukkhepaṃ pava]ttitha N, °ukkhepa (°paṃ M) pavattayuṃ Z. — 54. etam atthaṃ mam' akkhâhi? — °ânugaṃ ABG2, °ânugâ G1Zn. — 57. aññamaññe kaṃkhanti vihârehirâjeti idha ABG2, aññamaññaṃ pamodanti vihâro hissatî (hiraññati G1) idha G1N; in Z the hemistich is wanting. aññamaññaṃ pamodenti vihâro hessatî idha? — 59. lâbhâ?

sutvâ therassa vacanaṃ râjâpi tuṭṭhamânaso
upanâmesi therassa râjâ pupphaṃ varuttamaṃ, |
thero ca pupphaṃ âdâya aparokâse pamuñcayi,
tatthâpi paṭhavî kampi sattamaṃ paṭhavikampanaṃ. |
disvâ acchariyaṃ sabbe râjasenâ saraṭṭhakâ
celukkhepaṃ pavattiṃsu kampite dharaṇîtale. |
kimatthâya mahâpañña sattamaṃ paṭhavikampanaṃ?
byâkarohi mahâpañña, gaṇaṃ kaṅkhâ vitâratha. |
yâvatâ imasmiṃ vihâre âvasanti supesalâ
bhattaggaṃ bhojanasâlaṃ idh' okâse bhavissati. |

bhâṇavâraṃ terasamaṃ.

XIV.

Therassa vacanaṃ sutvâ râjâ bhiyyo pasîdati,
aladdhâ campakaṃ pupphaṃ therassa abhihârayi. |
thero campakapupphâni pamuñcittha mahîtale,
tatthâpi paṭhavî kampi aṭṭhamaṃ paṭhavikampanaṃ. |
imaṃ acchariyaṃ disvâ râjasenâ saraṭṭhakâ
ukkuṭṭhisaddaṃ pavattiṃsu, celukkhepaṃ pavattitha. |
kimatthâya mahâvîra aṭṭhamaṃ paṭhavikampanaṃ?
byâkarohi mahâpañña, suṇoma tava bhâsato. |
tathâgatassa dhâtuyo aṭṭha doṇâ sârîrikâ,
ekaṃ doṇaṃ mahârâja âharitvâ mahiddhikâ |
idh' okâse niharitvâ thûpaṃ kâhanti sobhanaṃ
saṃvegajananaṭṭhânaṃ bahujanapasâdanaṃ. |
samâgatâ janâ sabbe râjasenâ saraṭṭhakâ
ukkuṭṭhisaddaṃ pavattiṃsu mahâpaṭhavikampane. |
Tissârâme vasitvâna vîtivattâya rattiyâ
nivâsanaṃ nivâsetvâ pârupetvâna cîvaraṃ |
tato pattaṃ gahetvâna pâvisi nagaraṃ puraṃ.
piṇḍacâraṃ caramâno râjadvâraṃ upâgami. |
pâvisi nivesanaṃ rañño, nisîditvâna âsane

---

63. gaṇi BG, gaṇi A, gaṇaṃ N, jana° Z. — vihâratha ABG, vitâratha N, vinodatha Z.

XIV, 3. In Y the second hemistich runs thus: celukkhepe pavattittha aggârâmo bhavissati. — 6. nîharitvâ BG, niharitvâ N, nidahitvâ AZ. — kârenti Y. — vv. 7. 8 are wanting in Y. — 8. pârupitvâna?

10 bhojanaṃ tattha bhuñjitvâ pattaṃ dhovitvâna pâṇinâ |
bhuttâvi anumodetvâ nikkhamitvâ nivesanâ
nagaramhâ dakkhiṇadvârâ uyyâne Nandane tadâ |
kathesi tattha suttantaṃ aggikkhandhaṃ varuttamaṃ.
tattha pâṇasahassânaṃ dhammâbhisamayo ahû. |
desayitvâna saddhammaṃ uddharitvâna pâṇinaṃ
uṭṭhâya âsanâ thero Tissârâme punâvasi. |
tattha rattiṃ vasitvâna vîtivattâya rattiyâ
nivâsanaṃ nivâsetvâ pârupitvâna cîvaraṃ |
tato pattaṃ gahetvâna pâvisi nagaraṃ puraṃ.
15 piṇḍacâraṃ caramâno râjadvâraṃ upâgami. |
pâvisi nivesanaṃ rañño, nisîditvâna âsane
bhojanaṃ tattha bhuñjitvâ pattaṃ dhovitvâna pâṇinâ |
bhuttâvi anumoditvâ nikkhami nagarâ purâ.
divâvihâraṃ karitvâ Naudanuyyânamuttame |
kathesi tattha suttantaṃ âsivisûpamaṃ subhaṃ.
pariyosâne sahassânaṃ pañcamâbhisamayo ahû. |
desayitvâna saddhammaṃ bodhayitvâna pâṇinaṃ
âsanâ vuṭṭhahitvâna Tissârâmaṃ upâgami. |
bhiyyo râjâ pasanno 'si aṭṭhamaṃ paṭhavikampane.
20 haṭṭho udaggo sumano râjâ therânam abravî: |
patiṭṭhito vihâro ca saṃghârâmaṃ mahârahaṃ
abhiññâpâdakaṃ bhante mahâpaṭhavikampane. |
na kho râja ettâvatâ saṃghârâmo patiṭṭhito.
sîmâsammannanaṃ nâma anuññâtaṃ tathâgato. |
samânasaṃvâsakasîmaṃ avippavâsaṃ ticîvaraṃ
aṭṭhahi sîmânimittehi kittayitvâ samantato |
kammavâcâya sâventi saṃghâ sabbe samâgatâ,
evaṃ baddhâni sîmâni ekâvâso 'ti vuccati;
vihâraṃ thâvaraṃ hoti ârâmo suppatiṭṭhito. |

---

17. anumodetvâ! — karitvâ N, katvâna Y. — 18. saccâbhisamayo N. — 20. aṭṭhamaṃ AG1, paṭhamaṃ N, aṭṭhame BZ. aṭṭhahi paṭh°? aṭṭhapaṭh°? — 21. abhiññâpâdaka, as is seen from several passages of the Samantap., is an epithet of the fourth jhâna which an Arahat enters upon when desiring to produce a miracle, for instance an earth-quake. — 22. kho N, vo AG1, ve BG2Z. — anuññâtaṃ AG1N, aññâtaṃ Z, anuññâto B, anuññatâ G2. — tathâgate G1. See 12, 64. — 24. kammavâcaṃ A. kammavâcâyo? — Between v. 24 and 25 Z inserts the following words: idaṃ vutte ca therena râjâpi etad abruvi.

mama puttâ ca dârâ ca sâmaccâ saparijjanâ
sabbe upâsakâ tuyhaṃ pâṇena saraṇaṃ gatâ. | 25
yâcâmi taṃ mahâvîra, karohi vacanaṃ mama,
antosîmamhi okâse âvasantu mahâjanâ; |
mettâkaruṇâparetâya sadârakkho bhavissati.
pariccâgañ ca janeti râjâ tuyhaṃ yadicchakaṃ, |
saṃgho katapariccâgo sîmaṃ sammannayissati.
Mahâpadumo Kuñjaro ca ubho nâgâ sumañgalâ |
sovaṇṇanañgale yuttâ paṭhamaṃ Koṭṭhamâlake,
caturañginî mahâsenâ saha therehi khattiyo |
suvaṇṇanañgalasîtaṃ dassayanto arindamo,
samalaṃkataṃ puṇṇaghaṭaṃ nânârâgaṃ dhajaṃ subhaṃ | 30
nânâpupphadhajâkiṇṇaṃ toraṇañ ca mahâlaṃghiyâ,
bahucandijalamâlâ, suvaṇṇanañgale kasi. |
mahâjanapasâdâya saha therehi khattiyo
nagaraṃ padakkhiṇaṃ katvâ nadîtîraṃ upâgami. |
mahâsîmapariccâgâ sîtâ suvaṇṇanañgale
yaṃ yaṃ paṭhaviyaṃ yattha agamâ Koṭṭhamâlakaṃ. |
sîmaṃ sîmena ghaṭite mahâjanasamâgame
akampi paṭhavî tattha paṭhamaṃ paṭhavikampanaṃ. |
disvâ acchariyaṃ sabbe râjasenâ saraṭṭhakâ
aññamaññaṃ pamodiṃsu: sîmârâmo bhavissati. | 35

---

27. °paretâ Z. mettâkaruṇâparittâya? — sadârakkho AG1N, °kkhâ BG2Z. — janesi C. — râja ABG2R2, râjâ G1Zn. — Mahinda asks the king to point out what direction the boundary line should take (see Mahâvaṃsa, p. 98, l. 5). This does not imply an act of liberality (pariccâga) on the part of the king, for the ground included by the boundary line does not become *locus sacer*. Now we see that the MSS. have confounded at vv. 33. 36 the words „pariccâga“ and „paricchedа“. I therefore believe that a similar confusion has taken place here also, and I propose to read: paricchedañ ca jânâhi râjâ tuyhaṃ yadicchakaṃ, saṃgho kate paricchede .. — 29. caturañginîmahâseno? (see Mahâv., p. 99, ll. 1. 2.) — 30. samalaṃkataṃ N, sumalaṃgha G1, sumâlagghi (°ggi MR) Y. — 31. mahâlaṃghiyâ BGZn, mahagghiyaṃ A. mâlagghiyaṃ? — bahucandijalamâlâ BGZn, bahuṃ ca dîpamâlâsu A. bahuṃ ca dîpaṃ jalamânaṃ (comp. 6, 75)? — 32. mahâjanaṃ pasîdâya N, mahâjana pasâdiya G1, mahâjanâpasâdâya Z. — 33. mahâsîmaparitogâ ABG2, °paricchedâ Z, °pariccâgo N, °pariccâgâ G1. — sîtaṃ N, sita G1. I propose to correct this stanza thus:

mahâsîmaparicchedaṃ sîtaṃ suvaṇṇanañgale
kasaṃ paṭhaviyaṃ tattha agamâ Koṭṭhamâlakaṃ. —

34. sîmaṃ sîmena (°me G1) G1N, sîmâya sîmaṃ Y. — mahâjane (°naṃ G1, °na Z) samâgate Y, [mahâjanasamâga]mo N.

yâvatâ sîmaparicchede nimittaṃ bandhiṃsu mâlake
paṭivedesi therânaṃ Devânampiyaissaro. |
katvâ kattabbakiccâni sîmassa mâlakassa ca
vihâraṃ thâvaratthâya bhikkhusaṃghassa phâsukaṃ |
mamañ ca anukampâya thero sîmâni bandhatu.
sutvâna rañño vacanaṃ Mahindo dîpajotako |
âmantayi bhikkhusaṃghaṃ: sîmaṃ bandhâma bhikkhavo.
nakkhatte uttarâsâḷhe sabbe saṃghâ samâgatâ, |
patiṭṭhapetvâ mâlakaṃ samânasaṃvâsakaṃ nâma sîmaṃ bandhittha cakkhumâ.
40 vihâraṃ thâvaraṃ katvâ Tissârâmaṃ varuttamaṃ |
Tissârâme vâsitvâ vîtivattâya rattiyâ
nivâsanaṃ nivâsetvâ pârupitvâna cîvaraṃ |
tato pattaṃ gahetvâna pâvisi nagaraṃ puraṃ.
piṇḍacâraṃ caramâno râjadvâraṃ upâgami. |
pavisitvâ nivesanaṃ rañño nisîditvâna âsane
bhojanaṃ tattha bhuñjitvâ pattaṃ dhovitvâna pâṇinâ |
bhuttâvi anumoditvâ nikkhami nagarâ purâ.
divâvihâraṃ karitvâna uyyâne Nandane vane |
kathesi tattha suttantaṃ âsivisûpamaṃ tadâ,
45 anamataggiyasuttaṃ ca cariyâpiṭakam anuttaraṃ |
gomayapiṇḍaovâdaṃ dhammacakkappavattanaṃ
Mahânandanamhi tatth' eva pakâsesi punappunaṃ. |
iminâ ca suttantena sattâhâni pakâsayi
aṭṭha ca saṃghasahassâni pañca jaṅghasatâni ca |
mocesi bandhanâ thero Mahindo dîpajotako.
ûnamâsaṃ vasitvâna Tissârâme sahaggaṇo |
âsâḷhiyâ puṇṇamâse upakaṭṭhe ca vassake
âmantayi nâgare sabbe: vassakâlo bhavissati. |

Mahâvihârapaṭiggahaṇaṃ niṭṭhitaṃ.

Senâsanaṃ saṃsâmetvâ Mahindo dîpajotako
50 pattacîvaraṃ âdâya Tissârâmamhâ nikkhami. |
nivâsanaṃ nivâsetvâ pârupitvâna cîvaraṃ

---

36. sîmapariccâgo G1N. — 37. sîmassa G1N, sîmâya Y. — 41. vâsitvâ N, vâsetvâ G1, vâsayitvâ ABG2Z. vasitvâna? — 44. anumodetvâ BG. — 47. imâni ca suttantâni? — aṭṭha jaṃghas° N. — pañca saṃghasatâni ca A.

tato pattaṃ gahetvâna pâvisi nagaraṃ puraṃ. |
piṇḍacâraṃ caramâno râjadvâraṃ upâgami,
pâvisi nivesanaṃ rañño, nisîdiṃsu yathâsane. |
bhojanaṃ tattha bhuñjitvâ pattaṃ dhovitvâna pâṇinâ
mahâsamayasuttantaṃ ovâdatthâya desayi. |
ovaditvâna râjânaṃ Mahindo dîpajotako
âsanâ vuṭṭhahitvâna anâpucchâ apakkami. |
nagaramhâ pâcînadvârâ nikkhamitvâ mahâgaṇî
nivattetvâ jane sabbe agamâ yena pabbataṃ. | 55
râjânaṃ paṭivedesuṃ amaccâ ubbiggamânasâ:
sabbe deva mahâtherâ gatâ Missakapabbataṃ. |
sutvâna râjâ ubbiggo sîghaṃ yojetvâna sandanaṃ
abhiruhitvâ rathaṃ khippaṃ saha devîhi khattiyo. |
gantvâna pabbatapâdaṃ Mahindathero sahaggaṇo,
Nagaracatukkaṃ nâma rahadaṃ selanimmitaṃ,
tattha nahâtvâ pivitvâna ṭhito pâsânamuddhani. |
sîghaṃ vegena sedâni nippâhetvâna khattiyo
dûrato addasa theraṃ pabbatamuddhani ṭhitaṃ. |
deviyo ca rathe ṭhatvâ rathâ oruyha khattiyo
upasaṃkamitvâ therânaṃ vanditvâ idam abravî: | 60
rammaṃ raṭṭhaṃ jahetvâna mamañ c' ohâya pâṇino
kimatthâya mahâvîra imaṃ âgami pabbataṃ? |
idha vassaṃ vasissâma tîṇi mâsaṃ anûnakaṃ
purimaṃ pacchimakaṃ nâma anuññâtaṃ tathâgate. |
karomi sabbakiccâni bhikkhusaṃghassa phâsukaṃ,
anukampaṃ upâdâya mam' atthaṃ anusâsatu. |
gâmantaṃ vâ araññaṃ vâ bhikkhuvassûpanâyiko
senâsane saṃvutadvâre vâsaṃ buddhena anûmataṃ. |
anuññâtam etaṃ vacanaṃ atthaṃ sabbaṃ sahetukaṃ,

---

54. anâpucchâ 'va pakkami A. — 57. yojetvâ Y. — abhiruhi? — 58[b] is wanting in BG2. — Nâñgacatakkaṃ A, Nagaraṃ catukkaṃ C1R1, Nagaraṃ catukkaṃ G1MN. Nâgacatukkaṃ? comp. Mahâv., p. 103, l. 2. — selanippitaṃ AG1. selanissitaṃ? — 59. pantitvâna A, nanipatitvâna BG2, nippahitvâna Z, nibbâhetvâna N, nipphaṃhitvâna G1. nibbattetvânâ? — 60. The words „deviyo ca rathe ṭhatvâ" are wanting in ABG2. — kovedjye G1Z, deviyo N. — rathe ṭhapetvâ? — 61. jahitvâna? — agami? — 62. tathâgatâ A, °to BG2, °te G1Zn. See 12, 64. — 64. °nâyiko GZn, °ka B, °kâ A. bhikkhuvassûpanâyikaṃ (adj. construed with vâsaṃ)? — anumataṃ CRG1, anûmataṃ Mn, anuññâtaṃ ABG2. — 65. anuññâtaṃ Zn, aññâtaṃ ABG. Comp. 15, 5.

65 ajj' evâhaṃ karissâmi âvâsaṃ vasaphâsukaṃ. |
gahaṭṭhasiddhiṃ sodhetvâ oloketvâ mahâyaso
therânaṃ paṭipâdesi: vasantu anukampakâ. |
sâdhu bhante imaṃ lenaṃ ârâmaṃ paṭipajjatu,
vihâraṃ thâvaratthâya sîmaṃ bandha mahâmuni. |
rañño bhaginiyâ putto Mahâriṭṭho 'ti vissuto
pañcapaññâsa khatteca kulejâtâ mahâyasâ |
upasaṃkamitvâ râjânaṃ abhivâdetvâ idaṃ abravuṃ:
sabbeva pabbajissâma varapaññassa santike, |
brahmacariyañ carissâma, taṃ devo anumaññatu.
70 sabbesaṃ vacanaṃ sutvâ râjâpi tuṭṭhamânaso |
therânaṃ upasaṃkamma ârocesi mahîpati:
Mahâariṭṭhapamukhâ pañcapaññâsa nâyakâ,
pabbâjehi anuññâtaṃ mahâvîra tav' antike. |
sutvâna rañño vacanaṃ Mahindo dîpajotako
âmantayi bhikkhusaṃghaṃ: sîmaṃ bandhâma bhikkhavo. |
samânasaṃvâsakâ c' eva avippavâsa ticîvaraṃ
vihâraṃ thâvaratthâya sîmaṃ bandhâsimâpana. |
sîmaṃ ca sîmantarikaṃ ca ṭhapetvâ Tumbamâlake
mahâsîmâni kittesi Mahindo dîpajotako. |
bandhitvâ mâlakaṃ sabbaṃ sîmaṃ bandhitvâna cakkhumâ
75 vihâraṃ thâvaraṃ katvâ dutiyaṃ Tissapabbate |
puṇṇâya puṇṇamâsiyâ âsâḷhamâse uposathe
nakkhatte uttarâsâḷhe sîmaṃ bandhitvâna pabbate |
pabbâjesi Mahâriṭṭhaṃ paṭhamaṃ dutiyamâlake,
upasampâdesi tatth' eva Tambapaṇṇikulissaro, |
pañcapaññâsa tatth' eva pabbajjâ upasampadâ.
battiṃsa mâlakâ honti paṭhamârâme patiṭṭhitâ, |

---

65. vassaphâsukam? — v. 66 is wanting in BG2Z. — °siddhi AG1, °saddhiṃ N. — sâdhetvâ? — 68. khattiyâ ca A, khatiyâ ca B, khatte ca ZGn. tatth' eva? comp. v. 78. — 71. pabbâjehi N, °jeti AG1, °jetu BG2Z. — 73. samânasaṃvâsakaṃ BG2, °kâ AG1Z, samânavâsakâ N. — avippavâsa ABG2Z, °sâ G1N. samânasaṃvâsakaṃ c' eva avippavâsaṃ ticîvaraṃ? Comp. v. 23. — bandhâsimâpana G, bandhasîmaṃ pana N, bandhâsiyâpana A, bandhâyimâpana B, bandhâma CR, bandhâma bhikkhave M. sîmaṃ bandhiṃsu mâlakaṃ? — v. 74 and the first hem. of v. 75 are wanting in Z. — 74. Tambamâlake BG2, Pattasamâlake G1, Tumbamâlake A, bâttiṃsa mâlake N. Comp. Mahâv., p. 108, l. 12. — mahâsîmâ ca kittesi ABG2. — Cetiyapabbate BG2. Cetiyapabbate? Missakapabbate? (see Mahâv., p. 106, l. 4.) — 77. °kulissaraṃ B, °râ AG2, °ro G1Zn.

dutiyârâme battiṃsa vihâre Tissapabbate,
avasesakhuddakârâme paccek' ekekamâlake. |
patiṭṭhapetvâ ârâmaṃ vihâraṃ pabbatuttame
dvâsaṭṭhi arahantâ sabbe paṭhamaṃ vass' upâgatâ. |

Cetiyapabbatapaṭiggahaṇaṃ niṭṭhitaṃ.
bhâṇavâraṃ cuddasamaṃ.

XV.

Gimhâne paṭhame mâse puṇṇamâse uposathe
âgatâ Jambudîpamhâ vasimhâ pabbatuttame. |
pañcamâse na vuṭṭhamhâ Tissârâme ca pabbate,
gacchâma Jambudîpânaṃ, anujâna rathesabha. |
tappema annapânena vatthasenâsanena ca,
saraṇaṃ gato jano sabbo, kuto vo anabhîrati? |
abhivâdanapaccupaṭṭhânaṃ añjaligarudassanaṃ
ciraṃ diṭṭho mahârâja sambuddhaṃ dipaduttamaṃ. |
aññâtaṃ vat' ahaṃ bhante, karomi thûpam uttamaṃ,
vijânâtha bhûmikammaṃ, thûpaṃ kâhâmi satthuno. |
ehi tvaṃ Sumana nâga Pâṭaliputtapuraṃ gantvâ
Asokaṃ dhammarâjânaṃ evaṃ ca ârocayâhi tvaṃ: |
sahâyo te mahârâja pasanno buddhasâsane,
dehi dhâtuvaraṃ tassa, thûpaṃ kâhasi satthuno. |
bahussuto sutadharo subbaco vacanakkhamo
iddhiyâ pâramippatto acalo suppatiṭṭhito |
pattacîvaraṃ âdâya khaṇe pakkami pabbatâ.
Asokaṃ dhammarâjânaṃ ârocesi yathâtathaṃ: |
upajjhâyassa mahârâja suṇohi vacanaṃ tuvaṃ,
sahâyo te mahârâja pasanno buddhasâsane,
dehi dhâtuvaraṃ tassa, thûpaṃ kâhati satthuno. |

---

79. Tissap° G1Zn, Missakap° AB2G2, Missap° B1. See v. 75. — avasese kh° BG1. °ârâmâ °mâlakâ?

XV, 2. vuṭṭhimha BG2. — Jambudîpânaṃ ABGMnR, °pantaṃ C, °pânnaṃ d'Alwis (Attanag., p. 184). Jambudîpavhaṃ? — 4. °paccuṭṭhânaṃ A. — ciradiṭṭho A. — sambuddho °uttamo? — Comp. Mahâv., p. 104, and Sam. Pâs.: „ciradiṭṭho no mahârâja sammâsambuddho, abhivâdanapaccuṭṭhânañjalikammasâmîcikammakaraṇaṭṭhânaṃ n' atthi." — 5. bhûmikampaṃ Y, bhûmikammaṃ N. bhûmibhâgaṃ? Sam. Pâs.: „karomi bhante thûpaṃ, bhûmibhâgaṃ dâni vicinatha." — karomi Y. — 7. kâhati BG2. — 8. acale Z, d'Alwis.

sutvâna vacanaṃ râjâ tuṭṭho saṃviggamânaso
dhâtu pattaṃ apûresi: khippaṃ gacchâhi subbata. |
tato dhâtuṃ gahetvâna subbaco vacanakkhamo
vehâsaṃ abbhuggantvâna agamâ Kosiyasantike. |
upasaṃkamitvâ subbaco Kosiyam etad abravî:
upajjhâyassa mahârâja suṇohi vacanaṃ tuvaṃ, |
Devânampiyo râjâ so pasanno buddhasâsane,
dehi dhâtuvaraṃ tassa, karissati thûpam uttamaṃ. |
sutvâna vacanaṃ tassa Kosiyo tuṭṭhamânaso
dakkhiṇakkhakaṃ pâdâsi: khippaṃ gacchâhi subbata. |
sâmaṇero ca Sumano gantvâ Kosiyasantike
dakkhiṇakkhakaṃ gahetvâna patiṭṭhito pabbatuttame. |
sampannahirottappako garubhâvo ca paṇḍito
pesito therarâjena patiṭṭhito pabbatuttame. |
sabhâtuko mahâseno bhikkhusaṃghe varuttame
paccuggami tadâ râjâ buddhaseṭṭhassa dhâtuyo. |
câtumâsaṃ komudiyaṃ divasaṃ puṇṇarattiyâ
âgato ca mahâvîro . . . |
. . . . gajakumbhe patiṭṭhito. |
akâsi so kuñcanâdaṃ kaṃsathâlaggiyâhataṃ,
akampi tattha paṭhavî paccante âgate muni. |
saṅkhapaṇavaninnâdo bherisaddo samâhato,
khattiyo parivâretvâ pûjesi purisuttamaṃ. |
pacchâmukho hatthinâgo pakkâmi pattisammukhâ,
puratthimena dvârena nagaraṃ pâvisi tadâ. |
sabbagandhaṃ ca mâlaṃ ca pûjenti naranâriyo.
dakkhiṇena ca dvârena nikkhamitvâ gajuttamo, |
Kakusandhe ca satthari Konâgamane ca Kassape
patiṭṭhite bhûmibhâge porâṇâ isayo pure |

---

11. dhâtuṃ Z, d'Alwis. This may be correct. — 13. subbato ABG2, °te G1Z, °co N. — 16. Kosiyasantikaṃ AN, °santike BGZ, d'Alwis. °santikâ? — 18. bhikkhusaṃghapurakkhato, d'Alwis. — 19. catumâsaṃ ABG, cât° Zn. — komudiyâṃ A2. D'Alwis: câtumâse komudiyâ divase punnarattiya. câtumâsikomudiyâ divasaṃ? — 19ᵇ. 20. These fragments do not form one hemistich, for „patiṭṭhita" does not refer to Sumana, but to the relic dish, see Mahâv., p. 106, l. 8. — 21. kaṃsapâtiṃ (°tî A) va âhataṃ ABG2, kaṃsithâlaggiyâbataṃ G1Z, kaṃsamâlaggiyâhataṃ N. D'Alwis: kaṃsatâlaṃ viyâhataṃ. — 22. purisuttame G1N. — 25. porâṇa ABG2Z, d'Alwis, porâṇâ G1M2n. — °issaro ABG2Z; issare G1, d'Alwis; isayo N. Comp. the Jâtaka quoted by Minayeff, Grammaire P., p. IX.

upagantvâ hatthinâgo bhûmisîsaṃ gajuttamo
dhâtuyo Sakyaputtassa patiṭṭhapesi narâsabho. |
saha patiṭṭhite dhâtu devâ tattha pamoditâ,
akampi tattha paṭhavî abbhutaṃ lomahaṃsanaṃ. |
sabhâtuko pasâdetvâ mahâmacce saraṭṭhake
thûpiṭṭhakaṃ ca kâresi sâmaṇero Sumanavhayo. |
paccekapûjaṃ akaṃsu khattiyâ thûpam uttamaṃ
vararatanehi saṃchannaṃ dhâtudîpaṃ varuttamaṃ. |
sachattaṃ paccekachattaṃ dvethanavekachattaṃ
tathârûpaṃ alaṃkâraṃ vâlavîjani dassaniyaṃ |
thûpaṭṭhâne catuddisâ padîpehi vibhâtakâ
sataraṃsi udente va upasobhanti samantato. |
pattharilâni dussâni nânârañgehi cittiyo
âkâso vigatabbho hi upari ca parisobhati, |
ratanamayaparikkhittaṃ aggiyaphalikâni ca
kañcanavitânaṃ chattaṃ sovaṇṇavâlikavicittaṃ. |
ayaṃ passati sambuddho Kakusandho vinâyako
cattâlîsasahassehi tâdîhi parivârito. |
karuṇâcodito buddho satte passati cakkhumâ
Ojadîpe 'bhayapure dukkhappatte ca mânuse |
Ojadîpe bahû satte bodhaneyye mahâjane
buddharaṃsânubhâvena âdicco padumaṃ yathâ. |
cattâlîsasahassehi bhikkhûhi parivârito
abbhuṭṭhito suriyo va Ojadîpe patiṭṭhito. |

---

26. hatthinâgo N, °nâṃgo A, °nâge BGZ. — gajuttame G1Z. — 28. dasa bhâtuke N. — saraṭṭhake N, karaṃḍake A, karaṭṭhake BG, varaṭṭhake Z, ca raṭṭhake d'Alwis. — The words „sâmaṇero Sumanavhayo" seem to belong to another passage, perhaps to v. 19. — v. 30 is wanting in BG2. — sachattaṃ AGN; setacchattaṃ Z, comp. Mahâv., p. 104, l. 11. — dvethanaveka- (°meka- A) chattaṃ (°jattaṃ A) AGZ, dvemanussadevachattaṃ N. veṭhanaṃ anekachattakaṃ? — vâlavîjaniṃ? — dassaneyyaṃ AGZ, dassaniyaṃ N. — 31. „padîpehi vibhâtakâ" is wanting in Y. — udantave A, udanteva BGZ. — 32. pattharilâni N, pakatikâni Y. — vigatabbho hi N, viya ahosi A, viya ahâsi G, viya abhâyi B, viya abbhâsi Z. — uparûpari sobhati AZ, upari ca paris° BG, upari ca pasobhati N. — I do not pretend fully to restore this stanza, but I will try at least to correct some of the blunders.

pattharitâni dussâni nânârañgehi cittiyâ (cetiye? see Mah., p. 108, l. 10 et seq.),
âkâso vigatabbho va uparûpari sobhati, |

33. aggiphalikâni ca A, aggiyathalikâni ca (°phalikâni ca M2) BGZ, [a]gghi-[yaphalikâni ca] N.

Kakusandho Mahâdevo Devakûṭo ca pabbato
Ojadîpe 'bhayapure Abhayo nâma khattiyo. |
nagaraṃ Kadambakokâse nadîto âsi mâpitaṃ
suvibhattaṃ dassaneyyaṃ ramaṇîyaṃ manoramaṃ. |
puṇṇakanarako nâma pajjaro âsi kakkhalo,
40 jano saṃsayam âpanno maccho va kuminâmukhe. |
buddhassa ânubhâvena pakkanto pajjaro tadâ.
desite amate dhamme patiṭṭhite jinasâsane |
caturâsîtisahassânaṃ dhammâbhisamayo ahû.
Paṭiyârâmo tadâ âsi dhammakarakacetiyaṃ. |
bhikkhusahassaparivuto Mahâdevo mahiddhiko,
pakkanto 'va jino tamhâ sayam ev' aggapuggalo 'ti. |
ayaṃ passati sambuddho Konâgamano mahâmuni
tiṃsabhikkhusahassehi sambuddho parivârito. |
dasasahassehi sambuddho karuṇâ pharati cakkhumâ,
45 Varadîpe mahâvîro dukkhite passati mânuse. |
Varadîpe bahû satte bodhaneyye mahâjane
buddharaṃsânubhâvena âdicco padumaṃ yathâ. |
tiṃsabhikkhusahassehi sambuddho parivârito
abbhuṭṭhito suriyo va Varadîpe patiṭṭhito. |
Konâgamano Mahâsumano Sumanakûṭo ca pabbato,
Varadîpe Vaḍḍhamâne Samiddho nâma khattiyo. |
dubbuṭṭhiyo tadâ âsi dubbhikkhi âsi yonakâ,
dubbhikkhadukkhite satte macche vappodake yathâ |
âgate lokavidumhi devo sammâbhivassati,
50 khemo âsi janapado, assâsesi bahû jane. |
Tissatalâkasâmante nagare dakkhiṇâmukhe
vihâro Uttarârâmo kâyabandhanacetiyaṃ. |
caturâsîtisahassânaṃ dhammâbhisamayo ahû.

---

43. Mahâdevo patiṭṭhito pakkanto ca jino? comp. vv. 53. 64. — 44[b]. sambuddho AG1nZ, tâdihi BG2. — 45. dasasahassehi AG1N, dasasahassî ca BG2Z. — karuṇâ passati Y. karuṇâya pharati? comp. v. 56. — 49. dubbhikkhaṃ (°kkha A) setaṭṭhikaṃ ABG2, dubbhikkhi âsi yonakâ G1N, dubbhikkhe bhayapîlite Z. dubbuṭṭhikâ tadâ âsi dubbhikkhaṃ âsi châtakam? comp. Cariyâ Piṭaka: „avuṭṭhiko janapado dubbhikkho châtako mahâ"; Sam. Pâs.: „Varadîpe dubbuṭṭhikâ ahosi dubbhikkhaṃ dussassaṃ, sattâ châtakarogena anayavyasanaṃ âpajjanti." — maccho N. — appodake? comp. Suttanipâta: „phandamânaṃ pajaṃ disvâ macche appodake yathâ." — 50. jannssavo ABG2, °ve Z, °do G1. — 51. nagaradakkh° G1N.

desite amate dhamme suriyo udito yathâ |
bhikkhusahassaparivuto Mahâsumano patiṭṭhito
pakkanto ca mahâvîro sayam ev' aggapuggalo 'ti. |
ayaṃ passati sambuddho Kassapo lokanâyako
vîsatibhikkhusahassehi sambuddho parivârito. |
Kassapo ca lokavidû voloketi sadevakaṃ
visuddhabuddhacakkhunâ bodhaneyye ca passati. |
Kassapo ca lokavidû âhutînaṃ paṭiggaho
pharanto mahâkaruṇâya vivâdaṃ passati kuppitaṃ |
Maṇḍadîpe bahû satte bodhaneyye ca passati
buddharaṃsânubhâvena âdicco padumaṃ yathâ. |
gacchissâmi Maṇḍadîpaṃ jotayissâmi sâsanaṃ
patiṭṭhapemi sammâbhaṃ andhakâre va candimâ. |
bhikkhugaṇehi parivuto âkâse pakkamî jino,
patiṭṭhito Maṇḍadîpe suriyo abbhuṭṭhito yathâ. |
Kassapo Sabbanando ca Subhakûṭo ca pabbato,
Visâlaṃ nâma nagaraṃ, Jayanto nâma khattiyo, |
Khematalâkasâmante nagare pacchime mukhe
vihâro Pâcînârâmo, cetiyaṃ dakasâṭikaṃ. |
assâsetvâna sambuddho samagge katvâna bhâtuke
desesi amataṃ dhammaṃ patiṭṭhapesi sâsanaṃ. |
desite amate dhamme patiṭṭhite jinasâsane
caturâsîtisahassânaṃ dhammâbhisamayo ahû. |
bhikkhusahassaparivuto Sabbanando mahâyaso
patiṭṭhito Maṇḍadîpe, pakkanto lokanâyako 'ti. |
ayaṃ hi loke sambuddho uppanno lokanâyako:
sattânaṃ anukampâya târayissâmi pâṇinaṃ. |
so 'vapassati sambuddho lokajeṭṭho narâsabho
nâgânaṃ saṃgâmatthâya mahâsenâ samâgatâ. |
dhûmâyanti pajjalanti verâyanti caranti te

---

52. suriye Y. — udite Y (except G1). — 53. ca Y, va N. — 54. sambuddho G1nZ, tâdîhi ABG2. — 58. patiṭṭhissâmi ABG2, patiṭṭhapemi GZ, [patiṭṭhape]si N. — sammâ A, sammâbhâ B, sammâbhaṃ G2, sattânaṃ (°nnaṃ G1) G1N, yaṃ dhâtuṃ Z. — 59. suriye (°yo R) abbhuṭṭhite yathâ Y (except G1). — 61. pacchimâmukhe? comp. v. 88: uttarâmukho. — °sâṭakaṃ? Comp. 17, 10. — 62. bhâtuke ABG2Z, bhâsite G1, tâsike N. Comp. Mahâv., p. 93, l. 13. — 65. târayanto (°nto ca BG2) pâṇino ABG2, târayissâmi pâṇinaṃ G1N, desesi dhammaṃ uttamaṃ Z. — 66. so va° ABG, so ca Z, te so N. — 67. dhûpâyanti? see Mahâvagga, I, 15. — verâyanti Z, verayanti ABG2, verânañ ca G1N.

mahâbhayan ti vipulaṃ dîpaṃ nâsenti pannagâ. |
agamâ ekîbhûto 'va: gacchâmi dîpam uttamaṃ
mâtulaṃ bhâgineyyaṃ ca nibbâpessâmi pannage. |
ahaṃ Gotamasambuddho, pabbate Cetiyanâmake,
Anurâdhapure ramme Tisso nâmâsi khattiyo. |
Kusinârâyaṃ bhagavâ Mallânaṃ Upavattane
70 anupâdisesâya sambuddho nibbuto upadhikkhaye. |
dve vassasatâ honti chattiṃsa ca vassâ tathâ,
Mahindo nâma nâmena jotayissati sâsanaṃ. |
nagarassa dakkhiṇato bhûmibhâge manorame
ârâmo ca ramaṇîyo Thûpârâmo 'ti suyyare. |
Tambapaṇṇîti sutvâna dîpo abbhuggato tadâ.
sârîrikaṃ mama dhâtuṃ patiṭṭhissaṃ diputtame. |
buddhe pasannâ dhamme ca saṃghe ca ujudiṭṭhikâ
bhave cittaṃ virâjeti Anulâ nâma khattiyâ. |
deviyâ vacanaṃ sutvâ râjâ theraṃ id' abravî:
75 buddhe pasannâ dhamme ca saṃghe ca ujudiṭṭhikâ |
bhave cittaṃ virâjeti, pabbâjehi Anûlakaṃ.
akappiyâ mahârâja itthipabbajjâ bhikkhuno, |
âgamissati me râjâ Saṃghamittâ bhaginiyâ,
Anulaṃ pabbâjetvâna mocesi sabbabandhanâ. |
Saṃghamittâ mahâpaññâ Uttarâ ca vicakkhaṇâ
Hemâ ca Mâsagallâ ca Aggimittâ mitâvadâ
Tappâ Pabbatachinnâ ca Mallâ ca Dhammadâsiyâ, |
ettakâ tâ bhikkhuniyo dhutarâgâ samâhitâ
odâtamanasaṃkappâ saddhammavinaye ratâ |
khîṇâsavâ vasî pattâ tevijjâ iddhikovidâ
80 uttamante ṭhitâ tattha âgamissanti tâ idha. |
mahâmattaparivuto nisinno cintiye tadâ

---

67. muhuṃ bhayanti (bhây° A) ABG2. — vepullaṃ Zn. pharanti te mahâbhayaṃ ativipulaṃ? — vv. 69—76 are wanting in BG2. — 69. ayam? — pabbato °nâmako? — 72. suyyate? — 73. patiṭṭhissa N, patiṭṭhassaṃ CG, patiṭṭhissaṃ AMR. sârîrikâ m° dhâtû patiṭṭhissanti? — vv. 74—77 are given in the MSS. with a number of omissions and transpositions which it is superfluous here to indicate. — 77. mocesi AG1Zn, moceti BG2. — 78. Comp. 18, 11. 12. — Mâsâ BGZ, Mâyâ A, Hemâ N. — Mâragallâ N. — Tappâ Pabbatachinnâ ca N, Sabbatâ (subb° ABG2) Sinnâ va (ca M) Y. — Mâlâ Y. — Dhammatasiyâ Y, Dhammadâpiyâ N. — 80. uttamatthe AZ. This may be the correct reading. — 81. nisinne BG2Z. — cintiye G1Z, cintaye N, khattiye AB, khantiye G2.

mantitukâmo nisîditvâ mattânaṃ etad abravî. |
Ariṭṭho nâma khattiyo sutvâ devassa bhâsitaṃ |
therassa vacanaṃ sutvâ uggahetvâna sâsanaṃ
dâyakaṃ anusâsetvâ pakkâmi uttarâmukho. |
nagarassa ekadesamhi gharaṃ katvâna khattiyâ
dasa sîle samâdinnâ Anulâdevîpamukhâ |
sabbâ pañcasatâ kaññâ abhijâtâ jutindharâ
Anulaṃ parikkarontâ sâyampâto bahû janâ. | 85
nâvâtitthaṃ upagantvâ âropetvâ mahânâvaṃ
sâgaraṃ samatikkanto thale patvâ patiṭṭhito. |
Viñjhâṭaviṃ atikkanto mahâmatto mahabbalo
Pâṭaliputtaṃ anuppatto gato devassa santike. |
putto deva mahârâja atrajo Piyadassano
Mahindo nâma so thero pesito tava santikaṃ. |
Devânampiyo so râjâ sahâyo Piyadassano
buddhe abhippasanno so pesito tava santike. |
bhâtuno vacanaṃ tuyhaṃ âmantesi mahâ isi.
râjakaññe Saṃghamitte Anulâ nâma khattiyâ | 90
sabbâ taṃ apalokenti pabbajjâya purakkhakâ.
bhâtuno sâsanaṃ sutvâ Saṃghamittâ vicakkhaṇâ |
turitâ upasaṃkamma râjânaṃ idam abravî:
anujâna mahârâja, gacchâmi dîpalañjakaṃ. |
bhâtuno vacanaṃ mayhaṃ âmantesi mahâ isi.
bhâgineyyo ca Sumano putto ca jeṭṭhabhâtu te |
gatâ tava piyo mayhaṃ gamanaṃ vârenti dhîtuyâ.
bhârikaṃ me mahârâja bhâtuno vacanaṃ mama, |
râjakaññâ mahârâja Anulâ nâma khattiyâ
sabbâ maṃ apalokenti pabbajjâya purakkhakâ. | 95

bhâṇavâraṃ pannarasamaṃ.

---

81. mantetukâmo? — khattiyaṃ Z, khattaṃ ABG, mattânaṃ N. (a)maccânaṃ? mantînaṃ? — 83. dâsakaṃ Z, dây° ABG, dâr° N. ayyakaṃ abhivâdetvâ? Comp. Mahâv., p. 110, l. 6. — 85. parikkharontâ? — 86. âruhitvâ? — thale patvâ N, ṭhapetvâna N. — 88. putto deva N, putto (°tte A) te ABG, putto te deva Z. — Piyadassana BG2. — 89. Piyadassana B. — vv. 90 and 91[a] are wanting in BG2Z, 90[b] also in AG1. — 90. bh° vacanaṃ tassâ âmantesi mahâ isi? — râjakaññâ? comp. v. 95. — 91. purakkhakâ Y, purakkhikâ N (the same at v. 95). purekkharâ? Comp. Sam. Pâs.: „Anulâpi khattiyâ itthisahassaparivutâ pabbajjâpurekkhârâ maṃ paṭimâneti.“ — vv. 93[b] and 94[a] are wanting in BG2Z. — 93. jeṭṭhabhâtâ te (*i. e.* Mahinda)? — gatâ tava piyo N, laddhâ ca pitaro (pitayo F) AFG. gatâ tava piye? — vâresi AFG. — 95. purekkharâ? see v. 91.

XVI.

Caturaṅginiṃ mahâsenaṃ sannayhitvâna khattiyo
tathâgatassa sambodhiṃ âdâya pakkamî tadâ. |
tîsu rajjesu atikkanto Viñjhâṭavîsu khattiyo
atikkanto brahâraññaṃ anuppatto jalasâgaraṃ. |
caturaṅginî mahâsenâ bhikkhunîsaṃghasâvikâ
mahâsamuddaṃ pakkantâ âdâya bodhim uttamaṃ. |
upari devânaṃ turiyaṃ heṭṭhato ca manussakaṃ
câtudisâmânusaturiyaṃ, pakkanto jalasâgare. |
muddhani avaloketvâ khattiyo Piyadassano
5 abhivâdayitvâ taṃ bodhiṃ imaṃ atthaṃ abhâsatha: |
bahussuto iddhimanto sîlavâ susamâhito
dassane akappiyaṃ mayhaṃ atappaneyyaṃ mahâjanaṃ. |
tattha kanditvâ roditvâ oloketvâna dassanaṃ
khattiyo paṭinivattetvâ agamâ sakanivesanaṃ. |
udake ca nimmitâ nâgâ devatâkâse ca nimmitâ
rukkhe ca nimmitâ devâ nâgânivâsanam pi ca |
parivârayiṃsu te sabbe gacchantaṃ bodhim uttamaṃ.
amanâpâ ca pisâcâ bhûtakumbhaṇḍarakkhasâ
bodhiṃ paccantam âyantaṃ parivâriṃsu amânusâ. |
tâvatiṃsâ ca yâmâ ca tusitâpi ca devatâ
10 nimmânaratino devâ ye devâ vasavattino |
bodhiṃ paccantaṃ âyantaṃ tuṭṭhahaṭṭhâ pamoditâ,
tettiṃsâ ca devaputtâ sabbe Indapurohitâ |
bodhiṃ paccantaṃ âyantaṃ appoṭhenti hasanti ca.
Kuvero Dhataraṭṭho ca Virûpakkho Virûḷhako |
cattâro te mahârâjâ samantâ caturodisâ
parivârayiṃsu sambodhiṃ gacchantaṃ dîpalañjakaṃ. |
mahâmukhapaṭahâro divillâtatadindimâ
bodhiṃ paccantaṃ ayantaṃ sâdhu kîlanti devatâ. |
pâricchattakapupphaṃ ca dibbamandâravâni ca

XVI, 3. bhikkhunîsaṃghapâmukhâ? — 4. catuddisâmân° ABG. câtuddisamânusaturiyaṃ? — 5. apaloketvâ N, acaloketvâ F, avaloketvâ Y. — 6. I do not try to correct the second hemistich. — 7. paṭinivattitvâ A. — v. 8 is wanting in BG2. — nâgâ (nâṃgâ A) nivesaṇam pi ca AGZ, nâgâ nivâsanam pi ca F, nâgâdhivâsanâ pi ca N. nâganivâsane pi ca? — 9c. parivârayiṃsu A. — v. 14 is wanting in BG2Z. — °paṭahâ ca?

dibbacandanacuṇṇaṃ ca antalikkhe pavassati,
bodhiṃ paccantaṃ âyantaṃ pûjayanti ca devatâ. |
campakâ sallâ nimbâ nâgapunnâgaketakâ
jalasâgare mahâbodhiṃ devâ pûjenti satthuno. |
nâgarâjâ nâgakaññâ nâgapotâ bahû janâ
bhavanato nikkhamitvâ pûjenti bodhim uttamaṃ. |
nânâvirâgavasanâ nânârâgavibhûsitâ
jalasâgare mahâbodhiṃ nâgâ kîlanti sâdhu no. |
uppalapadumakumudanîlâni satapattakaṃ
kallahâraṃ kuvalayaṃ adhimuttamadhugandhikaṃ |
takkârikaṃ koviḷâraṃ pâṭaliṃ bimbajâlakaṃ
asokaṃ sâlapupphaṃ ca missakaṃ ca piyaṅgukaṃ
nâgâ pûjenti te bodhiṃ sobhati jalasâgare. |
âmoditâ nâgakaññâ nâgarâjâ pamoditâ
bodhiṃ paccantaṃ âyantaṃ nâgâ kîlanti sâdhu no. |
tattha maṇimayâ bhûmi muttâphalikasanthatâ,
ârâmapokkharaṇiyo nânâpupphehi vicittâ. |
sattâhakaṃ vasitvâna sadevâ sahamânusâ
bhavanato nikkhamantaṃ pûjenti bodhim uttamaṃ. |
mâlâdâmakalâpâ ca nâgakaññâ ca devatâ
âvijjhanti ca celâni sambodhiparivâritâ. |
bodhiṃ paccantaṃ âyantaṃ sâdhu kîlanti devatâ.
pâricchattakapupphaṃ ca dibbamandâravâni ca
dibbacandanacuṇṇaṃ ca antalikkhe pavassati. |
nâgâ yakkhâ ca bhûtâ ca sadevâ sahamânusâ
jalasâgaram âyantaṃ sambodhiparivâritâ |
tattha naccanti gâyanti vâdayanti hasanti ca
poṭhenti diguṇaṃ bhujaṃ te bodhiparivâritâ. |
nâgâ yakkhâ ca bhûtâ ca sadevâ sahamânusâ
kittenti maṅgalaṃ sotthiṃ nîyate bodhim uttamaṃ. |
nâgâ dhajapaggahitâ nîlobhâsâ manoramâ
kittenti bodhim uttamaṃ patiṭṭhitaṃ dîpalañjake. |
Anurâdhapurâ rammâ nikkhamitvâ bahû janâ

16[a]. One syllable is wanting. We should probably for „sallâ“ read „salalâ“ or „sallakâ“; comp. Apadâna (Phayre MS., fol. kû'): „campakâ salaḷâ nimbâ nâna- (sic) punnâgaketakâ.“ — 18. sâdhu no Zn, sâdhuyo AFG, sâdhuso B. — 19. atimuttaṃ m°? — 21. sâdhu no N, sâdhuso BG2, sâdhuyo AFG1Z. — 22. tattha ABG2Z, tassa G1X. — 28. nîyate AZ, niyataṃ B, niyate F2G, niyato F1, nîyâte N. nîyantaṃ? — °uttame F, °uttamaṃ Yn.

30 sambodhiṃ upasaṃkantâ saha devehi khattiyo |
parivârayiṃsu sambodhiṃ saha puttehi khattiyo
gandhamâlaṃ ca pûjesuṃ gandhagandhânam uttamaṃ. |
vîthiyo ca susammaṭṭhâ aggbiyâ ca alaṃkatâ.
saha patiṭṭhite bodhi kampittha paṭhavî tadâ 'ti. |
dâpesi râjâ aṭṭhaṭṭha khattiyesu pan' aṭṭhasu
sabbajeṭṭhaṃ bodhiguttaṃ rakkhituṃ bodhim uttamaṃ. |
adâsi sabbaparihâraṃ sabbâlaṃkâraphâsukaṃ,
soḷasa laṃkâ mahâlekhâ dharaṇî bodhigâravâ. |
tathâ susiñcattharaṃ câpi mahâlekhaṭṭhâne ṭhape.
35 so kulasahassakaṃ katvâ ketuchâditta pâlanaṃ, |
suvaṇṇabheriyâ raṭṭhaabhisekâdimaṅgale.
ekañ janapadaṃ datvâ Candaguttaṃ ṭhapesi ca |
Devaguttapâsâdaṃ bhûmi cekaṃ yathârahaṃ,
kulânan tâdaññesaṃ vâ gâmabhoge pariccaji. |
Rañño pañcasatâ kaññâ aggajâtâ yasassinî
pabbajiṃsu ca tâ sabbâ vîtarâgâ samâhitâ. |
kumârikâ pañcasatâ Anulâparivâritâ
pabbajiṃsu ca tâ sabbâ vîtarâgâ samâhitâ. |
Ariṭṭho nâma khattiyo nikkhanto bhayaanduto
pañcasataparivâro pabbaji jinasâsane.
40 sabbeva arahattappattâ sampuṇṇâ jinasâsane. |
hemante paṭhame mâse supupphite dharaṇîruhe
âgato so mahâbodhi patiṭṭhito Tambapaṇṇike 'ti. |

bhâṇavâraṃ soḷasamaṃ.

XVII.

Battiṃsa yojanaṃ dîghaṃ aṭṭhârasahi vitthataṃ
yojanasataâvaṭṭaṃ sâgarena parikkhitaṃ |

---

30. saha devîhi? — 31. gandhagandhânam N, gandho gandhânam (°ram F) AF, gandho gandhâdim (°dam G1) BG, gandhodakam Z. gandhâgandhânaṃ? — 33. bodhiguttiṃ? — vv. 34—37 are wanting in BG2Z. — 34. sabbâlaṃkârupâgatâ N, sabbâlaṃkâram âgataṃ F, sabbâlaṃkârapâsukaṃ AG1. — laṃkâ AG1N, saṃghâ F. — mahâlekhaṃ AFG. — dharaṇi AF. soḷas' akâ mahâlekhâ dharaṇî (locative) bodhigâravâ? — 35. tathâpi supiñcattharâpiñcâpi AG, tathâ susiñcatthañ câpi N, tathâ susañcittharañ câpi F. tathâ sucisantharañ câpi (comp. Mahâv., p. 118, l. 4)? — kulayakaṃ AG, kulasahassakaṃ N, kusalassakaṃ F. — ketuṃ châdittha (°tta G) AFG. I do not try any conjecture. — 36. °bheriyo? — raṭṭhu AG. — datvâ datvâ Cand° AG. — 37. Dev° ca bhûmiccâgaṃ? — dadaññesaṃ vâ F, tarasaṃvâsâ AG. tadaññesañ ca? — 40. bhayañcuto Y, bhayaanduto N, bhayaañcuto F.

Laṅkâdîpavaraṃ nâma sabbattha ratanâkaraṃ
upetaṃ nadîtalâkehi pabbatehi vanehi ca. |
dîpaṃ purañ ca râjâ ca upaddutañ ca dhâtuyo
thûpaṃ dîpañ ca pabbataṃ uyyânaṃ bodhi bhikkhunî |
bhikkhu ca buddhaseṭṭho ca terasa honti te tahiṃ;
ekadese caturonâmaṃ suṇâtha mama bhâsato. |
Ojadîpaṃ Varadîpaṃ Maṇḍadîpan ti vuccati
Laṅkâdîpavaraṃ nâma Tambapaṇṇîti ñâyati. | 5
Abhayapuraṃ Vaḍḍhamânaṃ Visâlaṃ Anurâdhapuraṃ
purassa caturonâmaṃ catubuddhâna sâsane. |
Abhayo ca Samiddho ca Jayanto ca narâdhipo
Devânampiyatisso ca râjâno honti câturo. |
rogadubbuṭṭhikañ c' eva vivâdayakkhâdhivâsanaṃ
caturo upaddutâ ete catubuddhavinoditâ. |
Kakusandhassa bhagavato dhâtu dhammakarako ahû,
Konâgamanassa buddhassa dhâtu kâyabandhanaṃ ahû, |
Kassapassa sambuddhassa dhâtu udakasâṭakaṃ,
Gotamassa sirîmato doṇadhâtu sârîrikâ. | 10
Abhayapure Paṭiyârâmo, Vaḍḍhamânassa Uttarâ,
Visâle Pâcînârâmo, Thûpârâmo 'nurâdhassa
dakkhiṇe caturo thûpâ catubuddhâna sâsane. |
Kadambakassa sâmantâ nagaraṃ Abhayapuraṃ,
Tissatalâkasâmantâ nagaraṃ Vaḍḍhamânakaṃ, |
Khematalâkasâmantâ Visâlaṃ nagaraṃ . . .,
. . . . . Anurâdhapuraṃ,
. . . . tatth' eva caturodîpavicâraṇaṃ. |
Devakûṭo Sumanakûṭo Subhakûṭo 'ti vuccati,
Sîlakûṭo nâma dâni catupaṇṇatti pabbate. |
Mahâtitthaṃ nâma uyyânaṃ Mahânâmañ ca Sâgaraṃ
Mahâmeghavanaṃ nâma vasantaṃ ariyâpathaṃ
caturolokanâthânaṃ paṭhamaṃ senâsanaṃ ahû. | 15

XVII, 3. thûpaṃ dahañ ca? — 4. ekadese caturo (cattâro BG2) nâma ABFG, ekadesena vakkhâmi Z, ekadesaṃ caturonâmaṃ N. — 8. catubuddhâ vin° BGFZ; this may be the correct reading. — 11. Uttaro A1. — dakkhiṇo ABG, °ne ZFn. — 13. After the words „Visâlaṃ nagaraṃ" N inserts „puraṃ", Z: „ahu". Evidently some words are wanting. — tath' eva caturodisâvicâraṇaṃ? — 14. Silâkûṭo Z. — 15. Mahânomaṃ N, Mahânopañ F. (Comp. Mahâv., pp. 92. 93.) — pasatthaṃ? — catunnaṃ lok° ABG2.

Kakusandhassa bhagavato sirîsabodhim uttamaṃ
âdâya dakkhiṇaṃ sâkhaṃ Rucânandâ mahiddhikâ
Ojadîpe Mahâtitthe ârâme tattha ropitâ. |
Konâgamanassa bhagavato udumbarabodhim uttamaṃ
âdâya dakkhiṇaṃ sâkhaṃ Kandanandâ mahiddhikâ |
Varadîpe Mahânomamhi ârâme tattha ropitâ.
Kassapassa bhagavato nigrodhabodhim uttamaṃ |
âdâya dakkhiṇaṃ sâkhaṃ Sudhammâ nâma mahiddhikâ
Sâgaramhi nâma ârâme ropitaṃ dumacetiyaṃ. |
Gotamassa bhagavato assatthabodhim uttamaṃ
âdâya dakkhiṇaṃ sâkhaṃ Saṃghamittâ mahiddhikâ |
Mahâmeghavane ramme ropitâ dîpalañjake.
Rucânandâ Kanakadattâ Sudhammâ ca mahiddhikâ |
bahussutâ Saṃghamittâ chaḷabhiññâ vicakkhaṇâ
catasso tâ bhikkhuniyo sabbâ ca bodhim âharuṃ. |
sirîsabodhi Mahâtitthe, Mahânâme udumbaro,
Mahâsâgaramhi nigrodho, assattho Meghavane tadâ |
acale caturârâme catubodhi patiṭṭhitâ.
acale senâsanaṃ rammaṃ catubuddhâna sâsane. |
Mahâdevo chaḷabhiñño Sumano paṭisambhido
mahiddhiko Sabbanando Mahindo ca bahussuto
ete therâ mahâpaññâ Tambapaṇṇipasâdakâ. |
Kakusandho sabbalokaggo pañcacakkhûhi cakkhumâ
sabbalokaṃ avekkhanto Ojadîpavar' addasa. |
puṇṇakanarako nâma ahû pajjarako tadâ.
tasmiṃ samaye manussânaṃ rogo pajjarako ahû. |
rogena phuṭṭhâ bahujanâ bhantamacchâ va thalamhi ṭhitâ socanti dummanâ |
bhayaṭṭitâ na labhanti cittasukhasâtam attano.
disvâna dukkhite satte rogabandhena dûsite |
cattâlîsasahassehi Kakusandho lokanâyako

---

17. Kanakadattâ A, Kandanandâ (°ntâ G1) G1N, Kanandâ BFG2, Nandâ nâma Z. — 18. Mahânâmamhi A, Majaṃgânomamhi BG, Janomambhi Z, Mahânomamhi X. — 19. ropitâ? — 21. Kandanandâ X, Kandânandâ G1. — 22. sabbâ va F. — 23. Mahânome XG1. — 24. caturorâme YF. — catubodhi? — 24[b]. acalo Y, ajalo F. — sâsanaṃ G1N, °ne YF. — 28. bhantam° X, pantam° G1, matťam° A, pattâ m° BG2Z. — ṭhitâ N, uṭṭhitâ Y, uṭṭhito uṭṭhito F. — 29. rogabhayena A, rogabhantena BGZ, rogabandena F, rogabandhena N.

rogânaṃ bhindanatthâya Jambudîpâ idhâgato. | 30
cattâlîsasahassehi chaḷabhiññâ mahiddhikâ
parivârayiṃsu sambuddhaṃ nabhe candaṃ va târakâ. |
Kakusandho lokapajjoto Devakûṭamhi pabbate
obhâsetvâna devo va patiṭṭhâsi sasâvako. |
Ojadîpe Devakûṭamhi obhâsetvâ patiṭṭhitaṃ
devo 'va maññanti sabbe na jânanti tathâgataṃ. |
udentaṃ aruṇuggamamhi puṇṇamâse uposathe
ujjâletvâna taṃ selaṃ jalamânaṃ sakânanaṃ |
disvâna selaṃ jalamânaṃ obhâsentaṃ catuddisaṃ
tuṭṭhahaṭṭhâ janâ sabbe sarâjâ Abhaye pure. | 35
passantu maṃ janâ sabbe Ojadîpagatâ narâ
iti buddho adhiṭṭhâsi Kakusandho lokanâyako. |
isisammato Devakûṭo manusse abhipatthito.
upaddave pajjarake manussabalavâhanâ |
nikkhamitvâ janâ sabbe sarâjâ nagarâ purâ
tattha gantvâ namassanti Kakusandhaṃ naruttamaṃ. |
abhivâdetvâna sambuddhaṃ râjasenâ saraṭṭhakâ
devâ 'ti taṃ maññamânâ âgatâ te mahâjanâ. |
anuppattâ janâ sabbe buddhaseṭṭhaṃ narâsabhaṃ.
adhivâsetu me bhagavâ saddhiṃ bhikkhugaṇe saha | 40
ajjatanâya bhattena, gacchâma nagaraṃ puraṃ.
adhivâseti sambuddho tuṇhî râjassa bhâsitaṃ. |
adhivâsanaṃ viditvâna râjasenâ saraṭṭhakâ
pûjâsakkârabahute tadâ puraṃ upâgamuṃ. |
mahâ ayaṃ bhikkhusaṃgho, janakâyo anappako,
nagarake atisambâdhe akatabhûmi pure mama. |
atthi mayhaṃ bahuyyâṇaṃ Mahâtitthaṃ manoramaṃ
asambâdhaṃ adûraṭṭhaṃ pabbajitânulomikaṃ |
paṭisallânasâruppaṃ paṭirûpaṃ tathâgataṃ
tatthâhaṃ buddhapamukhaṃ saṃghaṃ dassâmi dakkhiṇaṃ. | 45

---

30. bhindanatthâya N, bandhan° BG, bandan° F, mocanatthâya AZ. — 31. °sahassâ hi BG2. °sahassâni? — vv. 33[a]—35[a] are wanting in A. — 33. devo va X, na (omitting devo) YF; devo ti (comp. v. 39)? — 34. udayâ aruṇ° N. — 37. manusse abhipatiṭṭhito Y, m° abhipaṭṭhito F. manusseh' abhipatthito? — upaddute N. — manussabalavâhane N, °naṃ FG1Z, °nâ ABG2. — 39. devo 'ti? — 41. adhivâsesi AZ. — 42. pûjâsakkâraṃ katvâna te ABG2, °kkârabahunâ te Z, °kkârabahute N, °kkâ bahu ca te (va te) FG1. pûjâsakkârabahulâ? — 44. bahuyyânaṃ FG1Zn, brahuyyânaṃ ABG2.

sabbo jano passeyya taṃ buddhaṃ saṃghañ ca dassanaṃ.
cattâlîsasahassehi bhikkhusaṃghapurakkhato |
Kakusandho lokavidû Mahâtitthamhi pâpuṇi.
patiṭṭhite Mahâtitthamhi uyyâne dipaduttame |
akâlapupphehi sañchannâ yaṃ kiñci ca latâ dumâ.
sovaṇṇamayabhiṅkâraṃ samâdâya mahîpati |
onojetvâna Laṃkatthaṃ jalaṃ hatthe akârayi.
im' âhaṃ bhante uyyânaṃ dadâmi buddhapâmukhe.
saṃghassa phâsuvihâram rammaṃ senâsanaṃ ahû. |
paṭiggahesi uyyânaṃ Kakusandho lokanâyako,
50 pakampi dharaṇî tattha paṭhamaṃ senâsanaṃ tadâ. |
paṭhavîacalaṃ kampetaṃ ṭhito lokagganâyako:
aho nûna Rucânandâ bodhiṃ haritvâ idhâgatâ. |
Kakusandhassa bhagavato cittaṃ aññâya bhikkhunî
gantvâ sirîsamahâbodhimûle ṭhatvâ mahiddhikâ, |
buddho ca icchati bodhi Ojadîpamhi rohanaṃ,
manusâ cintayaṃ tattha bodhiṃ âharituṃ gamâ. |
anumataṃ buddhaseṭṭhena anukampâya pâṇino
mama iddhânubhâvena dakkhiṇasâkhâ pamuccatu. |
Rucânandâ imaṃ vâkyaṃ yâcamânâ katañjali
55 muccitvâ dakkkiṇasâkhâ patiṭṭhâsi kaṭâhake. |
gahetvâna Rucânandâ bodhiṃ suvaṇṇakaṭâhake
pañcasatabhikkhunîhi parivâresi mahiddhikâ. |
tadâpi paṭhavî kampi sasamuddaṃ sapabbataṃ
âloko 'va mahâ âsi abbhuto lomahaṃsano. |
disvâ attamanâ sabbe râjasenâ saraṭṭhakâ
añjaliṃ paggahetvâna namassanti bodhim uttamaṃ. |
âmoditâ marû sabbe devatâ haṭṭhamânasâ
ukkuṭṭhisaddaṃ pavattesuṃ disvâ bodhivaruttamaṃ. |

---

47. patiṭṭhe N, titthite A, saha patiṭṭhite BGZ, saha patiṭṭhe F. — 48. saṃchantaṃ kiṃci ca A. — Instead of „yaṃ kiñci" we should expect a preterite ending in -iṃsu. — 49. laṃkattha R, laṃtattha C, laṃtatthaṃ M, laṃkataṃ F. — âkiri A. — rammaṃ N, maṃ F, imaṃ Y. — 50. ahû A (instead of tadâ). Perhaps we should transpose ahû (v. 49), and tadâ (v. 50). — 51. [pa]tha[vî]âja[laṃ] N, pathavîajalaṃ F. — kampento ABG2. — 52. Y omits gantvâ. — 53. rohanaṃ (sic) BG, ropanaṃ AZ, rûhanaṃ X. — manusâ N, manasâ F, manussâ ABG, manussa Z. — cintayaṃ Zn, cintayan G1, cintayuṃ ABG2, cittayan F. — manusâcintiyaṃ tattha bodhiṃ âharituṃ gamâ? — 57. sasamuddâ Z. — âloko ca AGZ. — 59. marû ABG, maru Z, manu F, narâ N.

cattâro ca mahârâjâ lokapâlâ yasassino
ârakkhaṃ sirîsabodhissa akaṃsu devatâ tadâ. | 60
tâvatiṃsâ ca ye devâ ye devâ vasavattino
Yamo Sakko Suyâmo ca Santusito Sunimmito
sabbe te parivâriṃsu sirîsabodhim uttamaṃ. |
añjaliṃ paggahetvâna devasaṃghâ pamoditâ
Rucânandâya sah' eva pûjenti bodhim uttamaṃ. |
sirîsabodhiṃ âdâya Rucânandâ mahiddhikâ
bhikkhunîsaṃghaparibbûḷhâ Ojadîpavaraṃ gami. |
devâ naccanti hasanti poṭhenti diguṇaṃ bhujaṃ
Ojadîpavaraṃ yantaṃ sirîsabodhim uttamaṃ. |
devasaṃghaparibbûḷhâ Rucânandâ mahiddhikâ
âdâya sirîsabodhiṃ Kakusandhaṃ upâgami. | 65
tamhi kâle mahâvîro Kakusandho lokanâyako
Mahâtitthamhi uyyâne bodhiṭṭhâne patiṭṭhito. |
Rucânandâ sayaṃ bodhiṃ obhâsentaṃ na ropayi,
disvâ sayaṃ Kakusandho paggahi dakkhiṇaṃ bhujaṃ. |
bodhiyâ dakkhiṇaṃ sâkhaṃ Rucânandâ mahiddhikâ
buddhassa dakkhiṇahatthe ṭhapayitvâbhivâdayi. |
parâmasitvâ lokaggo Kakusandho narâsabho
adâsi rañño 'bhayassa: imaṃ ṭhânamhi ropaya. |
yamhi ṭhânamhi âcikkhi Kakusandho lokanâyako
tamhi ṭhânamhi ropesi Abhayo raṭṭhavaḍḍhano. | 70
patiṭṭhite sirîsabodhimhi bhûmibhâge manorame
buddho dhammaṃ adesayi catusaccaṃ saṇhakâraṇaṃ. |
pariyosâne satasahassaṃ cattâlîsa sahassiyo
abhisamayo manussânaṃ, devânaṃ tiṃsa koṭiyo. |
sirîsabodhi Kakusandhassa, Konâgamanassa udumbaro,
Kassapassâpi nigrodho tayobodhivihâraṇâ. |
Sakyaputtassa asamassa bodhi assattham uttamaṃ
âharitvâna ropiṃsu Mahâmeghavane tadâ. |

Muṭasîvassa atrajâ ath' aññe dasa bhâtaro
Abhayo Tisso Nâgo ca Utti Mattâbhayo pi ca | 75
Mitto Sîvo Aselo ca Tisso Khîro ca bhâtaro,

---

71. °ccaṃ saṇhakâraṇaṃ G1X, °ccappakâsanaṃ A, °ccaṃ sattakâraṇaṃ BG2, °ccappakâsato Z. — 73. tayo bodhim idh' âharuṃ (°raṃ B) ABG2Z, tayobodhivihâraṇâ (°rakâ N, °ruṇâ G1) FG1N. tayobodhivicâraṇaṃ? comp. v. 18. — 74. bodhiṃ? — 76. Sivo AG. — Kiro ca?

anudevî Anulâ ca Muṭasîvassa dhîtaro. |
tadâ ca bilayo agâ Lañkâdîpavaruttamaṃ
yadâ abhisitto râjâ Muṭasîvassa atrajo
etthantare yaṃ gaṇitaṃ vassaṃ bhavati kittakaṃ? |
dve satâni ca vassâni chattiṃsa ca saṃvacchare
sambuddhe parinibbute abhisitto Devânampiyo. |
âgatâ râjaiddhiyo abhisitte Devânampiye,
pharati puññatejâni Tambapaṇṇimhi issaro. |
ratanâkaraṃ tadâ âsi Lañkâdîpaṃ varuttamaṃ,
80 Tissassa puññatejena uggatâ ratanâ bahû. |
disvâna ratanaṃ râjâ haṭṭho saṃviggamânaso
paṇṇâkâraṃ karitvâna Asokadhammassa pâhiṇi. |
disvâna taṃ paṇṇâkâraṃ Asoko attamano ahû,
abhisekaṃ nânâratanaṃ puna pâhesi Devânampiyassa. |
vâlavîjaniṃ uṇhîsaṃ chattaṃ khaggañ ca pâdukaṃ
veṭhanaṃ sârapâmañgaṃ bhiñkâraṃ nandivaṭṭakaṃ |
sivikaṃ sañkhavataṃsaṃ adhovimaṃ vatthakoṭikaṃ
sovaṇṇapâtikaṭacchuṃ mahagghaṃ hatthapuñchanaṃ |
Anotattodakaṃ kâjaṃ uttamaṃ haricandanaṃ
85 aruṇavaṇṇamattikaṃ añjanaṃ nâgamâhaṭaṃ |
harîtakaṃ âmalakaṃ mahagghaṃ amatosadhaṃ
saṭṭhivâhasataṃ sâliṃ sugandhaṃ sukamâhaṭaṃ
puññakammâbhinibbattaṃ pâhesi Asokasavhayo. |
Lañkâbhisekatisso ca Asokadhammassa pesito
abhisitto dutiyâbhisekena Tambapaṇṇimhi issaro. |
dutiyâbhisittaṃ Tissaṃ atikkami tiṃsa rattiyo
Mahindo gaṇapâmokkho Jambudîpâ idhâgato. |
kârâpesi vihâraṃ so Tissârâmaṃ varuttamaṃ,
patiṭṭhapesi mahâbodhiṃ Mahâmeghavane tadâ, |
patiṭṭhapesi so thûpaṃ mahantaṃ râmaṇeyyakaṃ,
90 akâsi Devânampiyo ârâmañ Cetiyapabbate, |
Thûpârâmaṃ akâresi vihâraṃ Tissaârâmaṃ,

---

76. anudevî G1N, adudevî F, ahudevî BG2, âhud° Z, ahûd° A. — Anulâdevî Sîvalâ ca (comp. 10, 7)? — 77. pilayo N. yadâ ca Vijayo agâ (comp. 6, 19)? — yadâ câbhisitto? — 79. °tejena G1X. — 87. Lañkâbhisekatissassa BG2. Lañkâbhiseke Tisso ca .. pesite? — 88. atikkami Y, atiggayha N, atikkayha F. atikkamma? — 91. Tissaârâmaṃ N, Tissaâgamaṃ F, Pissaârâmaṃ ABG2, Vissaâr° G1, Missakârâmaṃ Z. The Tissârâma having been mentioned in v. 89, I propose to read vihâraṃ Issarasamaṇaṃ, comp. Mahâv., p. 119, l. 14; p. 128, ll. 8. 9.

Vessagiriñ ca kâresi Colakatissanâmakaṃ, |
tato yojaniko ârâmo Tissarâjena kârito.
patiṭṭhapesi mahâdânaṃ mahâpelavaruttamaṃ.
cattârîsam pi vassâni rajjaṃ kàresi khattiyo 'ti. |
Muṭasîvassa atrajâ ath' aññe catubhâtaro,
Uttiyo dasavassamhi rajjaṃ kâresi khattiyo. |
aṭṭhavassâbhisittassa nibbuto dîpajotako.
akâsi sarîranikkhepaṃ Tissârâme puratthime. |
paripuṇṇadvâdasavasso Mahindo ca idhâgato,
saṭṭhivasse paripuṇṇe nibbuto Cetiyapabbate. | 95
samalaṃkaritvâna puṇṇaghaṭaṃ toraṇañ ca mâlagghiyaṃ
padîpâ ca jalamânâ nibbuto dîpajotako |
râjâ kho Uttiyo nâma kûṭâgâraṃ varuttamaṃ
dassaneyyaṃ akâresi, pûjesi dîpajotakaṃ. |
ubho devâ manussâ ca nâgâ gandhabbadânavâ
sabbeva dukkhitâ hutvâ pûjesuṃ dîpajotakaṃ. |
sattâhaṃ pûjaṃ katvâna Cetiye pabbatuttame
ekacce evam âhaṃsu: gacchâma nagaraṃ puraṃ. |
ath' ettha vattati saddo tumulo bheravo mahâ,
idh' eva jhâpayissâma Laṅkâya dîpajotakaṃ. | 100
râjâ sutvâna vacanaṃ janakâyassa bhâsato:
mahâthûpaṃ karissâmi Tissârâmapuratthime. |
âdâya sakûṭâgâraṃ Mahindaṃ dîpajotakaṃ
nagaraṃ puratthimadvâraṃ pâvisiṃsu sarâjikâ. |
majjhena nagaraṃ gantvâ nikkhamitvâna dakkhiṇe
Mahâvihâre sattâhaṃ mahâpûjaṃ akaṃsu te. |
katvâna gandhacitakaṃ ubho devâ ca mânusâ
ṭhapayiṃsu râjuyyâne: jhâpayissâma subbataṃ. |
sakûṭâgâraṃ gahetvâna Mahindaṃ dîpajotakaṃ
vihâraṃ padakkhiṇaṃ katvâ vandâpesuṃ thûpam uttamaṃ. | 105
ârâmâ puratthimadvârâ nikkhamitvâ mahâjanâ

---

92. yojanikâ ârâmâ .. kâritâ? comp. Mahâv., p. 120, l. 2. — mahâmeghavaruttamaṃ Y, mahâpelavaruttamaṃ N, mahâpelagaruttamaṃ F. Comp. Mahâv., p. 225, l. 15; on p. 202, l. 13 we have the following remark in the Ṭîkâ: „mahâpelabhattâdi paṭhamaṃ saṃghanavakânaṃ dâpayîti attho." — 93. dasavassâpi N. dasa vassâni? — 94. Tissârâmapuratthime? comp. v. 101. — 96ᵇ. va X, ca Y. — nibbute °jotake A2BG2. — 97. pûjesi N, pûjesuṃ FZ, pûjetuṃ ABG. — 101. Tissârâmapuratthito XG1. Comp. v. 93; Mahâvaṃsa, p. 125, l. 5. — 103. dakkhiṇâ B, dakkhinâ A. — 105. kûtâgâraṃ Y, kûṭâkâraṃ F.

akaṃsu sarîranikkhepaṃ bhûmibhâge samantato. |
ârûḷhâ citakaṃ sabbe rodamânâ katañjalî
abhivâdetvâna sirasâ citakaṃ dîpayiṃsu te. |
sadhâtum eva tathâsesaṃ jhâyamâno mahâgaṇî.
akaṃsu thûpavaraṃ sabbe ârâme yojanike tadâ. |
kataṃ sarîranikkhepaṃ Mahindaṃ dîpajotakaṃ
Isibhûmîti taṃ nâmam samaññâ paṭhamaṃ ahû. |
bhâṇavâraṃ sattarasamaṃ.

XVIII.

Idâni atthi aññe pi therâ ca majjhimâ navâ
vibhajjavâdâ vinaye sâsane paveṇipâlakâ, |
bahussutâ sîlasampannâ obhâsenti mahiṃ imaṃ,
dhutaṅgâcârasampannâ sobhanti dîpalañjake. |
Sâkyaputtâ bahû c' ettha saddhammavaṃsakovidâ.
bahunnaṃ vata atthâya loke uppajji cakkhumâ,
andhakâraṃ vidhametvâ âlokaṃ dassesi so jino. |
yesaṃ tathâgate saddhâ acalâ suppatiṭṭhitâ
sabbaduggatiyo hitvâ sugatiṃ upapajjare. |
ye ca bhâventi bojjhaṅgaṃ indriyâni balâni ca
satisammappadhâne ca iddhipâde ca kevalaṃ |
ariyaṃ aṭṭhaṅgikaṃ maggaṃ dukkhûpasamagâminaṃ,
chetvâna Maccuno senaṃ te loke vijitâvino 'ti. |
Mâyâdevî ca kaniṭṭhâ sahajâtâ ekamâtukâ
bhagavantaṃ thanaṃ pâyesi mâtâ va anukampikâ |
kittitâ agganikkhittâ chaḷabhiññâ mahiddhikâ
Mahâpajâpatî nâma Gotamî iti vissutâ. |
Khemâ Uppalavaṇṇâ ca ubho tâ aggasâvikâ
Paṭâcârâ Dhammadinnâ Sobhitâ Isidâsikâ |
Visâkhâ Soṇâ Sabalâ ca Saṃghadâsî vicakkhaṇâ
Nandâ ca dhammapâlâ ca vinaye ca visâradâ
etâ Jambudîpavhaye vinayaññû maggakovidâ. |

---

107. dîpayiṃsu te Y, dîpisu teja G1, dîpiṃsu (dîpisu F) te janâ X. — 108. jhâpayamânâ N, jhâyyamâno F, jhâyamâne Z.

XVIII, 1. therâ pi Y. — vibhajjavâdî A. — vv. 3—44 are wanting in BG2. — 8. Sâkyaputtâ N, Saky° YF. Sâkyaputtiyâ? (or Sâkyaputtî? see schol. Kacc., p. 186, ed. Senart.) — 10. Soṇâ X, Sokâ AG, Yokâ Z. — Sapalâ ca YF.

therikâ Saṃghamittâ ca Uttarâ ca vicakkhaṇâ
Hema Pasâdapâlâ ca Aggimittâ ca Dâsikâ |
Pheggu Pabbatâ Mattâ ca Mallâ ca Dhammadâsiyâ
etâ daharabhikkhuniyo Jambudîpâ idhâgatâ. |
vinayaṃ vâcayiṃsu piṭakaṃ Anurâdhapuravhaye
vinaye pañca vâcesuṃ satta c' eva pakaraṇe. |
Saddhammanandi Somâ ca Giriddhi pi ca Dâsiyâ
Dhammâ ca dhammapâlâ ca vinaye ca visâradâ |
dhutavâdâ ca Mahilâ Sobhaṇâ ca Dhammatâpasâ
Naramittâ mahâpaññâ vinaye ca visâradâ |
theriyovâdakusalâ Sâtâ Kâlî ca Uttarâ,
etâ tadâ bhikkhuniyo upasampannâ dîpalañjake. |
abhiññâtâ ca Sumanâ saddhammavaṃsakovidâ,
etâ tadâ bhikkhuniyo dhutarâgâ samâhitâ |
sudhotamanasaṃkappâ saddhammavinaye ratâ
vîsatibhikkhunîsahassehi Uttarâ sâdhusammatâ
sujâtâ kulaputtena Abhayena yasassinâ. |
vinayaṃ tâva vâcesuṃ piṭakaṃ Anurâdhasavhaye
nikâye pañca vâcesuṃ satta c' eva pakaraṇe. |
abhiññâtâ ca Mahilâ saddhammavaṃsakovidâ
Samantâ Kâkavaṇṇassa etâ râjassa dhîtarâ |
purohitassa dhîtâ ca Girikâlî bahussutâ
Dâsî Kâlî tu dhuttassa dhîtaro sabbapâpikâ, |
etâ tadâ bhikkhuniyo sabbapâli durâsadâ
odâtamanasaṃkappâ saddhammavinaye ratâ |
vîsatibhikkhunîsahassehi saha Rohanam âgatâ,
pûjitâ naradevena Abhayena yasassinâ
vinayaṃ vâcayiṃsu piṭakaṃ Anurâdhapuravhaye. |

---

11. 12. Comp. 15, 77. 78. — 11. Hema AGZn, Soma F. Hemâ? — Pasâdapâlâ N, Pâsâdassalâ FY. — 12. Sallâ YF. — ekâdasa bhikkhuniyo? Comp. Mahâvaṃsa, p. 115, l. 10. — 13. nikâye pañca (comp. vv. 19. 33)? — 14. Saddhammanandi N, Sadhammanavantaṃga F, Saddhammacandabbâ (°bâ A) Y. — Naramittâ (Narâm° F) mahâpaññâ X, Nagamissâma Y. — 18. Uttarâ sâdhusammatâ X, Uttarâ sâmasammatâ Z, Uttarâ sâsammatâ (sâsamattâ A1) AG. We probably ought to read thus: vîsatibhikkhunîsahassehi saha ... âgatâ. Comp. vv. 23. 25. 32. — pûjitâ kulaputtena? (comp. vv. 23. 26. 37.) — 20. dhîtaro? — 21. Dâsikâlâsâguttassa Y, Dâsikâlî tu dhuttassa N, Dâsikâlâbu bhuttassa F. — dhîtaro sabbapâlikâ? — 22. sabbapâlî? — 23. As the Bhikkhunîs mentioned here lived in Anurâdhapura, I believe that we ought to read: Rohanamh[â] âgatâ. Probably these Bhikkhunîs came from Rohana to Anurâdhapura at the time when

Mahâdevî ca Padumâ Hemâsâ ca yasassinî Unnalâ Añjalî
Sumâ |
etâ tadâ bhikkhuniyo chaḷabhiññâ mahiddhikâ
25 soḷasabhikkhunîsahassehi saha Saṃghamittâgatâ, |
pûjitâ Tissarâjena Devânampiyayasassinâ
vinayaṃ vâcayiṃsu piṭakaṃ Anurâdhapuravhaye. |
Mahâsoṇâ ca Dattâ ca Sîvalâ ca vicakkhaṇâ
Rûpasobhiṇî appamattâ pûjitâ Devamânusâ |
Nâgâ ca Nâgamittâ ca Dhammaguttâ ca Dâsiyâ
cakkhubhûtâ Samuddâ ca saddhammavaṃsakovidâ |
Sapattâ Channâ Upâlî ca Revatâ sâdhusammatâ
etâ venayaggînaṃ aggâ Somanadevassa atrajâ |
Mâlâ Khemâ ca Tissâ ca dhammakathikamuttamâ
30 vinayaṃ tâva vâcayiṃsu paṭhamaṃ apagate bhaye. |
Sîvalâ ca Mahâruhâ saddhammavaṃsakovidâ
pasâdikâ Jambudîpâ sâsanena bahû janâ |
vîsatibhikkhunîsahassehi saha Jambudîpâgatâ
yâcitâ naradevena Abhayena yasassinâ. |
vinayaṃ vâcayiṃsu piṭakaṃ Anurâdhapuravhaye
nikâye pañca vâcesuṃ satta c' eva pakaraṇe. |
sa-Samuddanavâ devî Sîvalâ râjadhîtaro
visâradâ Nâgapâlî Nâgamittâ ca paṇḍitâ |
Mahilâ bhikkhunîpâlâ ca vinaye ca visâradâ
Nâgâ ca Nâgamittâ ca saddhammavaṃsakovidâ,
35 etâ tadâ bhikkhuniyo upasampannâ dîpalañjake |
sabbâ 'va jâtisampannâ sâsane vissutâ tadâ
soḷasannaṃ bhikkhunîsahassânaṃ uttamâ dhurasammatâ |
pûjitâ Kuṭikaṇṇena Abhayena yasassinâ
vinayaṃ vâcayiṃsu piṭakaṃ Anurâdhapuravhaye. |
Cûlanâgâ ca Dhannâ ca Soṇâ ca sâdhusammatâ
abhiññâtâ ca Saṇhâ ca saddhammavaṃsakovidâ |

Abhaya Duṭṭhagâmaṇi, whose father Kâkavaṇṇa had been king of Rohana, and whose sister was the chief of these Bhikkhunîs, transferred his residence to Anurâdhapura, after the defeat of Elâra.

24. Unalâ YF. — 25. saha Saṃghamittâ idhâgatâ N. This passage is hopelessy corrupted. The names both of Saṃghamittâ and of Devânampiya (v. 26) seem to be out of place here. — 29. venayikânaṃ aggâ? — Chandâ Y. — 30. apagato Y. — 31. pâsâdikâ CM. — pasâditâ Jambudîpe sasanena bahû jane? — 34. °samuddanâvâ Z. — 38. Dhannâ ca N, Dhammâ ca F; these words are wanting in Y.

Gamikadhîtâ mahâpaññâ Mahâtissâ visâradâ
Cûlasumanâ Mahâsumanâ Mahâkâlî ca paṇḍitâ |
sambhâvitâ kule jâtâ Lakkhadhammâ mahâyasâ,
Dîpanayâ mahâpaññâ Rohane sâdhusammatâ | 40
abhiññâtâ ca Samuddâ saddhammavaṃsakovidâ
vibhajjavâdi vinayadharâ ubho tâ saṃghasobhaṇâ, |
etâ c' aññâ ca bhikkhuniyo upasampannâ dîpalañjake
odâtamanasaṃkappâ saddhammavinaye ratâ |
bahussutâ sutadharâ pâpabâhirakâ ca tâ
jalitvâ aggikkhandhâ va nibbutâ tâ mahâyasâ. |
idâni atthi aññâyo therikâ majjhimâ navâ
vibhajjavâdî vinayadharâ sâsane paveṇipâlakâ
bahussutâ sîlasampannâ obhâsenti mahiṃ iman ti. |
Sivo ca dasa vassâni rajjaṃ kâresi khattiyo,
patiṭṭhapesi ârâmaṃ vihâraṃ Nagaraṅgaṇaṃ. | 45
Sûratisso dasa vassâni rajjaṃ kâresi khattiyo,
kâresi pañcasatârâmaṃ uḷâraṃ puññaṃ anappakaṃ. |
Sûratissaṃ gahetvâna Damilâ Senaguttakâ
duve dvâdasa vassâni rajjaṃ dhammena kârayuṃ. |
atrajo Muṭasîvassa Aselo Senaguttake
hantvâna dasa vassâni rajjaṃ kâresi khattiyo. |
Elâro nâma nâmena Aselaṃ hantvâna khattiyo
catutâlîsa vassâni rajjaṃ dhammena kârayi. |
chandâgatiṃ agantvâna na dosabhayamohâgatiṃ
tulâbhûto va hutvâna dhammena anusâsi so. | 50
hemantam pi ca gimhânaṃ vassânam pi na vassati,
sataṭaṃ megho vassati sattasattâham pi vassati. |
tîṇi adhikaraṇâni âsi .. vinicchi bhûpati,
rattiṃ 'va vassati megho divâ pana na vassati. |
Kâkavaṇṇassa yo putto Abhayo nâma khattiyo
dasayodhaparivâro, vâraṇo Kaṇḍulo tahiṃ, |
hanitvâ battiṃsa râjânaṃ vaṃsaṃ katvâna ekato,
catuvîsati vassâni rajjaṃ kâresi khattiyo. |

bhâṇavâraṃ aṭṭhârasamaṃ. mahâvâraṃ niṭṭhitaṃ.

---

40. Rohane X, Rosâmano Z, Rosâmane (°ṇe G) AG. — 41. vibhajjavâdî? — 44. vibhajjavâdi Y, °dâ X. — obhâsenta A, obhâseti GX, obhâsenti Z. Comp. v. 2. — 45. Sivo BF, Sivo AGZn. — vv. 47. 48 are wanting in YF. — vv. 51—53 are wanting in BG2Z. — 51. vuṭṭhahi X, vaṭṭhati (corrected into vassati) G1, vassati A. — 52. ca AFG, va N.

XIX.

Pâsâdaṃ mâpayi râjâ ubbedhaṃ navabhûmikaṃ
anagghikañ catumukhaṃ, pariccâgâ tiṃsa koṭiyo. |
sudhâbhûmi thûlaselaṃ mattikaṃ iṭṭhakâya ca
visuddhabhûmikâ c' eva ayojâlaṃ tato marumpaṃ |
îsasakkharapâsâṇâ aṭṭhaaṭṭhalikâ silâ phalikarajatena dvâdasa, |
etâni bhûmikammâni kârâpetvâna khattiyo
bhikkhusaṃghaṃ samodhânetvâ cetiyâvattasammiti. |
Indagutto Dhammaseno Piyadassî mahâkathî
5 Buddho Dhammo ca Saṃgho ca Mittanno ca visârado |
Anattano Mahâdevo Dhammarakkhito bahussuto
Uttaro Cittagutto ca Indagutto ca paṇḍito |
Suriyagutto mahânâgo paṭibhânavisârado,
ete kho cuddasa sabbe Jambudîpâ idhâgatâ. |
Siddhattho Mañgalo Sumano Padumo câpi Sîvalî
Candagutto Suriyagutto Indagutto ca Sâgaro
Mittaseno Jayaseno Acalena ca dvâdasa, |
Suppatiṭṭhito Brahmâ ca Nandisena Sumanadevî ca
putto mâtu pitu c' eva gihibhûtâ tayo janâ. |
kârâpesi Mahâthûpaṃ mahâvihâram uttamaṃ
10 anagghaṃ vîsati datvâ pariccâgo . . . |

XIX. vv. 2—4 are wanting in BG2. — 2. mattikâ A. — paruppaṃ G, parupapaṃ ca Z, marumpaṃ N, badumaṃ F, pari A. We ought to read marumbaṃ; comp. Mahâvaṃsa, p. 169, l. 8 (with the correction, p. XXIV); Thûpavaṃsa (MS. Burnouf 142, fol. kho'): „tassopari ayojâlaṃ, tassopari khîṇâsavasâmaṇerehi Himavantato âhaṭaṃ sugandhamârumbaṃ." — 3. °pâsâṇa N, °pâsâna G. — aṭṭhaaṭṭhâlikâ (aṭṭha + âli) silâ? — 4. cetiyâcattasamîti A, °âvattasammuti Z, °âvattasamiti G, °avatthasamiti F, °âvattasammiti N. cetiyâvaṭṭa[ṃ] sammitaṃ? comp. Mahâv., p. 172, l. 10; p. 178, l. 1. — 5. Mittako (°ke G1) Y, Mittano F, Ttunno (*sic*, instead of [Mi]ttunno?) N. Mahâv. Ṭîkâ: Mittaṇṇa. — 9. Nandiseno. — mâtâ pitâ c' eva? Comp. Mahâv. Ṭîkâ, fol. ṭâm: „paṭhavikampanâdîhi acchariyehi vimhito râjâ attano samîpe ṭhitaṃ paribbhamaṇadaṇḍakagâhakaṃ amaccaputtaṃ tvaṃ konâmo tâtâ 'ti pucchi. ahaṃ Suppatiṭṭhitabrahmâ nâma mahârâjâ 'ti âha. tava pitâ ko nâma tâtâ 'ti vatvâ mayhaṃ pitâ Nandiseno nâma mahârâjâ 'ti vutte, tava mâtâ kânâmâ 'ti pucchi. mama mâtâ Sumaṇadevî nâma mahârâjâ 'ti âha. tenâhu porâṇâ:

Suppatiṭṭhitabrahmâ ca Nandiseno Sumaṇadeviyâ
putto mâtâ pitâ c' eva gihîbhûtâ tayo janâ 'ti." —

10. The end of the verse may be written thus: pariccâgaṃ cattâri ca; see Mahâv., p. 195, l. 8.

gamikavattaṃ suṇitvâ bhikkhusaṃghassa bhâsato
adâsi gamikabhesajjaṃ phâsuvihâraṃ .... |
bhikkhunînaṃ vaco sutvâ harikâle subhâsitaṃ
adâsi c' eva bhikkhunînaṃ yadicchaṃ râjaissaro. |
silâkathûpaṃ akâresi vihârañ Cetiyapabbate
kâresi âsanasâlaṃ Jalakaṃ nâma uttamaṃ. |
Girinâmanigaṇṭhassa vuṭṭhokâse tahiṃ kato
Abhayagirîti paññatti vohâro samajâyatha. |
Âlavatto Sâbhiyo ca Panayo Palaya-Dâṭhikâ
cuddasavassaṃ satta mâsâ pañca râjâno kârayuṃ. |
Saddhâtissassâyaṃ putto Abhayo nâma khattiyo
Dâṭhikaṃ Damilaṃ hantvâ rajjaṃ kâresi khattiyo. |
Abhayagiriṃ patiṭṭhapesi silâthûpaṃ cetiyamantare.
dvâdasavassaṃ pañca mâsâni rajjaṃ kâresi khattiyo. |
satta yodhâ Abhayassa ârâmaṃ pañca kârayuṃ;
Uttiyo ca Sâliyo ca Mûlo Tisso ca Pabbato
Devo ca Uttaro c' eva ete kho satta yodhino. |
vihâraṃ Dakkhiṇaṃ nâma Uttiyo nâma kârayi,
Sâliyo Sâliyârâmaṃ, Mûlo ca Mûlaâsayaṃ, |
Pabbato Pabbatârâmaṃ, Tisso Tissârâmaṃ kare,
Devo ca Uttaro c' eva Devâgâraṃ akaṃsu te. |
Kâkavaṇṇassa atrajo Mahâtisso mahîpati
dinne kathikaṃ katvâna sâlikkhette mahîpati
adâsi Summatherassa santacittassa jhâyino. |
yantaṃ kathikaṃ katvâna tîṇi vassaṃ anûnakaṃ
mahâdânaṃ pavattesi bhikkhu koṭisahassiyo. |
katapuñño mahâpañño Abhayo Duṭṭhagâmani
kâyassa bhedâ sappañño tusitaṃ kâyaṃ upâgami. |
bhâṇavâraṃ ekûnavîsatimaṃ.

XX.

Kâkavaṇṇassa yo putto Tisso nâmâ 'ti vissuto
kârâpesi mahâthûpaṃ Tisso vihâram uttamo. |

---

11. gamikavatthaṃ Y, kamikavattaṃ F, gamikavattakaṃ N. — 12. hâni-kâle N, mârikâle F. I do not understand this word. — 13. silâthûpaṃ A, comp. Mahâv., p. 202, l. 1. — vihâre A. — 14. vuṭṭhokâse N, phuṭṭhokâse F, puṭṭhokâse BGZ, vutthokâse A. Comp. Mahâv., p. 203, l. 6. — gato BFGZ, kato AN. — 15. The first two names ought to be Pulahattho and Bâhiyo. — sattamâsaṃ? satta mâsâni? — 17. Abhayagiri YF. — 22. yante? — bhikkhû koṭ°? — 23. mahâpuñño FY.

vihâraṃ kârâpayati Kallakâlena uttamaṃ
aññañ ca bahu vihâraṃ Saddhâtissena kâritaṃ. |
caturâsîtisahassâni dhammakkhandhaṃ mahârahaṃ,
ekekadhammakkhandhassa pûjaṃ ekekaṃ akârayi. |
pâsâdañ ca akârayi manuññaṃ sattabhûmikaṃ,
lohiṭṭhakena châdesi Saddhâtisso mahâyaso; |
Lohapâsâdakaṃ nâma samaññâ paṭhamaṃ ahû.
5 kârâpesi kharâpiṇḍaṃ, Mahâthûpe varuttame |
hatthipâkâraṃ kâresi parivâraṃ manoramaṃ,
caturassañ ca kâresi talâkaṃ tâvakâlikaṃ. |
aṭṭhârasâni vassâni rajjaṃ kâresi khattiyo.
katvâ aññaṃ bahu puññaṃ datvâ dânaṃ anappakaṃ
kâyassa bhedâ sappañño tusitaṃ kâyaṃ upâgami. |
Saddhâtissassa atrajo Thûlathano 'ti vissuto
kârâpesi mahârâmaṃ vihâraṃ Alakandaraṃ.
dasâhaṃ ekamâsañ ca rajjaṃ kâresi khattiyo. |
Saddhâtissassa atrajo Lañjatisso 'ti vissuto
navavassaṃ chamâsaṃ ca issariyaṃ anusâsi so. |
kârâpesi tilañcanaṃ Mahâthûpe varuttame,
10 patiṭṭhâpesi ârâmaṃ Kumbhilâdhimanoramaṃ, |
kârâpesi Dîghathûpaṃ Thûpârâmapuratthito,
silâkañcuke kâresi Thûpamârâmamuttame. |
Lajjitissamhi uparate kaniṭṭho tassa kârayi
rajjaṃ chaḷ eva vassâni Khallâṭanâganâmako. |
kam Mahârattako nâma hantvâ Khallâṭakaṃ camûpati
rajjaṃ kâresi dinekaṃ paduṭṭho akataññuko. |
tassa rañño kaniṭṭho tu Vaṭṭagâmaninâmako
duṭṭhaṃ senâpatiṃ hantvâ pañcamâsaṃ rajjaṃ kari. |
Pulahattho tu Damilo tîṇi vassâni kârayi.

XX, 2. Gallakâlena ABG, Gallakâlenaṃ Z, Kallahâlena N, Kallakâlena F. Kallakâlenaṃ? comp. Mahâv., p. 200, l. 10. — aññaṃ G1X, aññe Y. — bahû AB, bahu GFZn. — vihâraṃ G1XZ, vihâre ABG2. — 7. bahuṃ ABG2. — 9. Lañcatisso FG1Z, Lañjatisso N, Lajjîtisso, Lajjitisso BG2 (comp. Mah., pp. 201. 202.) — 10. Kumbhilâdim° Z, Kumbhilâdiṃ m° A, Kumbhilâdhim° BGX. Kumbhilâtimanoramaṃ? See Mah., p. 201, l. 6. — 12. Lañjatissamhi N, Lañcatissamhi FG1, Lajjikat° ABG2, Lajjit° Z. — 13. Mahârantako AB, Kammahârattako ZG1, Kammahârantako G2, Kammahârathako F, Kammahâratthako N. — Khallâṭabhûpatiṃ ABG2Z. taṃ Mahârattako nâma hantvâ Khallâṭakaṃ camûpati? Comp. Mahâv., p. 202, l. 10; the excellent Mahâvaṃsa MS. of the India Off. Library (no. 91) reads Mahârattako.

duve vassâni Bâhiyo camûpati rajjaṃ kari. |
hantvâ taṃ Panayamâro satta vassâni kârayi.
taṃ hantvâ Palayamâro satta mâsâni kârayi. |
taṃ hantvâ Dâṭhiyo nâma duve vassâni kârayi.
ete pañca Damilajâtâ antarikâ ca bhûpati
satta mâsâni cuddasa vassâni kârayuṃ rajjaṃ. |
Vaṭṭagâmani mahârâjâ âgantvâna mahâyaso
Dâṭhikaṃ Damilaṃ hantvâ sayaṃ rajjaṃ akârayi. |
Vaṭṭagâmani Abhayo so evaṃ dvâdasa vassâni
pañcamâsesu âdito râjâ rajjaṃ akârayi. |
piṭakattayapâliñ ca tassâ aṭṭhakatham pi ca
mukhapâṭhena ânesuṃ pubbe bhikkhu mahâmati. |
hâniṃ disvâna sattânaṃ tadâ bhikkhu samâgatâ
ciraṭṭhitatthaṃ dhammassa potthakesu likhâpayuṃ. |
tass' accaye Mahâcûli Mahâtisso akârayi
rajjaṃ cuddasa vassâni dhammena ca samena ca. |
saddhâsampanno so râjâ katvâ puññâni nekadhâ
catuddasannaṃ vassânaṃ accayena divaṃ agâ. |
Vaṭṭagâmanino putto Coranâgo 'ti vissuto
rajjaṃ dvâdasa vassâni coro hutvâ akârayi. |
Mahâcûlissa yo putto Tisso nâmâ 'ti vissuto
rajjaṃ kâresi dîpamhi tîṇi vassâni khattiyo. |
Sîvo nâma yo râjâ Anulâdeviyâ saṃvasi,
ekavassañ ca dvemâsaṃ issariyaṃ anusâsi so. |
Vaṭuko nâma yo râjâ Damilo aññadesiko
ekavassañ ca dvemâsaṃ issariyaṃ anusâsi so. |
Tisso nâmâsi so râjâ kaṭṭhabhatîti vissuto,
ekavass' ekamâsañ ca rajjaṃ kâresi tâvade. |
Niliyo nâma nâmena Damilarâjâ 'ti vissuto
kâresi rajjaṃ temâsaṃ issariyaṃ anusâsi so. |
Anulâ nâma sâ itthi hanitvâna naruttame
catumâsaṃ Tambapaṇṇimhi issariyaṃ anusâsi sâ. |
Kuṭikaṇṇatisso nâma Mahâcûlissa atrajo

17. antarikâ ca bh° ABGR, antanikâ va bh° F, anantarikâ ca bh° CMn. antarikâ camûpati? — 19. °mâsesu FY, °mâsehi N. — 20. °katham pi ca XG, °kathâni ca M, °katâni ca CR, °kathâ pi ca AB. bhikkhû mahâmatî! — 21. bhikkhû! — 26. Sivo AC. — S° ca (or: 'ti) nâma? — so Y. — 27ª. so AZ. — 30ª. sâ BFGZn, yâ A and the stanza of the Porâṇâ, Introd., p. 6.

uposathagharaṃ kâresi vihâre Cetiyapabbate, |
gharassa purato kâresi silâthûpaṃ manoramaṃ,
ropesi bodhiṃ tatth' eva, mahâvatthuṃ akârayi. |
bhikkhunînaṃ dadatthâya jantâgharaṃ akârayi,
Padumassare ca uyyâne pâkârañ ca akârayi, |
nagarassa gopanatthâya parikhaṃ khanâpesi so,
pâkârañ ca akâresi sattahatthaṃ anûnakaṃ. |
Khemaṃ va Duggaṃ gaṇhâpesi talâkaṃ vatikâlikaṃ,
Setuppalâdi gaṇhâpesi Vaṇṇakâlaṃ manoramaṃ.
35 dvevîsati ca vassâni rajjaṃ kâresi khattiyo. |

bhâṇavâraṃ vîsatimaṃ.

XXI.

Kuṭikaṇṇassa atrajo Abhayo nâma khattiyo
Mahâthûpavare ramme sayaṃ dassanam âgami. |
khîṇâsavâ vasî pattâ vimalâ suddhamânasâ
sajjhâyanti dhâtugabbhamhi pûjanatthâya gaṇhati. |
râjâ sutvâna sajjhâyaṃ dhâtugabbhe manorame
thûpaṃ padakkhiṇaṃ katvâ catudvâresu nâddasa. |
samantato namassitvâ narindo sajjhâyam uttamaṃ
iti râjâ vicintesi: sajjhâyaṃ tattha gaṇhati? |
catudvâre na gaṇhati, bahiddhâpi na gaṇhare,
5 anto pi dhâtugabbhasmiṃ sajjhâyaṃ gaṇhanti pesalâ. |
aham pi daṭṭhukâmo 'mhi dhâtugabbhaṃ varuttamaṃ

---

33. atthâya AZB2G2, adatthâya B1G1F, dadatthâya N. tad(â) atthâya? — 35. setuppalâdiṃ AB. — vaṇṇamâlaṃ Z. — I conjecture:

Khemaṃ ca Duggaṃ khanâpesi (or: gaṇhâpesi? see 22, 64) talâkaṃ tâvakâlikaṃ,
Setuppalavâpiṃ khanâpesi (gaṇhâpesi?) Vaṇṇakâliṃ manoramaṃ.

Comp. 21, 17; 20, 6; Mah., p. 210, l. 10.

XXI, 1. saṃghaṃ dassanam âgami? comp. v. 6; 13, 15. — 2. sajjhâyaṃ dhâtug°? — „gaṇhati“ is said here and at v. 4 *metri causa* instead of „gaṇhanti“. Comp. Therîgâthâ (Phayre MS., fol. ña):

„ko nu te idaṃ akkhâsi ajânantassa ajânato?“

Saṃy. Nikâya (Phayre MS. vol. I, fol. ku):

„akkheyyasaññino sattâ akkheyyasmiṃ patiṭṭhitâ,
akkheyyaṃ apariññâya yogaṃ âyanti maccuno,
akkheyyaṃ ca pariññâya akkhâtâraṃ na maññati.“ —

4. tattha X, tassa Y. kattha? — 5a. gaṇhanti?

sajjhâyam pi suṇissâmi bhikkhusaṃghañ ca dassanaṃ. |
rañño saṃkappam aññâya Sakko devânam issaro
pâturahû dhâtugabbhasmiṃ there hi ajjhabhâsatha: |
râjâ bhante daṭṭhukâmo dhâtugabbhassa dassanaṃ.
saddhânurakkhanatthâya dhâtugabbhaṃ nayiṃsu te. |
disvâ dhâtugharaṃ râjâ vedajâto katañjali
akâsi dhâtusakkâraṃ mahâpûjâ ca sattâhaṃ. |
madhubhaṇḍapûjaṃ kâresi sattakkhattuṃ varuttamaṃ,
akâsi sabbapûjañ ca sattakkhattuṃ anagghikaṃ, | 10
aññam pûjañ ca kâresi sattakkhattuṃ yathârahaṃ,
sattakkhattuṃ ca kâresi dîpapûjaṃ punappunaṃ, |
pupphapûjaṃ akâresi sattakkhattuṃ manoramaṃ,
pûritajalapûjaṃ sattâhaṃ dakapûjañ ca sattâhaṃ. |
pavâḷamayajâlañ ca kârâpesi anagghikaṃ
Mahâthûpe paṭimukka cîvaram iva pârutaṃ. |
daḷhaṃ katvâ dîpadaṇḍaṃ thûpapâdasamantato
sappinâliñ ca pûretvâ dîpañ jalâpesi sattadhâ. |
telanâliṃ pûretvâ thûpapâdasamantato
teladîpañ jalâpesi cuddasakkhattuṃ punappunaṃ. | 15
gandhodakena pûretvâ kilañjaṃ katvâna matthake
patthaaretvâ uppalahatthe sattakkhattuṃ akârayi. |
thûpassa pacchimokâse talâke Khemanâmake
yojetvâ yantakaṃ tattha udakapûjaṃ akârayi. |
samantâ yojanaṃ sabbaṃ kusumânañ ca ropayi,
akâsi pupphagumbañ ca Mahâthûpe varuttame. |
makulapupphitaṃ pupphaṃ samânetvâna khattiyo
akâresi pupphagumbaṃ cuddasakkhattuṃ punappunaṃ. |
nânâpupphaṃ samocitvâ sâlindaṃ sahapâkâraṃ
pupphathambhaṃ kâretvâna sattakkhattuṃ punappunaṃ. | 20
. . . addasa nânârûpaṃ vicitrakaṃ

---

7. there hi X, there ti G, there AB, therânaṃ Z. — 8. saddhânurakkhaṇatthâya C. te XG1, taṃ Y. — 9. mahâpûjañ ca N, mahapûjâni Z. — 10b. sabbapûjaṃ ABG2Z, gabbhapûjaṃ G1X. sappipûjaṃ? — 11. añjanapûjaṃ ca kâresi? Comp. Mahâv., p. 212, l. 2. — 12. thûpapûjaṃ G1X. — ekapûjaṃ Y, dakapûjaṃ X. — 13. paṭimukkaṃ? — pârutaṃ N, pâruto AFG1Z, pârutâ BG2. — 16. pattharitvâ AZ. — 17. Tissanâmake ABG2Z. — dakapûjaṃ N. — 18. kusumâni (which may be the correct reading) ABG2, kusumânaṃ FG1Z, kusumâgaṃ N. — akâresi N. — 19. makulap° G1X, vakulap° Y. — akâsi FY. — 20. samocinitvâ Z.

... akâsi samânarûpâni khattiyo. |
sudhâkammaṃ akâresi Mahâthûpe varuttame.
abhisekaṃ karitvâna akâsi sudhâmañgalaṃ. |
Sakyaputto mahâvîro assatthadumasantike
sabbadhammapaṭividdho akârayi anuttaro. |
ṭhito Meghavane ramme yo rukkho dîpajotano
taṃ bodhim pi abhisekaṃ khattiyo akâsi sînanaṃ. |
vassaṃ vutthâ pavâresuṃ bhikkhusaṃghasukhâvahâ,
25 pavâraṇânuggahâya pavâraṇadânaṃ akâsi so. |
adâsi candanaṃ dânaṃ bhikkhusaṃghe gaṇuttame,
balabheriñ ca adâsi Mahâthûpe varuttame. |
lañkâmadamadâ c' eva seṭṭhakanaṭanâṭakâ
sabbesaṃ saṃkharitvâna Mahâthûpe adâsi so. |
visâkhamâse puṇṇamâyaṃ sambuddho upapajjatha,
taṃ mâsaṃ pûjanatthâya aṭṭhavîsati akârayi. |
Mahâmeghavane ramme Thûpârâme varuttame
kâresi uposathâgâraṃ ubhovihâramantare. |
akâ aññaṃ bahuṃ puññaṃ dânañ câpi anappakaṃ,
30 aṭṭhavîsati vassâni rajjaṃ kâresi khattiyo. |
Kuṭikaṇṇassa yo putto Nâganâmo 'ti khattiyo
kâresi ratanamayaṃ iṭṭhakâdiṃ varuttame, |
dhammâsanañ ca sabbattha Ambatthalathûpamuttame.
giribhaṇḍagahaṇaṃ nâma mahâpûjaṃ akârayi. |
yâvatâ Lañkâdîpamhi bhikkhû atthi supesalâ
sabbesañ cîvaraṃ datvâ bhikkhusaṃghe gaṇuttame,
dvâdasâni so vassâni rajjaṃ kâresi khattiyo. |
Mahâdâṭhikassa putto Âmaṇḍagâmani nâma Abhayo iti vissuto

---

21. samânar° X, sammâni r° G1Z, sabbâni r° G2B, sammâr° A. — 22. akâresi ABG2, ca kâresi Z, karissanti XG1. — vv. 22ᵇ—28 are wanting in B. — subham° N, sudhâm° F, thûpam° Z, mañgalaṃ AG. Comp. Mahâv., p. 212, l. 7. — 23. pakâsesi Z. akârayi is corrupted; at 13, 50 we have instead of it: „buddho âsi“. — 24. ṭhite N, piṭṭhito (°te M) AFGZ. — yo F, gho AGZn. — dîpajotako AZ. — sînanaṃ N, dhinnâmanaṃ (°taṃ A) AFG, bhûpati Z. sinâpanaṃ? — 25. bhikkhusaṃghâ sukhâvahâ? — pavâraṇâd° C. — adâsi Z. — 27. laṃkâmamadâ Y, laṃkâmamadasadâ F. Comp. 6, 69. V. 27ᵇ seems to be a conglomeration of fragments of two different verses, the first beginning (comp. 6, 69): „sabbe saṃ[ghaṃ] ...“ — 28. vesâkhamâse. — 31. iṭṭhakâdiṃ N, °di YF. — 32. girigaṇhigahanan F, giribhaṇḍikan BG2, giribhaṇḍikakan Z, girigaṇḍikakan G1, giriṃ bhaṇḍikaṃ A. Comp. Mahâv., p. 214, l. 2. — 34. °nâmako Y.

khanâpesi udapânaṃ Gâmeṇḍitalâkam pi ca, |
Rajatalenaṃ kâresi, thûpassa rajatâmayaṃ
chattâtichattaṃ kâresi Thûpârâme varuttame, | 35
Mahâvihâre Thûpârâme ubhopâsâdamuttame
bhaṇḍâgâraṃ akâresi bhaṇḍalenaṃ ca sabbaso, |
mâghâtañ ca akâresi Tambapaṇṇitale pi ca.
nava vass' aṭṭha mâsâni rajjaṃ kâresi khattiyo. |
tass' eva kaniṭṭhako râjâ Kaṇirajânû 'ti vissuto
paripuṇṇatîṇi vassâni rajjaṃ kâresi khattiyo. |
Âmaṇḍagâmaniputto Cûlâbhayo 'ti vissuto
patiṭṭhâpesi so râjâ Gaggarârâmam uttamaṃ. |
rajjaṃ kâresi vass' ekaṃ Cûlâbhayo mahîpati.
Sîvalî nâma sâ itthi Revatî iti vissutâ | 40
catumâsaṃ rajjaṃ kâresi rañño Âmaṇḍadhîtaro.
Âmaṇḍabhâgineyyo tu Sîvaliṃ apanîya taṃ |
Ilanâgo 'ti nâmena rajjaṃ akârayi pure.
Ilanâgo nâma râjâ suṇitvâ kapijâtakaṃ |
Tissadûratalâke ca khanâpesi arindamo.
chahi vassehi so rajjaṃ kâresi dîpalañjake. |
Sîvo 'ti nâma nâmena Candamukho 'ti vissuto
akâsi Manikârâmaṃ vihâre Issaravhaye. |
tassa rañño mahesî ca Damilâdevîti vissutâ
tañ ñeva gâme attano vaṭṭaṃ adâsi ârâme.
satta mâs' aṭṭha vassâni rajjaṃ kâresi khattiyo. | 45
Tisso ca nâma so râjâ Yasalâlo 'ti vissuto
satta mâs' aṭṭha vassâni râjâ rajjaṃ akârayi. |
dvârapâlassa atrajo Subharâjâ 'ti vissuto
kârâpesi Subhârâmaṃ Villavihâraṃ manoramaṃ, |
pariveṇâni kâresi attanâmena samakaṃ.
chamhi vassamhi so râjâ issariyaṃ anusâsi so. |

bhâṇavâraṃ ekavîsatimaṃ.

---

34. pi ca ABG2, ca kârayi Z, iva G1, idha X. — 36. bhaṇḍagharaṃ (instead of bhaṇḍalenaṃ) X. — 38. tasseva kaniṭṭhako N, Tisso nâma so (yo C) YF. — 41. I believe that dhîtaro ought to be corrected into dhîtikâ which looks very much like it in Burmese characters. — 44. Manikârâmaṃ Mn, Maṇik° ABCGR, Saṇik° F. Manikâragâmaṃ? Comp. Mahâv., p. 218, l. 9. — 45b.c is wanting in BG2. — taññeva gâme N, tañecagâme F, taññekome AG1Z. — vaṭṭaṃ F, vattaṃ N, vannaṃ A, vaṇṇaṃ G1Z. — 47. Mahâv.: Vallivihârakaṃ. — 48. samakaṃ YF, sâmakaṃ N. — chahi AZ, chamhi BGX. — vassehi C. chahi vassehi? comp. v. 43.

XXII.

Vasabho nâma so râjâ vihâre Cetiyapabbate
dasa thûpâni kâresi kittiphalavaruttame. |
Issariye nâma ârâme vihâram ca manoramam
kâresi uposathagharam dassaneyyam manoramam. |
balabheriñ ca kâresi Mucelam vihâram uttamam.
sampatte tîṇi vassâni chaḷâni cîvaram adâ. |
sabbattha Laṅkâdîpasmim ârâme santi jiṇṇake,
kâresi sabbattha âvâsam dhammikapûjam mahâraham. |
cetiyagharam kâresi Thûpârâme varuttame.
5 kâresi pûjayî râjâ catucattâlîsa anûnakam. |
Mahâvihâre Thûpârâme vihâre Cetiyapabbate
paccekâni sahassâni teladîpañ jalâpayi. |
Mayantim Râjuppalavâpim Vaham Kolambanâmakam
Mahânikkhavaṭṭivâpim Mahârâmettim eva ca |
Kehâlam Kâlivâpiñ ca Jambuṭiñ Câthamaṅganam
Abhivaḍḍhamânakañ ca icc ekâdasa vapiyo. |
dvâdasa mâtikañ c' eva subhikkhatthaṃ akârayi.
puññam nânâvidham katvâ pâkâram parikham pure, |
dvâraṭṭâlam akârayi, mahâvatthuñ ca kârayi.
10 tahim tahim pokkharaṇî khanâpesi nagare pure, |
ummaggena pavesayi udakam râjakuñjaro.
catucattâlîsa vassâni rajjam kâresi issaro 'ti. |
Vasabhassa atrajo putto Tisso 'ti vissuto
ârâmam Maṅgalanâmakam kârâpesi mahîpati.
kâresi rajjam dîpasmim tîṇi vassâni tâvade 'ti. |
Tissassa atrajo putto Gajâbâhukagâmani
kârâpesi mahâthûpam Abhâyârâme manorame. |

XXII, 1. kittipâlo v° BG2, kittipalav° AG1. Possibly we should correct: Cittalakûṭe varuttame. Comp. Mahâv., p. 221, l. 2. — 3. chalâni ABFZ, chaḷâni G, [chalâ]nam N. A chacîvaram instead of the ticîvara is mentioned in the Mah., p. 229, l. 6. — 4. santi Y, panti X. saṃkhari? — 5. pûjâyo? — 7. Mayenti A, Mayanti BG1, Yanti ZG2, Cayantim N, Vassanti F. — Kolambagâmakam, Mahâv. and Mahâv. Ṭîkâ. — Mahânikkaviṭṭivâpim ca A, Mahâṇikavidhivâpim Mahâv. — Mahârâmettim X, Mahâmettiyam Y, Mahâgâmadvim Mahâv. — 8. Koḷivâsam Mahâv. — Jambûdim F, Jambuṭim G1N, Jambuṭṭim Z, Jambuttham B, Jambuvim A. Cambuddhim Mahâv. — Vâtamaṅganam Mahâv. — 9. parikhâpâkâram pure Y, parinapâkâram pure F.

mâtattham Gâmaninâmam talâkam kâresi nâyako,
kârâpesi ca ârâmam Rammakam nâma issaro.
dvevîsati vassâni dîpe rajjam akârayîti. |
Mahallanâgo 'ti nâmena Tambapannimhi issaro
Sâjîlakandakârâmam, dakkhine Gotapabbatam, | 15
Dakapâsânaârâmam, vihâram Sâlipabbatam
kârâpesi Tanavelim, Rohane Nâgapabbatam. |
ârâmam Girisâlikam kârâpesi vinâyako.
chavassam rajjam kâretvâ gato so âyusamkhaye 'ti. |
Mahallanâgassa yo putto Bhâtutisso 'ti vissuto
Mahâmeghavanuyyânam kârâpanatthâya issaro |
parikkhepesi parikkhepam pâkâram dvârattâlakam
kârâpesi ca so râjâ ârâmam Varanâmakam. |
Gâmanim nâma talâkam khanâpetvâ vinâyako
pâdâsi bhikkhusamghassa Bhâtutisso vinâyako. | 20
khanâpesi talâkam tam Randhakandakanâmakam,
kâres' uposathâgâram Thûpârâme manorame. |
mahâdânam pavattesi bhikkhusamghe vinâyako
catuvîsati vassâni rajjam dîpe akârayîti. |
tassa kanittho nâmena Tisso iti suvissuto
kâresi uposathâgâram Abhayârâme manorame. |
kâresi dvâdasatthânam Mahâvihâramuttame,
vihâram kâresi so thûpam Dakkhinârâmasavhaye, |
tato aññam bahu puññam kalyâne buddhasâsane.
atthârasâni vassâni issariyam akârayîti. | 25
Tissassa atrajo putto râjârahâ dve bhâtukâ
rajjam kâresu dîpamhi tîni vassâni nâyakâ. |

Vañkanâsikatisso tu Anurâdhapure rajjam
tîni vassâni kârayi puññakammânurûpavâ. |
Vañkanâsikatissassa accaye kârayi suto

---

14. mâtattham N, yatthâva FGZ, yatthâ ca AB. Comp. Mahâv., p. 223, l. 9. — 15. Sajilakandakârâmam N, Pajilakandak° F, Sajîlakandhak° BG. Mahâv.: Pejalaka. — Gotapabbatam X, Golapabbatam G1, Kotip° BG2. Mahâv.; Golap° A, Holakapabbate Z. — 16. Mahâv.: Naceli. — 17. Girihâlikam F. Mahâv.: Antogiririhâlikam. — 18. Âhutisso Y. — Bhavaran° F. Gavaran°? Comp. Mahâv., p. 224, l. 10. — 21. Rannakanandakanâmakam F, Rannakandakan° B, Rattakandakan° A, Rannakanandakan° G, Rannakannakan° Z. — 24. dvâdasatthâne A, comp. Mahâv., p. 225, l. 6. — 25. bahum A. — 26. atrajâ puttâ? — vv. 27—31 are wanting in N.

rajjaṃ dvâvîsa vassâni Gajâbâhukagâmani. |
Gajâbâhuss' accayena pasuro tassa râjino
rajjaṃ Mahallakanâgo chabbassâni akârayi. |
Mahallanâgass' accayena putto Bhâtikatissako
30 catuvîsati vassâni Laṅkârajjaṃ akârayi. |
Bhâtikatissaccayena tassa kaniṭṭha-Tissako
aṭṭhârasa samâ rajjaṃ Laṅkâdîpe akârayi. |
Kaniṭṭhatissaccayena tassa putto akârayi
rajjaṃ dve yeva vassâni Khujjanâgo 'ti vissuto. |
Khujjanâgakaniṭṭho taṃ râjâ ghâtiya bhâtikaṃ
ekavassaṃ Kuñjanâgo rajjaṃ Laṅkâya kârayîti. |
Sirinâgo laddhajayo Anurâdhapure vare
Laṅkârajjaṃ akâresi vassân' ekûnavîsati. |
Sirinâgo nâma nâmena Mahâthûpaṃ varuttamaṃ
35 pûjesi ratanamâlena, chattaṃ thûpe akârayi. |
kâresi posathâgâraṃ Lohapâsâdaṃ uttamaṃ,
ûnavîsati vassâni rajjaṃ kâresi khattiyo 'ti. |
Sirinâgassa atrajo Abhayo nâma mahîpati
adâsi bhikkhusaṃghassa dvesatasahassarûpiyâ. |
pâsâṇavedim akâsi mahâbodhivaruttame.
dvâvîsa vassâni râjâ issariyaṃ anusâsi so 'ti. |
tassa kaniṭṭho râjâ tu Tissako isi vissuto
Abhayârâme Mahâthûpe kâresi chattam uttamaṃ, |
Mahâmeghavane ramme Abhayârâme manorame
40 akâsi suvaṇṇathûpaṃ ubhovihâramuttame. |
sutvâ gilânasuttantaṃ Devatherassa bhâsato
adâsi gilânabhesajjaṃ pañcâvâsaṃ varuttamaṃ. |
rattiṃ acchariyaṃ disvâ ârâmaṃ Dassamâliniṃ,
mahâbodhimanorame dîparûpe patiṭṭhasi. |
tassa rañño tu vijite dîpanti akappiyaṃ bahuṃ,
vitaṇḍavâde dîpetvâ dûsesuṃ jinasâsanaṃ. |
disvâna râjâ pâpabhikkhu dûsentaṃ jinasâsanaṃ

28. dvâvîsati BGZ. — 29. pasuro Z, payuro F, sapasuro ABG. sasuro? — 33. râjâ ABG2Z, râja G1, râjaṃ N, bhajaṃ F. — Kuñjanâgo G1Zn, Kuñcanâgo F, Khujjanâṃgo A, Kujjanâgo BG2. — 37. rûpiyaṃ A. — vv. 42. 43 are wanting in BG2Z. — 42. rattiṃ acch° N, rattinicch° F, vârassa acch° AG. — Dîpamâliniṃ N, Dassamâliṇi (°ni F) AFG. — dîparûpe (°ruse F) X, disarûpe AG. — patiṭṭhayi A, patiṭṭhasi GX. patiṭṭhapi? — 43. cipanti AG, dîpanti X. dîpenti? — 44. °bhikkhuṃ Mn. °bhikkhû? — dussente A, dûsente BG2, dûsentaṃ G1Zn, dûsantaṃ F.

Kapilâmaccaṃ âdâya akâsi pâpaniggahaṃ. |
vitaṇḍavâdaṃ madditvâ jotayitvâna sâsanaṃ
Hatthapaṇhîhi pâsânaṃ adâ Meghavanodanaṃ.
dvevîsati tu vassâni rajjaṃ kâresi issaro 'ti. | 45
Tissassa atrajo putto Sirinâgo 'ti vissuto
rajjaṃ kâresi dîpamhi dve vassâni anûnakaṃ. |
mahâbodhissa sâmantâ pâkârañ câta maṇḍapaṃ
akârayi pâsâdikaṃ Sirinâgavhayo ayaṃ. |
Asañgatisso 'ti nâmena Mahâthûpe varuttame
sovaṇṇamayâni chattâni kâresi thûpamatthake. |
maṇimayaṃ sikhâthûpaṃ Mahâthûpe varuttame
tassa kammassa nissande pûjâ kâresi tâvade. |
Andhakavindasuttantaṃ Devatherassa bhâsato
catudvâre dhuvayâguṃ paṭṭhapesi arindamo. | 50
Vijayakumârako nâma Sirinâgassa atrajo
pituno accaye rajjaṃ ekavassaṃ akârayi. |
rajjaṃ cattâri vassâni Saṃghatisso akârayi,
Mahâthûpamhi chattaṃ so hemakammañ ca kârayi. |
Saṃghabodhi nâma nâmena râjâ âsi susîlavâ,
dve vassân' eva so râjâ rajjaṃ kâresi khattiyo. |
ramme Meghavanuyyâne dhuvayâguṃ arindamo
paṭṭhapesi salâkaggaṃ Mahâvihâramuttame. |
Abhayo nâma nâmena Meghavaṇṇo 'ti vissuto
kâresi silâmaṇḍapaṃ Mahâvihâramuttame. | 55
padhânabhûmiṃ kâresi Mahâvihârapacchato,
kâresi bodhiparivâraṃ silâvedim anuttamaṃ, |
silâparikhañ ca kâresi toraṇañ ca mahârahaṃ,
kâresi silâpallañkaṃ mahâbodhigharuttame. |
uposathagharaṃ kâresi Dakkhiṇârâmamantare.
adâsi so mahâdânaṃ bhikkhusaṃghagaṇuttame. |

---

45. vetullavâdaṃ Y (except G1). This may be the correct reading (see Mahâv., p. 227, l. 6). — Hatthapaṇhîhi N, Hatthapâṇihi F, Hatthipannîhi (°ntîhi M) Z, Hatthipaṇṇihi (°ṇṇîhi B) ABG. — pâsâṇaṃ B, sâhanaṃ F, bâlânaṃ N. Hattha- (or: Satta-) paṇṇikapâsâdaṃ? comp. Mahâv., p. 226, l. 11. — 47. câtha? — I give this stanza according to N, the reading of which is confirmed by Mahâv., p. 228, ll. 8. 9. YF (instead of the whole stanza): panakaṃ (patakaṃ Z; F omits this word) pâkâraṃ ca samaṇḍapaṃ akârayi pâsâdakaṃ. — 48[a] is wanting in N. — Asaṃgahatisso BG. Read: Saṃghatisso. — 52[b] is wanting in YF. — 57. mahâbodhivaruttame ABG2Z, °garuttame G1.

katvâ râjagharaṃ râjâ mahâvatthuṃ manoramaṃ
bhikkhusaṃghassa datvâna pacchâ râjâ paṭiggahi. |
vesâkhapûjaṃ kâresi râjâ Meghavane tadâ.
60 terasâni hi vassâni issariyaṃ akâsi so 'ti. |
atrajo Meghavaṇṇassa Jeṭṭhatisso mahîpati
rajjaṃ kâresi dîpamhi Tambapaṇṇimhi issaro. |
maṇiṃ mahagghaṃ pûjesi Mahâthûpe varuttame.
katvâna lohapâsâdaṃ pûjetvâ maṇim uttamaṃ |
Maṇipâsâdo 'ti paṇṇattiṃ kârâpesi narâsabho.
kârâpetvâna ârâmaṃ Pâcînatissapabbataṃ |
pâdâsi bhikkhusaṃghassa narindo Tissasavhayo.
Âlambagâmatalâkaṃ gaṇhâpetvâ mahîpati |
aṭṭha saṃvaccharaṃ pûjaṃ kârâpesi narâsabho.
65 rajjaṃ kâresi so râjâ dasa vassâni Tambapaṇṇike. |
Jeṭṭhatissaccaye tassa Mahâseno kaniṭṭhako
sattavîsati vassâni râjâ rajjaṃ akârayi. |
tadâ so râjâ cintesi sâsane dvîsu bhikkhusu
ke dhammavâdino bhikkhû ke ca adhammavâdino, ke lajjî
ke alajjino? |
vicinetvâ imaṃ atthaṃ gavesanto lajjipuggale
addasa pâpake bhikkhû assamaṇe paṭirûpake. |
pûtikuṇapasadise vattaṃ va nîlamakkhike
asante assamaṇake addasa paṭirûpake |
Dummittaṃ Pâpasoṇaṃ ca aññe ca alajjipuggale;
70 upento pâpake bhikkhû atthaṃ dhammañ ca pucchi so. |
Dummitto Pâpasoṇo ca aññe ca alajjipuggalâ
rahogatâ mantayanti dûsanatthâya subbate. |
ubhosamaggabhâvissaṃ anuññâtaṃ Kumârakassape
akappiyan ti dîpesuṃ dussîlâ mohapârutâ. |
Chabbaggiyânaṃ vatthusmiṃ ananuññâtaṃ dantavattakaṃ

---

64. As to „gaṇhâpetvâ“ (or „khaṇâpetvâ?“) comp. 20, 34. 35. — 68. vicintetvâ ABG2, viriyetvâ F, vicinetvâ G1Zn. vicinitvâ? — paṭirûpapake (sic) N, [pa]ṇâpaṭidûsake [„pa“ is expunged] F, pake G1, pâpake ABG2, pâpakâmike Z. — 69. vattaṃ va Y, vattava N, cattaṃ ca F. — 72. ubhosamaggabhâviyaṃ N, ubhosamaggaṃ bhâvissaṃ F, ubhosamaggaṃ vibhavissaṃ Y. The way for correcting these words is shown by the Mahâv. Ṭîkâ, fol. ṇṛî: „Kumârakassapavatthumhi (Mahâvagga, I, 75) anuññâtaṃ gabbhamâsena paripuṇṇavîsativassûpasampadam pi na vaṭṭatîti.“ I therefore conjecture: upasampadaṃ gabbhavîsaṃ (or: °vîse). — 73[a]. anuññâtaṃ Y. — dunnivatthakaṃ (°ttakaṃ BG) Y, dantavattakaṃ X. The reading

anuññâtan ti dîpesuṃ alajjî dantagaṇikâ. |
imañ c' aññaṃ bhikkhû atthaṃ aññe bahu akâraṇe
adhammo iti dîpesuṃ alajjî lâbhahetukaṃ. |
asâdhusaṃgamen' eva yâvajîvaṃ subhâsubhaṃ
katvâ gato yathâkammaṃ so Mahâsenabhûpati. | 75
tasmâ asâdhusaṃsaggaṃ ârakâ parivajjiya
ahiṃ vâsivisaṃ vâsi kareyy' atthahitaṃ bhave 'ti. |

Dîpavaṃsaṃ niṭṭhitaṃ.
nibbânapaccayo hotu.

---

of X is confirmed by the Mahâv. Ṭikâ, l. l.: „Chabbaggiyânaṃ bhikkhûnaṃ vatthumhi anuññâtaṃ (ananuññâte?) dantamaye vijanimhi." As to the reading of Y, compare the following passage of the Cullavagga (Paris MS., fonds Pâli 20, fol. ñṛî'): „tena kho pana samayena Chabbaggiyâ bhikkhû dunnivatthâ duppârutâ anâkappasampannâ bhattaggaṃ gacchanti" *etc.* For further details, see my note on this passage in the Translation.

73. dantagaṇhikâ X. dandhagaṇikâ? — 74. bahû? — 76. vasî? Comp. Mahâvaṃsa, p. 238, l. 5.

TRANSLATION.

Adoration to the venerable, holy, universal Sambuddha.

I.

1. I will set forth the history of Buddha's coming to the Island, of the arrival of the relic and of the Bo (branch), of the doctrine of the teachers who made the recensions (of Dhamma and Vinaya), of the propagation of the Faith in the Island, of the arrival of the chief of men (Vijaya); listen. 2. Listen attentively to (the history proclaimed by) me, which inspires joy and delight, which causes serenity and gladdens the mind, which comprises many various forms. 3. With elated minds, satisfied, delighted and joyful, attentively receive the faultless, auspicious discourse. 4. Listen all, giving your minds (to the subject); I will proclaim a history, handed down from generation to generation, highly praised, adorned in many ways, joined together in this (work), just as flowers of various kinds (form a garland). 5. Attend to this incomparable praise of the Island (Ceylon), which dwells upon the most excellent successions (of teachers and kings), which is new and unrivalled and well narrated, which has been handed down by Saints, which is praised by all good men and revered by the holy ones.

---

6. On the immovable, firm, unshaken throne, a place worthy of the eminent one, the highest of men sat down, establishing himself in the four branches (of fortitude). 7. Seated on this most excellent throne, at the foot of

the king of trees, the chief of men, the highest among human beings, like a fearless lion, did not tremble, when he saw Mâra with the hosts of his army. 8. Having overcome the dispute of Mâra and put him to flight together with his army, the Conqueror, full of joy, wise, tranquil, and steadfast, — 9. mastered the state of meditation which consists in spiritual insight, and the thorough perfection of attention, (and also the knowledge of) many various qualities, distinguished by manifold attributes. 10. Mastering the knowledge of former existences and the gift of supernatural vision, the enlightened great Sage spent three watches of the night. 11. Thereafter, in the last watch, he revolved (in his mind) the causes of existence; the glorious One fixed the mind on them in direct and reverse order. 12. Having thoroughly understood the Dhamma, the highly wise One, who had reached emancipation by the destruction of human passions, taught (created beings) the abandonment (of temporal obstacles) and the attainment of the path (to sanctification). 13. The great Sage obtained („*abhisambuddha*“) the most excellent knowledge of omniscience. Thus first arose the title „Buddha, Buddha“. 14. Having penetrated all qualities and uttered his proclamation (of triumph)[1], the light-giver then spent seven days on that most excellent throne. 15. He in whom all fear had ceased, who had performed his duties and was free from sin, delighted, glad, and joyful, thought many kind thoughts. 16. In one moment, in one instant a Buddha surveys the whole world; he unveiled his fivefold power of vision and looked down over many people. 17. The highest of men sent forth the irresistible power of his knowledge; the stainless teacher then saw the most excellent Lañkâdîpa, — 18. an exquisite country, endowed with a beautiful climate, fertile, a mine of treasures, which had been visited by former Buddhas and had been inhabited by multitudes of Saints. 19. Perceiving the most excellent island of Lañkâ, a fertile region, a dwelling-place

1) This proclamation of triumph is the famous stanza, Dhp., v. 153.

fit for Saints, the compassionate One who well understood the right and wrong time, thus thought: 20. „In the present time Yakkhas, Bhûtas and Rakkhasas (inhabit) Lañkâdîpa, who are all too low for (adopting the doctrine of) the Buddhas; their power I can outroot. 21. Having driven out the hosts of Yakkhas, the Pisâcas and Avaruddhakas, I will establish peace in the island and cause it to be inhabited by men. 22. ... Let those wicked beings fully live out their span of life; (afterwards) there, in the most excellent Lañkâdîpa, an opportunity will arise for (the propagation of) the Faith. 23. Having removed (those) beings, having comforted many people and taught them the way, the road, the path of Saints, — 24. I shall reach complete Parinibbâna like the setting sun. Four months after my Parinibbâna the first convocation will be held ...; 25. a hundred and eighteen years later[1]) the third convocation will take place, for the sake of the propagation of the Faith. 26. Then there will be a ruler over this Jambudîpa, a highly virtuous, glorious monarch known as Dhammâsoka. 27. This king Asoka will have a son, a clever man, Mahinda, the learned converter of Lañkâdîpa.“ 28. Having foreseen these circumstances which were full of importance, (and understanding) the right and wrong time, the blessed Buddha placed a (divine) guard over this island. 29. 30. The Jina, having performed his various duties during the seven-times seven days (at the following places, that is) the throne, the Animisa (Cetiya) the cloister, the jewel-house, the Ajapâla and Mucalinda trees, and seventhly near the Khîrapâla grove, the hero went to Bârâṇasî in order to establish the kingdom of the Truth. 31. When he established the kingdom of the Truth and preached the most excellent Truth, the conversion of eighteen koṭis of beings took place. 32. Kondañña, Bhaddiya, Vappa, Mahânâma, and Assaji, these five great Theras attained emancipation when

1) A mention of the second convocation, which was held a hundred years after Buddha's death, is wanting in the MSS.; the third is said to have been held 118 years after the second.

he had preached the Anattalakkhaṇa discourse. 33. Residing in Bârâṇasî, in Isipatana, the Jina released the four friends of Yasa and, besides, the fifty youths. 34. Having spent the rainy season in Bârâṇasî, the Tathâgata released in the Kappâsika grove the Bhaddavaggiyas. 35. Wandering thence from place to place, he came to Uruvelâ; there the stainless Teacher saw Uruvelakassapa, an ascetic of the Jaṭila sect. 36. In the room where Kassapa kept his sacred fire, the highest of men conquered a serpent. Witnessing this miracle they all invited the Tathâgata: 37. „Reside here, o Gotama, during the four winter months; we will daily provide you with rice.“ 38. The Tathâgata, the chief of men, residing during the winter in Uruvela, devoted himself to the conversion of the Jaṭilas together with their followers. 39. (Once, during that period,) both Aṅgas and Magadhas prepared a great sacrifice. (Kassapa), seeing that great gains (could be obtained) at this sacrifice, conceived the following ignoble thought: 40. 41. „The great Samaṇa possesses high (magical) powers and great faculties; if he shall perform miracles or preach in the great assembly, the fee will escape me and go to Gotama. Well, the great Samaṇa should not appear in the assembly.“ 42. The Tathâgata understands action and resolution, intention and desire, the sixteen constituent parts of thought. 43. Having understood the thought of the Jaṭila, the Sage, who looks through the minds of other men, went by his high (magical) power to (Uttara-) Kurudîpa collecting alms. 44. Near the Anotatta lake Buddha took his meal; there he gave himself up to meditation (jhâna) and compassionate thoughts.

45. With his Buddha-eye, the highest in the world looked over the universe; the stainless Teacher (then) saw the most excellent Laṅkâdîpa. 46. At that time the ground of Laṅkâ was covered with great forests and full of horrors; frightful, cruel, blood-thirsty Yakkhas of various kinds, — 47. and savage, furious, pernicious Pisâcas of various shapes and full of various (wicked) thoughts, all had assembled together. 48. „I shall go there, in their midst;

I shall dispel the Rakkhasas and put away the Pisâcas; men shall be masters (of the island).“

49. Having considered this matter full of compassion, the great hero rose into the air and came hither from Jambudîpa. 50. In the midst of the assembly of Yakkhas, above their heads, he was seen, standing in the air, holding his seat (in his hands). 51. The assembled hosts of Yakkhas saw the Sambuddha standing there, but they did not think that he was the Buddha; they supposed him to be another Yakkha. 52. On the bank of the river, near Mahiya Pokkhala, on the site of the Subhañgana Thûpa, there the highest of men stood, and entered upon the highest ecstatic meditation. 53. The Sage, the awakener of quick attention, speedily entered upon that meditation (by revolving) in a moment by one thought (the whole system of qualities). Suddenly he thence rose; he who had reached (all) perfections by his virtuous resolutions, ... finished his meditation. 54. There the hero stood, performing miracles by his (magical) power, lika a Yakkha of high (magical) power and great (supernatural) faculties; gathering (?) thick clouds, containing thousands of rain drops, he sent rain, cold winds, and darkness. 55. (He then spoke to the Yakkhas:) „I will send you heat; give unto me a place where I may sit down. I possess such power over the fire as will dispel these dangers.“ 56. (The Yakkhas replied: „If thou art able to dispel them, sit down whereever thou likest; we all consent; show thy power over the fire.“ 57. (Buddha replied:) „You all ask me for warmth; I shall quickly produce the great heat which you are desiring, a fierce, burning fire.“ 58. As the sun shines in summer at noon, so fearful heat penetrated the assembly of Yakkhas. 59. Like the heat spread by the four suns at the end of a Kappa, such and greater still was the glow sent forth by the seat of the Teacher. 60. As the rising sun cannot be restrained in the sky, thus (Buddha's) carpet of skin cannot be restrained in the air. 61. The carpet diffused great heat, like the fire at the end of the Kappa, as the sun (scorches) the earth,

or like a great flame of fire. 62. Diffusing heat like a heap of burning coals, the carpet appeared similar to a cloud, or to a glowing iron mountain. 63. It spread insupportable heat over the islands. The Yakkhas quickly fled in all ten directions, to the east, the west, the south, the north, above, and beneath. 64. „Whither shall we go for safety and refuge? How shall we be released from this fearful being? 65. If this powerful Yakkha assumes the form of the fiery element, and burns us, all of us Yakkhas will perish like a handful of chaff, like dust blown away by the wind.“ 66. And Buddha, the chief among Sages, the bringer of happiness, the compassionate, merciful great Sage, when he saw the afflicted, frightened Yakkhas, thought how to administer joy to the minds of these non-human beings. 67. (He) then (thought of) another island, similar to this, with low ground and high ground, with many various aspects, beautifully adorned by rivers, mountains, and lakes, the island of Giri, most similar to the country of Lañkâ. 68. (It was) free from danger, well protected, surrounded by the ocean, full of excellent food and rich grain, with a well tempered climate, a green, grassy land, the beautiful island of Giri, superior to this (island). 69. It was charming and delightful, green and cool, adorned by gardens and forests, exquisite; there were trees, full of blossoms and fruits; it was empty and solitary, subject to no master. 70. (It was situated) in the great sea, in the midst of the ocean and of the deep waters, where the waves incessantly break; around it there was a chain of mountains, towering, difficult to pass; to enter it against the wish (of the inhabitants) was difficult. 71. Full of desire and anger towards other beings, backbiting, pitiless, given to injuring other beings, cruel and furious, violent, merciless, . . . 72. (Buddha thus spoke:) „Ye Rakkhasas and ye wicked hosts of Yakkhas, I give unto you this island which is not far from Lañkâ, the whole old island of Giri; may they all inhabit it and multiply undisturbed. 73. This country of Lañkâ is a residence inhabited by men since remote Kappas;

may many men dwell in the country of Laṅkâ, as they did in former times in the Oja, Vara, and Manda island. 74. Adorned with these and other good qualities, a residence fit for men, auspicious in many ways, it will shine among the islands, when the Doctrine will have been brought there, like the full moon in the sky at the time of Uposatha." 75. Weighing the prosperity and the high happiness of the two, the Sage who knew all worlds, interchanged the two islands and the two (kinds of beings), men and Rakkhasas, (as a peasant) easily (interchanges) his pairs of bullocks. 76. Gotama by his (magical) power drew the island towards himself, like the headstalls of bullocks which are drawn (towards the driver) with a strong rope. The Sage drew together one island towards the other, like two ships which are surrounded by stout ropes. 77. Having joined the beautiful island to the other, the Tathâgata transported (?) the Rakkhasas, (saying:) „May all Rakkhasas dwell in Giridîpa . . ." 78. The eager Yakkhas ran to Giridîpa, like thirsty people in summer to a river; they all entered it never to return; the Sage (then) restored the island to its former place. 79. The highly satisfied Yakkhas and the highly pleased Rakkhasas, having received this excellent island which they desired, all began to laugh with great joy, and all went to celebrate the festival called Nakkhattamaha. 80. When Buddha saw that joy had been restored to these non-human beings, he the Jina, having exerted his benevolence towards them, pronounced the spell of protection. Having walked three times round the island, for the sake of its ever-lasting protection and the expulsion of the Yakkha hosts, — 81. having comforted the Pisâcas and (other) non-human beings, having established a guard and restored a lasting peace, having put down all distress in the island, the Tathâgata returned to Uruvela.

Here ends (Buddha's) subjection of the Yakkhas.

II.

1. Again, the holy, glorious Sambuddha (once) dwelt near the most excellent capital of Kosala, in the garden of Sudatta (Anâthapiṇḍika). 2. In this Jetavana garden Buddha, the light-giving king of the Truth, looking all over the world, saw beautiful Tambapaṇṇi. 3. When five years had elapsed (after he had attained Buddhahood), he went to the country of Tambapaṇṇi. By dispelling the Avaruddhaka (demons) he (once) himself had made the island empty. 4. (But) now the mountain serpents and the sea serpents fought a battle in the island, having arranged their arrays on both sides, an awful struggle. 5. All those Nâgas possessed great (magical) powers, all were frightfully venomous, all were wicked and violent, furious and filled with desire. 6. The Serpents were quick and excessively powerful, corrupt, cruel, and harsh, hasty, given to anger, longing for destruction (?). 7. Powerful Mahodara and resplendent Cûḷodara, both were valiant, both had an exceedingly brilliant appearance. 8. No one saw a way how peaceably to compose that struggle (?). Mahodara whose fierceness was furiously excited by pride, was destroying the island with its mountains and its forests: „I will kill all hostile serpents." 9. Cûḷodara, filled with pride, roared: „May thousand koṭis of Nâgas approach; I will slay all them who dare to enter the battle; I will change the island, all its hundred yojanas, into one desert." 10. The Serpents whose venomous fury could not be restrained, who possessed high (magical) powers, raged and sent forth flames (sent forth smoke and flames?); the Serpent kings, infatuated with anger, incited them to destroy the foes (who opposed them) in the battle.

11. Buddha, the blessed wanderer through the world, when he perceived the anger of the Serpent kings, (and saw) that the island was being destroyed, thought, in order to prevent this, many kind thoughts, for the sake of the highest bliss of (men) and gods. 12. (He thus reflected:) „If I do not go (to Lankâ), the Serpents will not

become happy; the island will be destroyed, and there will be no welfare in future time. 13. Out of compassion for the Nâgas, for the sake of happiness (of men) I shall go there; may the happiness of the island prosper (?). 14. I perceive the excellent qualities of Lañkâdîpa; the Serpents shall not destroy the island from which I formerly have driven out the Yakkhas, and to which I have done good.“ 15. Speaking thus the Sambuddha rose from his seat; he who possessed the gift of (supernatural) vision, left the Gandhakuṭî, and stood in the door (of the Jetavana garden). 16. All the gods who resided in the trees of the Jetavana garden, offered their services to him: „Let us go (with thee, o Sage who art) possessed of (supernatural) vision.“ 17. (Buddha replied:) „Nay, remain ye all, Samiddhi alone may go (with me).“ (Samiddhi) went, taking up the tree (where his residence was,) and holding it from behind (over Buddha's head). 18. Samiddhi, when he heard what Buddha had said, was delighted; he took up the tree, roots and all, and followed the Tathâgata. 19. The highly powerful king of gods gave shade to the Sambuddha, the highest among men, and held (the tree) from behind over the most excellent Buddha. 20. The highest of men went to the place where the Nâgas fought their battle; the merciful Teacher (there) stood in the middle of both noble Nâgas. 21. Going through the air over the heads of both Nâgas, the Sambuddha, the chief of the world, produced a deep, terrifying darkness. 22. There arose a thick darkness, caused by the great (magical) power of the lion (among men); he was covered and veiled (?) by the darkness, and the tree too (?). 23. The frightened, terrifyed Nâgas did not see each other, nor did they see the Jina (?), (or) to what side they should direct their attacks. 24. They all forsook the battle, threw down their weapons, and stood all with clasped hands, paying reverence to the Sambuddha. 25. When (Buddha) perceived that they were struck with horror, when he saw that the Nâgas were terrifyed, he sent forth his thoughts of kindness towards them, and emitted a warm ray of light. 26. A great sight it was, astonishing and terrifying; they all saw the Sambuddha like the bright moon in the sky. 27. Standing there, resplendent with all the six colours, shining in the air, illuminating the ten regions (of the world), he thus addressed the Nâgas: 28. „From what cause, o great king, did this contention among the Nâgas arise? Out of compassion towards yourself I have come speedily hither." 29. (They replied:) „This Nâga Cûḷodara and that Nâga Mahodara, the maternal uncle and the nephew, are quarrelling with each other, desirous of treasure." 30. The Sambuddha addressed a speech full of compassion to the savage Nâgas: „Anger which arises in the mind of the fool, begins small, and grows great. 31. For what reason do you undergo, all these many Nâgas, great suffering? Destroy that small throne, but do not destroy each other. Destroying one the other you are going to cause an unheard of destruction of life." 32. Then he who possessed the gift of (supernatural) vision, agitated the Nâgas by (the description of) the sufferings in hell; he unfolded to them the (laws of) birth in the worlds of men and devas, and the nature of Nibbâna. 33. As the Sambuddha, the highest of men, thus preached the true doctrine, all the Nâgas, casting themselves down, propitiated the Tathâgata. 34. All the Nâgas (then) came together, the Serpents reconciled themselves to each other, and all took their refuge (in Buddha), eighty koṭis of living beings. 35. (Thus they spoke:) „We might perish, all we Nâgas, on account of this throne." 36. The two Nâga (kings), for the sake of restoring peace, took that most excellent throne (and thus spoke to Buddha:) „Accept this throne out of compassion, (o Sage who art) gifted with (supernatural) vision." 37. The Sambuddha who possessed the gift of (supernatural) vision, accepted it by remaining silent. When they understood that he had accepted it, the two great Serpents were delighted. 38. (They thus addressed Buddha:) „May the blessed One sit down on this splendid, noble Veḷuriya throne which the Nâgas were longing for." 39. The

Nâgas placed that throne in the midst of the two islands. There, on that throne, the light-giving king of the Truth sat down. 40. When those eighty koṭis of Nâgas had propitiated the Sambuddha, the Nâgas there served to him a meal, food and drink. 41. When he had removed his hands from the bowl, the eighty koṭis of Nâgas, surrounding him, sat down near the supreme Buddha.

42. At the mouth of the Kalyâṇî river there lived a Nâga together with his children and with a great retinue of Nâgas; his name was Maṇiakkhika. 43. (He was) full of faith, and had taken his refuge (in Buddha), a true and righteous believer. When he came to that assembly of Nâgas, his faith still increased. 44. When this Nâga perceived the Buddha's power, his compassion, and the fear of the Serpents (?), he bowed to him, sat down, and thus entreated the Tathâgata: 45. „Out of compassion to this island thou hast first dispelled the Yakkhas; this kindness towards the Nâgas is thy second act of compassion towards the Island. 46. May the holy, great Sage show his compassion still another time; I shall attend and do service to thee.“ 47. Having heard what the Nâga said, Buddha, full of compassion for created beings, the blessed One, accepted (his invitation,) for showing kindness to Lañkâdîpa. 48. Having sat on the throne, the light-giver arose; the Sage then rested during the midday time in the interior of the island. 49. In the interior of the island the supreme light spent the day; he who possessed the gift of (supernatural) vision, entered upon the Brahmavihâra meditation. 50. At evening time the Jina thus spoke to the Nâgas: „Let the throne remain here; may the Khîrapâla tree[1]) station itself here. Worship, o Nâgas, all of you this tree and the throne.“ 51. Having spoken thus, and preached to the Serpents, and given them that sacred object used by (himself), the Sambuddha returned to the Jetavana.

Here ends the conquering of the Nâgas.

---

1) This is the tree which the god Samiddhi had taken to the island; see v. 17 et seq.

52. Again, in the eighth year (after Buddha had reached Sambodhi), the Nâga king Maṇiakkhika invited the great hero together with five hundred Bhikkhus. 53. (These Bhikkhus) whose senses were subdued, who possessed the high (magical) powers, surrounded the Sambuddha; the Sage rose up into the air in the Jetavana, and proceeding through the air, he came to Lañkâ, to the mouth of the Kalyâṇî river. 54. All the Serpents constructed a pavilion of precious stones on the ground, and covered it with garments of different colours, with divine clothes. 55. (There were) ornaments of various precious stones, various blossoms of many descriptions, many flags of various colours; the pavilion was adorned in many ways. 56. They spread (cloth over the) entire (floor) and prepared seats; (then) they introduced the Fraternity with Buddha at its head, and invited them to sit down. 57. Sitting down together with five hundred Bhikkhus, the Sambuddha entered upon ecstatic meditations; he diffused (the rays of) his kindness to all quarters (of the horizon). 58. Seven times Buddha together with his pupils attained mystical trance; at that place (subsequently) the Mahâthûpa was built, the most excellent Cetiya. 59. The Nâga king Maṇiakkhika distributed a great donation (to the Bhikkhus). Having accepted the donation of that Nâga, having taken food, and gladdened (the Nâgas by preaching to them,) the Sambuddha together with his pupils rose up into the air. 60. At the place of the Dîghavâpi Cetiya, Buddha, he who was full of compassion to the world, descended from the air and again entered upon mystical meditation. 61. Having arisen from the trance at that place, the light-giving king of the Truth together with his pupils, wandering through the air, then proceeded to the place where the Bo tree was to be stationed in the Mahâmeghavana garden. 62. The Bo trees of three former Buddhas (there also) had been established on the ground; to that place he went, and there he entered upon meditation. 63. (He thus prophesied:) „Three Bo trees (have stood) at this place at (the time of) the teaching of

three Buddhas; my Bo tree also will stand on this very spot in future time.“ 64. The highest being, the chief of men, having arisen from that meditation together with his pupils, went to the delightful Meghavana garden. 65. There also he plunged himself in meditation together with his pupils. Having arisen from that meditation, the light-giver proclaimed: 66. „This place first Kakusandha, the chief of the world, has accepted, sitting down on this spot where a throne has been erected. 67. This place secondly Konâgamana, the chief of men, has .... 68. This place thirdly Kassapa, the chief of the world, has ... 69. Myself, Sambuddha Gotama, the descendant of the Sakya tribe, the chief of men, have attained (trance), seated on this spot, where a throne is to be erected.“

III.

1. Setting aside the kings who reigned in the past kappa, to whatever forms of existence they may have passed, I shall completely enumerate the kings of the present kappa. 2. Their descent, their name and tribe, their age and (the length of) their reign, all that I will proclaim, listen to it according to the truth.

3. The first inaugurated king, a ruler of the earth, full of brilliancy, prince Mahâsammata by name, reigned over his kingdom. 4. His son was called Roja by name; (then followed) the prince called Vararoja, Kalyâṇa and Varakalyâṇa, Uposatha, the lord of the earth; — 5. the seventh of them was Mandhâtâ who reigned over the four Dîpas. (Then followed) Cara, king Upacara, and Cetiya, the lord of the earth; — 6. Mucala, Mahâmucala, Mucalinda, and also Sâgara, Sâgaradeva, and Bharata, the prince called Bhagîrasa, — 7. Ruci, and he who was called Mahâruci, Patâpa, and also Mahâpatâpa, Panâda, and Mahâpanâda, the king called Sudassana, — 8. he who was called Mahâsudassana, two Nerus, and Accimâ. These were twenty-eight kings by number; their age extended to an Asaṃkheyya (of years). 9. In Kusâvatî, in Râjagaha, in Mi-

thilâ, best of towns, these kings reigned; their age extended to an Asaṃkheyya (of years).

10. Ten times ten is one hundred; ten times a hundred is one thousand; ten times a thousand is ten thousand; ten times ten thousand is a hundred thousand; — 11. ten times a hundred thousand is one koṭi; (the following numerals are) pakoṭi, koṭippakoṭi, nahuta, and ninnahuta, abbuda, and nirabbuda, — 12. ababa, and also aṭaṭa, ahaha, and kumuda, sogandhika, uppala, puṇḍarîka, paduma. 13. All these numbers are numerable and calculable by the means of calculation; the stage (of numbers) beyond these is called *asaṃkheyya* (not calculable).

14. One hundred kings, sons of Accimâ, governed their great kingdom in the town called Pakula (?). 15. The last of these kings was the prince called Arindama; his sons and grandsons, fifty-six princes, governed their great kingdom in the town of Ayujjhanagara. 16. The last of these kings was Duppasaha, the lord of the earth; his sons and grandsons, sixty rulers of the earth, reigned over their great kingdom in Bârâṇasî, best of towns. 17. The last of these kings was the prince called Ajitajana; his sons and grandsons, eighty-four thousand by number, reigned over their great kingdom in the town of Kapilanagara. 18. The last of these kings was Brahmadatta, the lord of the earth; his sons and grandsons, thirty-six princes, reigned over their great kingdom in Hatthipura, best of towns. 19. The last of these kings was Kambalavasabha; his sons and grandsons, thirty-two princes, reigned there in the town of Ekacakkhu. 20. The last of these kings was Purindada, honoured by the surname Deva; his sons and grandsons, twenty-eight princes, reigned over their great kingdom in Vajirâ, best of towns. 21. The last of these kings was the prince called Sâdhina. His sons and grandsons, twenty-two royal princes, reigned over their great kingdom in Madhurâ, best of towns. 22. The last of these kings was valiant Dhammagutta; his sons and grandsons, eighteen princes, reigned there in the town of Ariṭṭhapura. 23. The last of these kings was the chief

of men called Siṭṭhi; his sons and grandsons, seventeen princes, reigned there in the town of Indapatta. 24. The last of these kings was Brahmadeva, the lord of the earth; his sons and grandsons, fifteen princes, reigned there in the town of Ekacakkhu. 25. The last of these kings was Baladatta, the lord of the earth; his sons and grandsons, fourteen royal princes, governed their great kingdom in the town of Kosambî. 26. The last of them was the king known as Bhaddadeva; his sons and grandsons, nine royal princes, reigned there in the town of Kaṇṇagoccha. 27. The last of them was the king renowned by the name of Naradeva; his sons and grandsons, seven royal princes, governed their great kingdom in the town of Rojânanagara. 28. The last of these kings was the prince called Mahinda; his sons and grandsons, twelve royal princes, governed their great kingdom in the town of Campânagara. 29. The last of these kings was Nâgadeva, the lord of the earth; his sons and grandsons, twenty-five princes, governed their great kingdom in the town of Mithilânagara. 30. The last of these kings was valiant Buddhadatta; his sons and grandsons, twenty-five princes, governed their great kingdom in Râjagaha, best of towns. 31. The last of these kings was the prince called Dîpaṃkara; his sons and grandsons, twelve royal princes, governed their great kingdom in Takkasilâ, best of towns. 32. The last of these kings was the prince called Tâlissara; his sons and grandsons, twelve royal princes, reigned over their great kingdom in Kusinârâ, best of towns. 33. The last of these kings was the prince called Purinda; his sons and grandsons, nine royal princes, reigned over their great kingdom in the town of Malitthiya (Tâmalitti?). 34. The last of these kings was Sâgaradeva, the lord of the earth; his son Makhâdeva was a great, liberal giver. 35. His sons and grandsons, eighty-four thousand by number, reigned over their great kingdom in the town of Mithilânagara. 36. The last of these kings was Nemiya, honoured by the surname Deva, a universal monarch, a lord of the whole earth which the ocean surrounds.

37. Nemiya's son was Kalârajanaka; his son was Samaṃkura; (then followed) king Asoka, an inaugurated prince. 38. His sons and grandsons, eighty-four thousand by number, reigned over their great kingdom in Bârâṇasî, best of towns. 39. The last of these kings was the lord of the earth called Vijaya; his son was high-born, brilliant Vijitasena; — 40. (then followed) Dhammasena, Nâgasena, the (king) called Samatha, Disampati, Reṇu, Kusa, Mahâkusa, Navaratha, and also Dasaratha, — 41. Râma, the (king) called Biḷâratha, Cittadassî, Atthadassî, Sujâta, and Okkâka, Okkâmukha, and Nipura, — 42. Candimâ, and Candamukha, king Sivi, Sañjaya, Vessantara, the ruler of men, Jâlî, and Sîhavâhana, prince Sîhassara, the wise preserver of royal succession. 43. His sons and grandsons, eighty-two thousand kings, reigned in the town called Kapila(vatthu). 44. The last of these kings was Jayasena, the lord of the earth; his son was high-born, brilliant Sîhahanu. 45. The sons of that (?) Sîhahanu were five brothers, Suddhodana, and Dhota (Dhotodana), prince Sakkodana, — 46. king Sukkodana, and king Amitodana; all these five kings had names containing the word *odana*. 47. He the son of Suddhodana, Siddhattha, the chief of the world, begot Râhulabhadda, and then left his home in order to strive for Buddhaship.

48. The total number of these highly powerful ... kings is four Nahutas, one hundred thousand, and three hundred more. 49. So many lords of the earth are mentioned who originated from the family of the Bodhisatta in this first (?) kappa, preservers of royal succession, rulers of men[1]). —

50. Perishable, alas! is whatever exists, subject to origin and decay; it appears and perishes; its extinction is bliss.

End of the great lineage of kings.

---

1) The last words, which I think belong to this place, form, in the MSS., the second part of v. 53.

51. The king called Suddhodana reigned in the town called Kapila(vatthu), he the royal son of Sîhahanu. 52. Amid the five mountains, in Râjagaha, best of towns, reigned the prince who was called king Bodhisa (Bhâtiya![1]). 53. Suddhodana and Bhâtiya were friends of each other. When (Bimbisâra) was eight years old, five wishes arose (in his mind): 54. „May my royal father instruct me in the duties of royalty; may he the Buddha, the highest of men, arise in my kingdom; — 55. may the Tathâgata show himself first to me (before going to other kings); may he preach to me the eternal Truth; may I penetrate that most excellent Truth.“ 56. These were the five wishes which arose in Bimbisâra's mind. When he was fifteen years old, he received the royal coronation after his father's death; — 57. he (Buddha) the chief of the world arose in his beautiful kingdom; the Tathâgata showed himself to him first; when he preached his eternal Truth, the lord of the earth apprehended it. 58. The great hero then was full thirty-five years old; Bimbisâra, the lord of the earth, was thirty years old. Gotama was five years older than Bimbisâra. 59. Fifty-two years this prince reigned; thirty-seven years he reigned after having formed that connection with the Buddha. 60. Prince Ajâtasattu reigned thirty-two years. Eight years after his coronation the Sambuddha reached Parinibbâna. 61. After the Parinibbâna of the Sambuddha, the highest One in the world, the chief of men, that prince reigned (still) twenty-four years.

IV.

1. The congregation of Bhikkhus, seven hundred thousand (in number), assembled, holy men who having subdued their passions and having become pure, had all attained the summit of perfection. 2. They all, having made enquiry and determined which were the most worthy, elected by vote of the congregation five hundred Theras.

1) The father of Bimbisâra.

3. Kassapa was the chief propounder of the Dhutaṅga precepts according to the doctrine of the Jina; Ânanda was the first of those learned (in the Suttas), wise Upâli was chief in the Vinaya, — 4. Anuruddha in the (supernatural) visions, Vaṅgîsa in promptly comprehending, Puṇṇa among the preachers of the Dhamma, Kumârakassapa among the students of various tales, — 5. Kaccâna in establishing distinctions, Koṭṭhita in analytical knowledge. There were, besides, many other great Theras who were original depositaries (of Buddha's doctrine). 6. By these and other saintly Theras who had fulfilled their duties, to the number of five hundred, was the collection of the Dhamma and of the Vinaya made; because it was collected by the Theras, it is called the doctrine of the Theras (*theravâda*). 7. The Bhikkhus composed the collection of Dhamma and Vinaya by consulting Upâli about the Vinaya, and by asking the (Thera) called Ânanda regarding the Dhamma. 8. Thera Mahâkassapa and the great teacher Anuruddha, Thera Upâli of powerful memory, and the learned Ânanda, — 9. as well as many other distinguished disciples, who had been praised by the master, who possessed analytical knowledge, firmness, the six (supernatural) faculties and the great (magical) powers, who had attained the mystic trance proceeding from self-concentration, who had completely mastered the true faith, — 10. all these five hundred Theras bore in their minds the nine-fold doctrine of the Jina, having acquired it from the best of Buddhas. 11. They who had heard and received from Bhagavat himself the whole Dhamma and Vinaya taught by the Buddha, — 12. they who knew the Dhamma, who knew the Vinaya, who all were acquainted with the Âgamas, who were unconquerable, immovable, similar to their master, ever worshipful, — 13. they who had received the perfect doctrine, first (among religions), from the first (among teachers), who were Theras and original depositaries (of the Faith), made this first collection. Hence this whole doctrine of the Theras is also called the first (or primitive) doctrine. 14. Assembled in

the beautiful Sattapaṇṇa cave, the five hundred Theras, the teachers, arranged the nine-fold doctrine of the Teacher. 15. The nine-fold doctrine of the Teacher (comprises) Sutta, Geyya, Veyyâkaraṇa, Gâthâ, Udâna, Itivuttaka, Jâtaka, Abbhuta, Vedalla. 16. The Theras who arranged this true imperishable doctrine, according to Vaggas, Paññâsakas, Saṃyuttas, and Nipâtas[1]), composed the collection of the Âgamas which is known by the name of the Suttas. 17. As long as the true doctrines remain, as long as the collection does not perish, so long — a long time — will the teaching of the Master last. 18. The immovable, firm, insubvertible earth quaked on the appearance of the Collection of the Vinaya and of the Dhamma, which is worthy of the Faith. 19. Nobody, may a Samaṇa come or a Brâhmaṇa of great learning, skilled in disputation and hair-splitting, can subvert it; firm it stands like Sineru. 20. Neither a deity nor Mâra nor Brahmâ nor any earthly beings can find in it even the smallest ill-spoken sentence. 21. Thus the collection of the Dhamma and of the Vinaya is complete in every part, well arranged and well protected by the omniscience of the Teacher. 22. 23. And those five hundred Theras, chief among whom was Mahâkassapa, as they knew the doubts of the people, composed the imperishable collection of the Vinaya and of the Dhamma, which is an incarnation of the Faith like the highest Buddha, the collection of the Dhamma. 24. The doctrine of the Theras, which is founded on true reasons, which is free from heresies, full of true meaning, and supports the true faith, will exist as long as the Faith. 25. As long as holy disciples of Buddha's faith exist, all of them will recognize the first Council of the Dhamma. 26. The five hundred pre-eminent Theras, noble by birth (?), laid the first firm, original, fundamental base (of the Faith).

Here ends the Council of Mahâkassapa.

---

1) These are the sections into which the Dîgha-, Majjhima-, Saṃyuttaka-, and Aṅguttara-Nikâya respectively are divided.

27. Sixteen years had elapsed after the protector of the world had entered Nibbâna; it was the twenty-fourth year of Ajâtasattu's (reign), and the sixteenth of Vijaya's; — 28. learned Upâli had just completed sixty years, (then) Dâsaka received the Upasampadâ ordination from Thera Upâli. 29. The entire sacred Dhamma texts which the most excellent Buddha had set forth, the whole of the nine-fold speeches of the Jina, Upâli recited. 30. Upâli received from Buddha and (afterwards) recited the entire, complete, and whole nine-fold doctrine contained in the Suttas. 31. Buddha spoke regarding the learned Upâli in the assembly (of the Bhikkhus): „Upâli is the first chief of the Vinaya in my church." 32. The great teacher, being thus installed in the midst of the Assembly, recited the three Piṭakas to a thousand (pupils), chief among whom was Dâsaka. 33. Upâli taught five hundred Theras whose passions had been extinguished, who were pure, holy, and speakers of truth, the (texts of the) faith. 34. After the Sambuddha had attained Parinibbâna, the great teacher Thera Upâli taught then the Vinaya full thirty years. 35. Upâli taught the clever Dâsaka the whole nine-fold doctrine of the Teacher, eighty-four thousand (divisions). 36. Dâsaka, having learned all the Piṭakas from Thera Upâli, taught it just as his teacher in the Faith (had done). 37. The great teacher (Upâli) entered Nibbâna, after having appointed his pupil, the clever Thera Dâsaka, (to be chief) of the Vinaya. 38. Prince Udaya reigned sixteen years; when Udayabhadda had completed six (years), Thera Upâli attained Nibbâna.

39. Sonaka, a respectable merchant who came from Kâsi, received the first ordination according to the doctrine of the Teacher at Giribbaja (Râjagaha) in the Veḷuvana (monastery). 40. Dâsaka, the leader of the school, dwelt at Giribbaja in the Magadha country, and in his seven and thirtieth year gave Sonaka the first ordination. 41. (When) clever Dâsaka had completed forty-five years, and Nâgadâsa had reigned ten years, and king Paṇḍu(vâsa) twenty, then Sonaka received the Upasampadâ ordi-

nation from Thera Dâsaka. 42. Thera Dâsaka taught Sonaka also the nine-fold (doctrine); he having learned it from his teacher, (again) taught it (to others). 43. Dâsaka in his turn, having made his pupil Thera Sonaka chief of the Vinaya, attained Nibbâna in his sixty-fourth year.

44. The Thera called Sonaka had just completed forty years; Kâlâsoka had then reigned ten years and half a month in addition; — 45. Pakuṇḍaka was a robber during seventeen years; (of this period) eleven years and six months more had passed, — 46. when Thera Sonaka, the chief of the school, admitted Siggava and Candavajjî to the Upasampadâ ordination.

47. At that time, when Bhagavat had been dead a hundred years, the Vajjiputtas of Vesâlî proclaimed at Vesâlî the ten indulgences: the practice of (keeping) salt in a horn is permissible; the two inch alternative is permissible; the practice of (taking food after the regular meal when going to) the village is permissible; the practice of (holding Uposatha in different) residences (within the same boundary) is permissible; the practice of (obtaining) the consent (of the Fraternity not before, but after an act) is permissible; the practice of (acting according to) example is permissible; the practice of (drinking) milk-whey is permissible; the practice of (drinking) toddy is permissible; sitting (on seats covered with clothes) without fringes is permissible; (the possession of) gold and silver is permissible.

48. When Sambuddha had entered Parinibbâna ten times ten years, the Vajjiputtas proclaimed at Vesâlî these ten indulgences. 49. They proclaimed (the allowableness of) impermissible practices which all had been forbidden by the Tathâgata. Sabbakâmî, and Sâḷha, and Revata, (and) Khujjasobhita, — 50. and Yasa, Sambhûta of Sâṇa, these Theras who had formerly seen the Tathâgata, the pupils of Thera Ânanda; — 51. Sumana and Vâsabhagâmi, who had formerly seen the Tathâgata, these two most excellent pupils of Anuruddha; — 52. these (and other) Bhikkhus, seven hundred in number, came to Vesâlî

and expressed their assent to the discipline as it had been established in the doctrine of the Buddha. 53. All these who had obtained a (supernatural) insight, who were expert in reaching meditation, who were quit of their load, and saved, assembled together.

Here ends the history of the second Council.

V.

1. At the time of the Parinibbâna (which Buddha attained) at Kusinârâ, best of towns, seven hundred thousand (spiritual) sons of the Jina assembled. 2. In this assembly Thera Kassapa was chief, he who resembled the Teacher, a great leader; on earth is not his equal. 3. Kassapa, after having selected five hundred amongst the Arahats, taking always the most worthy ones, composed the collection of the Dhamma. 4. Out of compassion for created beings, in order to establish the Faith for a long time, he made, after the lapse of three months, when the fourth month and the second beginning of the Vassa[1]) had arrived, the collection of the Dhamma. 5. At the entrance of the Sattapaṇṇa cave, in the Magadha town Giribbaja (Râjagaha), this first council was finished after seven months. 6. At this council many Bhikkhus (were present), the original depositaries (of the Faith), and who had all reached perfection in the doctrine of the protector of the world. 7. Kassapa was the chief propounder of the Dhutavâda precepts according to the doctrine of the Jina; Ânanda was the first of those learned (in the Suttas), (the Thera) called Upâli was chief in the Vinaya, — 8. Anuruddha in the supernatural visions, Vaṅgîsa in promptly comprehending, Puṇṇa among the preachers of the Dhamma, Kumârakassapa among the students of various tales, — 9. Kaccâna in establishing distinctions, Koṭṭhita in analytical knowledge. There were, besides, many other

---

1) See Mahâvagga, 3, 2.

great Theras who were original depositaries (of the Faith). 10. By these and other saintly Theras who had fulfilled their duties, to the number of five hundred, was the collection of the Dhamma and of the Vinaya made; because it was collected by the Theras, it is called the doctrine of the Theras (*theravâda*). 11. They composed the collection of the Dhamma and of the whole Vinaya by consulting Upâli about the Vinaya and learned Ânanda about the Dhamma. 12. 13. Both these, Thera Upâli and Ânanda who had obtained perfection in the true Doctrine, had learned the Dhamma and Vinaya from the Jina; and, clever in the Suttas, they proclaimed what had been taught in long expositions and also without exposition, the natural meaning as well as the recondite meaning. 14. Having received the perfect word (of Buddha), the first (among doctrines), from the first (among teachers), these Theras and original depositaries (of the Faith) made the first collection. Hence this doctrine of the Theras is also called the first (or primitive) doctrine. 15. The most excellent Theravâda remained pure and faultless for a long time, for ten times ten years.

16. When the first hundred years had been completed and the second century had begun, a great schism happened, a most violent one, in the doctrine of the Theras. 17. 18. Twelve thousand Vajjiputtas of Vesalî assembled and proclaimed at Vesâlî, best of towns, the ten indulgences in the doctrine of Buddha, viz.: the indulgence of (keeping) salt in a horn, of the two inches, of the village and the monastery, of residences, of (obtaining) consent, of example, of milk-whey, of toddy, of silver, of seats without fringes. 19. They proclaimed (a doctrine) which was against the Faith, against the discipline, and repugnant to the doctrine of the Teacher; splitting the (true) meaning and the Faith, they proclaimed what was contrary to it. 20. In order to subdue them, many pupils of Buddha, twelve hundred thousand (spiritual) sons of the Jina, assembled. 21. In this congregation the eight chief Bhikkhus, resembling the Master, great leaders, diffi-

cult to conquer, great teachers, were — 22. Sabbakâmî and Sâḷha, Revata, Khujjasobhita, Vâsabhagâmi and Sumana, Sambhûta who resided at Sâṇa, — 23. Yasa, the son of Kâkaṇḍaka, a sage praised by the Jina. In order to subdue those wicked men (the Vajjiputtas), they came to Vesâlî. 24. Vâsabhagâmi and Sumana were pupils of Anuruddha, the other Theras (pupils) of Ânanda; they had all formerly seen Tathâgata. 25. At that time Asoka, the son of Susunâga, was king; that prince ruled in the town of Pâṭaliputta. 26. The eight Theras of great (supernatural) power gained one party for themselves, and destroying (the doctrine of) the ten indulgences they annihilated those wicked ones. 27. 28. After having annihilated the wicked Bhikkhus and after having crushed the sinful doctrine, those eight Theras of great (supernatural) power, those Bhikkhus selected seven hundred Arahats, choosing the best ones, in order to purify their own doctrine, and held a council. 29. This second council was finished in eight months at Vesâlî, best of towns, in the hall called Kûṭâgâra.

30. 31. The wicked Bhikkhus, the Vajjiputtakas who had been excommunicated by the Theras, gained another party; and many people, holding the wrong doctrine, ten thousand, assembled and (also) held a council. Therefore this Dhamma council is called the Great Council (*mahâsaṃgîti*).

32. The Bhikkhus of the Great Council settled a doctrine contrary (to the true Faith). Altering the original redaction they made another redaction. 33. They transposed Suttas which belonged to one place (of the collection), to another place; they destroyed the (true) meaning and the Faith, in the Vinaya and in the five Collections (of Suttas). 34. 35. Those Bhikkhus, who understood neither what had been taught in long expositions nor without exposition, neither the natural meaning nor the recondite meaning, settled a false meaning in connection with spurious speeches of Buddha; these Bhikkhus destroyed a great deal of (true) meaning under the colour

of the letter. 36. Rejecting single passages of the Suttas and of the profound Vinaya, they composed other Suttas and another Vinaya which had (only) the appearance (of the genuine ones). 37. Rejecting the following texts, viz.: the Parivâra which is an abstract of the contents (of the Vinaya), the six sections of the Abhidhamma, the Paṭisambhidâ, the Niddesa, and some portions of the Jâtaka, they composed new ones. 38. Forsaking the original rules regarding nouns, genders, composition, and the embellishments of style, they changed all that.

39. Those who held the Great Council were the first schismatics; in imitation of them many heretics arose. 40. Afterwards a schism occurred in that (new school); the Gokulika and Ekabyohâra Bhikkhus formed two divisions. 41. Afterwards two schisms took place amongst the Gokulikas: the Bahussutaka and the Paññatti Bhikkhus formed two divisions. 42. 43. And opposing these were the Cetiyas, (another) division of the Mahâsaṃgîtikas. All these five sects, originating from the Mahâsaṃgîtikas, split the (true) meaning and the Doctrine and some portions of the Collection; setting aside some portions of difficult passages, they altered them. 44. Forsaking the original rules regarding nouns, genders, composition, and the embellishments of style, they changed all that.

45. In the orthodox school of the Theras again a schism occurred: the Mahiṃsâsaka and Vajjiputtaka Bhikkhus formed two sections. 46. In the school of the Vajjiputtakas four sections arose, viz.: the Dhammuttarikas, Bhaddayânikas, Channagarikas, and Sammitis. 47. In later times two divisions arose among the Mahiṃsâsakas: the Sabbatthivâda and Dhammagutta Bhikkhus formed two divisions. 48. The Sabbatthivâdas and Kassapikas, the Kassapikas and Saṃkantikas, and subsequently another section, the Suttavâdas, separated themselves in their turn. 49. These eleven schools which separated themselves from the Theravâda, split the (true) meaning and the Doctrine and some portions of the Collection; setting aside some portions of difficult passages, they altered them. 50. For-

saking the original rules regarding nouns, genders, composition, and the embellishments of style, they changed all that.

51. Seventeen are the heretical sects, and there is one orthodox sect; together with the orthodox sect they are eighteen at all. 52. The most excellent Theravâda which resembles a large banyan tree, is the complete doctrine of the Jina, free from omissions or additions. The other schools arose as thorns grow on the tree. 53. In the first century there were no schisms; in the second century arose the seventeen heretical schools in the religion of the Jina. 54. The Hemavatikas, Râjagirikas, Siddhatthas, Pubba- and Aparaselikas, and sixthly the Apara-Râjagirikas arose one after the other.

Here ends the description of the schools of the teachers.

(At the time of the second Council the Theras foresaw the following events[1]):

55. „In the future time, after a hundred and eighteen years, a certain Bhikkhu will arise, a Samaṇa able (to suppress the schisms of that time). 56. Descending from Brahma's world he will be born in the human race, originating from a Brâhmaṇa tribe, an accomplished master of all Mantras (Vedas). 57. His name will be Tissa, his surname Moggaliputta; Siggava and Candavajjî will confer on the youth the Pabbajjâ ordination. 58. Then, having received the Pabbajjâ ordination and attained the knowledge of the sacred texts, Tissa will destroy the Titthiya doctrines and establish the (true) faith. 59. A royal chief called Asoka will govern at that time in Pâṭaliputta, a righteous prince, an increaser of the empire."

60. All the seven hundred Bhikkhus, the Theras, having taught the (true) doctrine and destroyed (the heresy of) the ten indulgences, had attained Parinibbâna. 61. Descend-

---

1) Here follows an account of the birth and conversion of Tissa Moggaliputta who presided at the third Council. See Mahâvaṃsa, pp. 28—38.

ing from Brahma's world he was born in the human race; at the age of sixteen he had mastered the whole Veda.

62. (Once young Tissa thus addressed the Thera Siggava, who had come to his father's house:) „I ask the Samaṇa a question, answer these questions (concerning) the Ṛigveda, the Yajurveda, the Sâmaveda and also the Nighaṇṭu, and fifthly the Itihâsa"; — 63. and the Thera having given his permission, he asked an exceedingly difficult question. Siggava then spoke to the youth possessed of mature knowledge: 64. „I also will ask you, young man, a question set forth by the Buddha; if you are clever, answer my question truly." 65. When the question had been pronounced, (Tissa said:) „That I have neither seen nor heard; I will learn this Mantra, I desire to receive the Pabbajjâ ordination." 66. Leaving the narrow way of the life of a layman, the youth went forth into the houseless state and to the condition of calm, according to the Jina's faith. 67. The disciple, desirous of learning and full of reverence, was taught the nine-fold doctrine of the Teacher by learned Candavajjî. 68. Siggava who had vanquished the young man, conferred on him the Pabbajjâ ordination; learned Candavajjî taught the well trained (disciple), versed in the Vedas, the nine-fold (doctrine); (having done so,) these Theras attained Parinibbâna.

69.[1]) Two years of Candagutta, fifty-eight of king Pakuṇḍaka having elapsed, Siggava having just completed his sixty-fourth year, Moggaliputta received from Thera Siggava the Upasampadâ ordination. 70. Tissa Moggaliputta, having learned the Vinaya from Candavajjî, reached emancipation by the destruction of the substrata (of existence). 71. Siggava and Candavajjî taught the glorious Moggaliputta all the Piṭakas which are filled with collections referring to both (Bhikkhus and Bhikkhunîs) (*or:*

1) In the following account, some of the numbers mentioned are evidently wrong; I have preferred, however, not to correct them, since the cause of these errors may be attributed as well to the author as to copyists.

the Sutta collection, as it had been settled at the two convocations?). 72. Siggava, possessed of (true) knowledge, made the glorious Moggaliputta chief of the Vinaya, and attained Nibbâna after having completed seventy-six years. 73. Candagutta ruled twenty-four years; when he had completed fourteen years, Siggava attained Parinibbâna. 74. (Siggava was) a dweller in the forest, keeping the Dhutañga precepts, of limited desires, attached to forest life, full of goodwill, of subdued passions, and perfect in the true Doctrine. 75. In a remote, delightful abode, in the depth of a great forest, this hero (lived) alone without a companion, like a valiant lion in his mountain cave.

76. Sixteen years had elapsed after the protector of the world had attained Nibbâna, learned Upâli had completed sixty years; — 77. it was the twenty-fourth year of Ajâtasattu's (reign) and the sixteenth of Vijaya's, (when) Dâsaka received the Upasampadâ ordination from Thera Upâli. 78. The learned (Thera) called Dâsaka had completed forty years; ten years of Nâgadasa's (reign) and twenty of Pakuṇḍaka's (Paṇḍuvâsa's!) had elapsed, — 79. (when) Thera Sonaka received the Upasampadâ from Dâsaka. The wise Thera called Sonaka had completed forty years; — 80. ten years of Kâlâsoka's (reign) had elapsed; it was in the eleventh year of the interregnum in Tambapaṇṇi, (when) Siggava received the Upasampadâ ordination from Thera Sonaka. 81. Two years of Candagutta's (reign) had elapsed; Siggava had completed sixty-four, and king Pakuṇḍaka fifty-eight years, (when) Moggaliputta received the Upasampadâ ordination from Thera Siggava. 82. Six years of Asokadhamma's (reign), sixty-six of Moggaliputta, forty-eight (years) of king Muṭasîva had elapsed, (when) Mahinda received the Upasampadâ ordination from Moggaliputta.

83. Upâli received the Vinaya from Buddha, Dâsaka received the whole Vinaya from Thera Upâli and taught it just as his teacher in the Faith (had done). 84. Thera Dâsaka taught Sonaka also the Vinaya; (Sonaka) taught it,

after having learnt it from his teacher. 85. Wise Sonaka who well knew the Dhamma and the Vinaya, in his turn taught Siggava the whole Vinaya. 86. The pupils of Sonaka were Siggava and Candavajjî; the Thera taught both these pupils the Vinaya. 87. Tissa Moggaliputta, having learnt the Vinaya from Candavajjî, reached emancipation by the destruction of the substrata (of existence). 88. Teacher Moggaliputta taught his pupil Mahinda the whole Vinaya, the complete doctrine of the Theras.

89. After the Sambuddha had attained Parinibbâna, resplendent Thera Upâli taught the Vinaya full thirty years. 90. This great Sage, after having made his pupil, the learned Thera called Dâsaka, chief of the Vinaya, attained Nibbâna. 91. Dâsaka in his turn made his pupil Thera Sonaka chief of the Vinaya, and attained Nibbâna sixty-four years (after his Upasampadâ). 92. Sonaka who possessed the six supernatural faculties, after having made Siggava, the descendant of an Arya family, chief of the Vinaya, attained Nibbâna sixty-six years (after his Upasampadâ). 93. Wise Siggava made young Moggaliputta chief of the Vinaya and attained Nibbâna seventy-six years (after his Upasampadâ). 94. Tissa Moggaliputta made his pupil Mahinda chief of the Vinaya and attained Nibbâna eighty-six years (after his Upasampadâ).

95. Seventy-four years of Upâli, sixty-four of Dâsaka, sixty-six of Thera Sonaka, seventy-six of Siggava, eighty of Moggaliputta: this is the Upasampadâ of them all (*i. e.* the number of years which elapsed between their Upasampadâ and their death).

96. Learned Upâli was the whole time chief of the Vinaya, Thera Dâsaka fifty years, Sonaka fourty-four years, Siggava fifty-five years, the (Thera) called Moggaliputta sixty-eight years.

97. Prince Udaya reigned sixteen years; when six years of Udayabhadda's reign had elapsed, Thera Upâli attained Nibbâna. 98. The ruler Susunâga reigned ten years; after eight years of Susunâga's reign Dâsaka attained Parinibbâna. 99. After Susunâga's (Kâlâsoka's!)

death the ten brothers succeeded; they reigned all jointly twenty-two years. In the sixth year of their reign Sonaka attained Parinibbâna. 100. Candagutta reigned twenty-four years; after fourteen years of his reign Siggava attained Parinibbâna. 101. The son of Bindusâra, illustrious prince Asokadhamma, reigned thirty-seven years. 102. When twenty-six years of Asoka's reign had elapsed, the (Thera) called Moggaliputta, after having exalted the splendour of the Religion, attained the end of his life and reached Nibbâna.

103. Learned Thera Upâli, a great teacher, attained Nibbâna seventy-four years (after his Upasampadâ), after having made his pupil, the learned Thera Dâsaka, chief of the Vinaya. 104. Dâsaka attained Nibbâna sixty-four years (after his Upasampadâ), after having in his turn made his pupil, Thera Sonaka, chief of the Vinaya. 105. Sonaka who possessed the six (supernatural) faculties, attained Parinibbâna sixty-six years (after his Upasampadâ), after having made Siggava, the descendant of an Arya family, chief of the Vinaya. 106. Wise Siggava attained Nibbâna seventy-six years (after his Upasampadâ), after having made young Moggaliputta chief of the Vinaya. 107. Tissa Moggaliputta attained Nibbâna eighty years (after his Upasampadâ), after having made his pupil Mahinda chief of the Vinaya.

VI.

1. Two hundred and eighteen years after the Parinibbâna of the Sambuddha Piyadassana was anointed king. 2. When Piyadassana was installed, the miraculous faculties of royal majesty entered into him; he diffused the splendour which he had obtained in consequence of his merits, one yojana above and one beneath (the earth); the wheel of his power rolled through the great empire of Jambudîpa. 3. The Devas constantly brought to him (?) every day sixteen jars of water (?), filled with medical herbs of every description, from the Anotatta lake at the

top of the Himavat mountains. 4. The Devas then constantly brought every day fragrant teeth-cleansers made of the betel vine, which were grown in the mountains, soft, smooth, sweet, endowed with flavour, and delightful. 5. The Devas then constantly brought every day fragrant myrobalans, which were grown in the mountains, soft and smooth, endowed with flavour, desirable to great kings (?). 6. The Devas then constantly brought every day divine drinks and ripe mangos endowed with flavour and fragrance. 7. The Devas then constantly brought every day from the Chaddanta lake upper and under garments dyed with the five colours. 8. 9. The Nâga kings then constantly brought every day fragrant powder for washing the head, and also unguents, and fine seamless clothes to put on of the colour of jessamine, and precious collyrium; all these things (they brought) from the Nâga world. 10. The Devas then constantly brought every day sugar cane, quantities of Areca-nuts, yellow towels. 11. The parrots brought nine thousand loads of hill paddy which was picked out by rats; the bees made honey; the bears forged with sledge-hammers. 12. Heaven-born birds, sweet-voiced cuckoos constantly sang to men, (attracted) by the splendour of Asoka's merit. 13. The great Nâga whose age endures through a Kappa, the attendant of four Buddhas, wearing a golden chain, came, (attracted) by the splendour of (Asoka's) merit. 14. The glorious Piyadassi honoured him with garlands of jewels. Splendid rewards were received for alms (given to religious mendicants).

15. This grandson of Candagutta, the son of Bindusâra, (king Asoka), whilst a mere prince, was subking of Ujjenî, charged with collecting the revenue (of that province). During his progress he came to the town of Vedissa. 16. There the daughter of a Seṭṭhi, known by the name of Devî, having cohabited with him, gave birth to a most noble son. 17. Mahinda and Saṃghamittâ chose to receive the Pabbajjâ ordination; having obtained Pabbajjâ, they both destroyed the fetter of (individual) existence.

18. Asoka ruled in Pâṭaliputta, best of towns; three

years after his coronation he was converted to Buddha's faith.

19. How great is the number of years between the time when the Sambuddha attained Parinibbâna in the Upavattana (at Kusinârâ), and when Mahinda, the issue of the Moriya family, was born? 20. Two hundred years and four years more had elapsed: just at that time Mahinda, the son of Asoka, was born.

21. When Mahinda was ten years old, his father put his brothers to death; then he passed four years reigning over Jambudîpa. 22. Having killed his hundred brothers, alone continuing his race, Asoka was anointed king in Mahinda's fourteenth year. 23. Asokadhamma, after his coronation, obtained the (above-mentioned) miraculous faculties; exceedingly splendid and rich in meritorious works (he was), universal monarch of (Jambu)dîpa. 24. They crowned Piyadassi after full twenty years (?); he passed three years doing honour to Pâsaṇḍa infidels. 25. (There were) adherents of the sixty-two false doctrines, ninety-six kinds of Pâsaṇḍas who proceeded from the Sassata and Uccheda doctrines, all of them established on these two principles; — 26. Nigaṇṭhas and Acelakas and other ascetics and other Brahmans and sectarians. 27. Searching where truth and where falsehood was, he invited the infatuated, infidel Nigaṇṭhas (?) and sectarians of the Sassata and Uccheda doctrines, and Pâsaṇḍa and Titthiya infidels of different creeds outside the Faith, sectarian people. 28. After having invited the numbers of Titthiyas and having introduced them into his palace and having bestowed on them great gifts, he asked them an exceedingly difficult question. 29. Being asked this question, they could not answer it by their own power; the ignorant people answered like a man who being asked about the mango tree, replies concerning the Lakucha tree. 30. They all were content with low seats (?) (in the royal hall) [1].

---

1) The king invited all the ascetics of different creeds to take the seats of which they deemed themselves worthy. All were content with lower seats, except Nigrodha, a Buddhist novice, who took his seat on the royal throne.

After having annihilated all the Pâsaṇḍas and defeated the sectarians, — 31. the king thought: „Which other men may we find who are Arahats in this world or see the path towards Arahatship? 32. (Surely) they are to be found in the world; this world cannot be void of them (?). How may I obtain the sight of such worthy men? If I hear his (*i. e.* such a man's) well spoken words, I will give up to him my paternal realm and my conquests." 33. The king, thinking thus, found nobody worthy of his presents; unceasingly the king searched after virtuous, clever men. 34. Walking about in his palace and looking at many people, he saw the Samaṇa Nigrodha who went along the road for alms. 35—41. When he saw Nigrodha whose walking, turning back and looking was graceful, who turned his eyes to the ground, who was adorned (by decent deportment), an Arahat, whose mind was peaceful, who had reached perfect self-control, who had subdued himself and protected and well defended himself (against human passions), who did not mix with noble people, who was stainless like the moon amidst clouds, fearless like a lion, brilliant like a fire-brand, venerable, unconquerable, firm, of a peaceful disposition, steadfast, who had destroyed his passions, had cleansed himself of all sins, who was the most excellent of men, who led a wandering life, the most excellent Samaṇa, who was endowed with all virtues, the thought occurred to him, that he had been his companion during a former life (?)[1]. (Seeing) that ascetic who led a life worthy of a Muni, who was happy in consequence of his meritorious deeds in former existences, who had reached the fruition which is obtained by the path of Arahats, walking along the road in search of alms, that wise man thought, full of longing: 42. „Indeed this Thera is one of the venerable ones; like Buddha, the holy One in this world, and like his disciples, he has reached the fruition which is obtained by the transcendent path, and has reached liberation and salvation."

---

1) See the story in the Mahâvaṃsa, p. 24.

43. (Asoka) obtained the enjoyment of the five-fold delight, high bliss; delighted, he who was comparable to Sakka rejoiced like a poor man who has found a treasure, like one who has gained the desire of his heart (?). 44. 45. He spoke to one of his ministers: „Well, quickly conduct hither that Bhikkhu, that handsome young man of tranquil appearance, who walks along the road like an elephant, fearless and endowed with the ornament of tranquillity.“ 46. The king felt great content; highly delighted he thought in his mind: „Without doubt this excellent person whom I have never seen before, has reached the highest perfection.“ 47. Thinking thus, he again spoke thus: „Well prepared seats are spread; sit down on the seat which is worthy of an ascetic; I grant thee whichsoever thou desirest.“ 48. After hearing the speech of the king, he took (the king's) right hand (?) and mounted the throne. Fearlessly he sat down on the most excellent seat, just as Sakka, king of the gods, seats himself on the Paṇḍukambala.

49. The king thought: „This most excellent boy is certainly immovable and fearless; him . . .

50. The king, recognizing that excellent tender boy who observed the customs of the Saints, (to be) well instructed and expert in Dhamma and Vinaya, again spoke thus, full of delight: 51. „Teach me the Faith which thou hast learnt; thou alone shalt be my teacher; I will obey the words which thou teachest me, o great Sage. Instruct me, I listen to thy preaching.“ 52. Having heard this exceedingly acute speech of the king, he who was well versed in the analytical distinctions of the nine-fold doctrine, thought over the precious Tipiṭaka and found the excellent sermon on Earnestness: 53.[1]) „Earnestness is the way to immortality, indifference is the way to death; the earnest do not die, the indifferent are like the dead.“ 54. When wise Nigrodha had pronounced this gladdening sentence, the king understood that highest motive

1) Dhammapada, v. 21.

(viz. earnestness): „This is the foundation of all doctrines whatsoever that have been preached by the omniscient Buddha. 55. To-day I choose as my refuge thee and Buddha with the Dhamma and the Saṃgha; together with my children and wives, with the number of my relatives I announce to thee my having become a lay-disciple. 56. Abiding together with children and wives in the refuge (of the Faith), in consequence of the arrival of Nigrodha, my spiritual guide, I offer four lacs of silver and eight (daily) portions of rice to the Thera."

57. (The king having asked, whether there are many ascetics like Nigrodha, he replied:) „There are many disciples of Buddha, versed in the three-fold science, possessed of (magical) power, well acquainted with the exposition of the qualities of mind, who have subdued their passions and reached Arahatship." 58. The king again spoke to the Thera: „I desire to meet with that precious Assembly; I will pay my respect to all (Bhikkhus) who come to the Assembly; I will listen to the Dhamma." 59. Sixty thousand ascetics assembled, and the messengers announced to the king: „A large congregation which is full of great joy, has assembled; go thou to see the congregation, as thou desiredst (to do)." 60. Asokadhamma, the ruler of the ẹarth, having heard what the messenger said, thus addressed the circle of his relations, his friends and counsellors and his kinsmen: 61. „We will offer presents on the occasion of the assembling of the great Saṃgha; we will show them attention as much as we can, as much as we are able. 62. Let them quickly make ready for me a hall, seats, water, attendants, gifts, and food, such as are worthy of being offered, and suitable. 63. Let the makers of curry and rice quickly make ready for me well cooked rice-milk, sweet, pure dishes. 64. I will bestow a great donation on the congregation of the Bhikkhus, the most excellent community. Let them beat the drums in the city, let them sweep the roads, let them scatter white sand and flowers of the five colours; — 65. let them place here and there garlands and trium-

phal arches, plantain trees, auspicious brimming jars, and let them place here and there ..., — 66. and let them make flags of cloth and fasten them here and there; let the people, adorned with flower garlands, make this city resplendent. 67. Khattiyas, Brahmans, and Vessas, Suddas, and people of different extraction, adorned with various ornaments, shall take clothes, ornaments, flowers, burning torches, and shall proceed to meet the Congregation. 68. All kinds of bands of music, well trained musicians of various schools who are pleasant to hear and sweet-voiced, shall play (various melodies) ... and proceed to meet the Congregation, (a) most meritorious (act). 69. ... dancers and acrobats in auspicious attitudes (?), all shall go to meet the Congregation and shall amuse them, when they have assembled. 70. And let them worship (the Assembly) with large heaps of flowers of different kinds, (aromatic) powder of various descriptions, and unguents. 71. Let them prepare in the city every kind of pomp (?) and desirable gifts. 72. The inhabitants of the kingdom, devoted (?) to the Fraternity, shall undertake to do homage (to the Saṃgha), and shall do so during the whole day and during all the three watches (?) of the night."

73—75. That night having elapsed, the illustrious prince, causing food of excellent flavour to be prepared in his own residence, gave the following orders to his counsellors and his attendants: „Let all people procure heaps of perfumed garlands and flowers, many flowers, parasols, flags, lamps burning in the day-time; let them procure as much as I have ordered. 76. Let all (people dwelling) in this city, the merchants from the four quarters of the horizon, and all the royal officers, with their oxen, troops, and vehicles, follow me to meet the congregation of Bhikkhus." 77. The best of kings proceeded with great pomp; the ruler of the earth shone like Sakka (when he goes) to the Nandana garden. 78. The king in whose mind wisdom had arisen, proceeding in great haste towards the Bhikkhu congregation, saluted them, raising his joined hands, and received greetings in return. 79. He spoke to the Bhikkhu congregation: „May (the Saṃgha) have compassion on me.“ 80. Taking the alms-bowl of the Thera, the Saṃgha's (spiritual) father, and paying reverence to him by (offering) various flowers, he entered the city. 81. Inviting them to enter his residence and to be seated, he offered to them with outstretched hands rice-milk and various highly precious food, hard and soft, as much as they wanted and desired. 82. When the congregation of Bhikkhus had finished their meal and removed their hands from the bowls, he offered to each Bhikkhu a suit of robes. 83. He distributed slippers (?), collyrium, oil, parasols, and also shoes, all the requisites of an ascetic, molasses and honey. 79[b]. 84. Introducing all the Bhikkhus, as many had assembled, into his interior appartments, Asokadhamma, the ruler of the earth, sat down. Sitting down the king invited the congregation of Bhikkhus (to accept) their gifts, (saying): 85. „I give as much as the Bhikkhus desire, whatever they choose.“ 86. After having gratified them with (a present of priestly) requisites and offered to them what was required (for their use), he asked them about the very profound, well propounded divisions of the Dhamma: 87. „Are there, venerable Sirs, sections taught by the kinsman of the Sun, by the indication of a certain number of divisions of the Dhamma, (according to) nouns, gender, and inflections, and also according to sections and to the composition?“ — 88. „It has been taught, o king, and has been numbered by the kinsman of the Sun; it is well divided, well promulgated, well explained, well taught, — 89. accompanied by reasons and replete with sense, well spoken without a fault: fixed attention, right exertion, the (magical) powers, the (five) organs (of spiritual life), — 90. the (ten) powers, the requisites for attaining supreme knowledge, and those leading to the supreme path, all of these are well divided and well taught: these are the seven divisions of the most excellent elements of supreme knowledge. 91. The doctrine preached by the Teacher, the highest among men, the supreme, transcendent Truth which has been expanded and well divided, consists of nine Aṅgas[1]). 92. Full eighty-four thousand sections of the Doctrine have been taught by the kinsman of the Sun out of compassion for created beings. 93. He has preached the highest Truth, the most excellent ambrosia, which frees from transmigration, which is the path leading to the extinction of all suffering and an ambrosia-like medicine.“ 94. After hearing the speech pronounced by the Congregation of the Bhikkhus, the king, the chief of men, filled with joy and mirth, wisdom having arisen in his mind, pronounced these words to his royal court: 95. „Full and complete eighty-four thousand most precious sections of the Truth have been taught by the most excellent Buddha; — 96. I will build eighty-four thousand monasteries, honouring each single section of the Truth by one monastery.“ 97. The prince expending ninety-six koṭis of treasure, he the king, gave immediately on that same day the order (for the erection of the buildings). 98. At that time there were in Jambudîpa eighty-four (thousand) towns; near each town he built one monastery. 99. And having completed the monasteries in three years' time, (the construction of) the Ârâmas being finished, the prince held during seven days a festival of offerings.

VII.

1. There was a great assemblage from all parts of Jambudîpa, eighty koṭis of Bhikkhus, ninety-six thousand Bhikkhunîs, the greater part of the Bhikkhus and Bhikkhunîs possessing the six (supernatural) faculties. 2. The Bhikkhus, by the greatness of their magical power levelling the surface of the earth, producing (the miracle called) the world-show, made visible the (84000 consecration-) festivals, worthy of veneration. 3. The king standing on

---

1) The Aṅgas of Buddha's doctrine are the well-known nine divisions, viz. Sutta, Geyya, Veyyâkaraṇa, Gâthâ, Udâna, Itivuttaka, Jâtaka, Abbhuta, Vedalla.

the Asokârâma, looked over (the whole of) Jambudîpa; by the Bhikkhus' magical power Asoka saw everything. 4. He saw all the Vihâras built all over the earth, the raised (?) flags, the flowers and arches and garlands, — 5. the plantains, the filled jars adorned with various flowers; he saw the whole extent of the great continent, the pomp all over the four quarters. 6. 7. Delighted, glad, looking at the festivals which were being celebrated, at the assembled fraternities of Bhikkhus and the assembled Bhikkhunîs and the beggars receiving rich alms which were prepared for them, seeing all the eighty-four thousand Vihâras, which were honoured (by festivals of consecration), — 8. Asoka joyfully made known to the fraternity of Bhikkhus: „I am, venerable Sirs, a relative of the religion of the teacher Buddha. 9. Great liberality has been shown by me out of reverence (?) for the Fraternity. 10. 11. By expending ninety-six koṭis, a great treasure, eighty-four thousand monasteries have been erected by me in honour of the (84000) sections of the Truth taught by the most excellent Buddha. I have daily made offerings of four lacs: — 12. one Cetiya offering, one to the (Bhikkhu) called Nigrodha, one to the preachers of the Religion, one for the requirements of the sick; boiled rice is distributed constantly every day, just as the Mahâgaṅgâ (gives her water). 13. I cannot find any other greater act of liberality. My faith is most firm; I am, therefore, a relation of the Faith.“ 14—16. After having heard the word spoken by king Asokadhamma, learned Moggaliputta who was well versed in the Scriptures, a clever decider of cases, answered the question of Asokadhamma, in order to secure a comfortable existence to the Fraternity, for the sake of the propagation of the Doctrine, and because he the wise one had learnt the future destiny (of the Faith): „The donor of the requisites (for the Bhikkhus) remains a stranger to the Faith, — 17. but that man who gives up his son or daughter, the issue of his body, and causes them to receive the Pabbajjâ ordination, becomes really a relation of the Faith.“ 18. 19. King

Asokadhamma, the ruler of the earth, having heard this speech, addressed both prince Mahinda, his son, and his daughter Saṃghamittâ: „I presently shall be a relation of the Faith." Both children hearing what their father had said, agreed, (saying:) — 20. „Well, Sire, we agree, we will do what you have said; make us quickly receive the Pabbajjâ ordination, become a relative of the Faith." 21. Mahinda, Asoka's son, had completed twenty years, and Saṃghamittâ might be eighteen years of age. 22. When Asoka had completed six years, both his children received the Pabbajjâ ordination, and Mahinda, the enlightener of the Island, received at once the Upasampadâ ordination; — 23. at the same time Saṃghamittâ began to exercise herself in the Sikkhâ precepts. He (Mahinda) was like Moggaliputta a great teacher of the doctrine of the Theras.

24. Fifty-four years (after Moggaliputta's Upasampadâ) Asokadhamma was crowned; (six years?) after Asoka's coronation, when Moggaliputta had completed sixty (?) years, Mahinda received the Pabbajjâ ordination from Moggaliputta. 25. Mahâdeva conferred the Pabbajjâ ordination on him and Majjhanta the Upasampadâ [1]); these were the chiefs who acted compassionately towards Mahinda in (those) three ways. 26. Moggaliputta, his Upajjhâya, taught Mahinda, the enlightener of the Island, all the Piṭakas, their whole meaning, and the Doctrine. 27. Ten years after Asoka's coronation Mahinda had completed four years (after his Upasampadâ), and had become a teacher of the whole scripture as handed down, and he had many pupils. 28. Mahinda studied and retained in his mind the well propounded, well divided Sutta (collection) as it had been settled at the two convocations, the doctrine of the Theras. 29. Moggaliputta instructed Mahinda, the son of Asoka, in the three sciences, (the doctrine regarding) the six (supernatural) faculties, the four analytical doctrines. 30. And Tissa Moggaliputta continuously taught Mahinda, his pupil, the whole Piṭaka of the Âga-

1) See Mahâvaṃsa, p. 37, l. 2.

mas (*i. e.* the Sutta-Piṭaka). 31. When (Asoka) had completed three years, (the story of) Nigrodha (happened), after the fourth year (he put his) brothers (to death), after his sixth year Mahinda, the son of Asoka, received the Pabbajjâ ordination. 32. Both sons of Kontî, the Theras Tissa and Sumitta, who possessed the great (magical) faculties, attained Parinibbâna after Asoka's eighth year. 33. Those royal children received the Pabbajjâ ordination, and both Theras attained Nibbâna.

34. Many Khattiyas and Brahmans declared their intention of becoming lay disciples, and great gain and honour accrued to the faith of Buddha; — 35. the schismatics and heretics lost both gain and honour. Paṇḍarañgas and Jaṭilas, Nigaṇṭhas, Acelakas, and others — 36. resided (in the Buddhist Vihâras) during seven years; the Uposatha ceremonies were performed by incomplete congregations; saintly, clever, and modest men did not appear at the Uposatha ceremonies. 37. When a hundred years and (another) hundred and thirty-six had elapsed (after the Parinibbâna of the Buddha), sixty thousand Bhikkhus dwelt in the Asokârâma. 38. Âjîvakas and sectarians of different descriptions ruined the Doctrine; all of them wearing the yellow robe injured the doctrine of the Jina. 39. Surrounded by one thousand Bhikkhus, Moggaliputta, the chief of the school, who possessed the six (supernatural) powers and the great (magical) faculties, convened a Council. 40. Wise Moggaliputta, the destroyer of the schismatic doctrines, firmly established the Theravâda and held the third Council. 41. Having destroyed the different (heretical) doctrines and subdued many shameless people and restored splendour to the (true) faith, he proclaimed (the treatise called) Kathâvatthu. 42. From that Moggaliputta Mahinda, who was the pupil of that teacher, learnt the true religion. 43. (Moggaliputta) taught him the five Nikâyas and the seven sections (of the Abhidhamma); he the hero, the clever one learnt from his teacher the two Vibhañgas of the Vinaya, the Parivâra, and the Khandhaka.

44. When the second century and thirty-six years more had elapsed (since the Buddha's death), again a most dreadful schism arose in the Theravâda. 45. In the city of Pâṭaliputta ruled prince Dhammâsoka, a great king, who was a believer in the faith of Buddha. 46. He bestowed great gifts on the Saṃgha, the best and most excellent of congregations; in one day he expended four lacs. 47. One he gave in honour of the Cetiyas, another for the preaching of the Dhamma, one for the requirements of the sick, one to the Saṃgha. 48. Infidels, sixty thousand in number, seeing this gain and these great honours, furtively attached themselves (to the Saṃgha). 49. The Pâtimokkha ceremonies in the monastery of the Asokârâma were interrupted; a minister who ordered the Pâtimokkha ceremonies to be performed, killed (some) of the Saints. 50. In order to destroy the infidels, many disciples of Buddha, sixty thousand sons of the Jina assembled. 51. At that convocation the son of Moggalî was the president, a great chief, similar to the Teacher; he had not his like on earth. 52. The king asked the Thera about the case of the slaughter of the Saints; having performed a miracle, he satisfied the desire of the king. 53. Having received the Doctrine from the Thera, the king destroyed the Bhikkhu emblems of those who had furtively attached themselves (to the Saṃgha). 54. The reckless infidels, performing the Pabbajjâ rite according to their own doctrine, injured the faith of the Buddha just as (men mix) pure gold (with baser metals). 55. They all were sectarian, opposed to the Theravâda; and in order to annihilate them and to make his own doctrine resplendent, — 56. the Thera set forth the treatise belonging to the Abhidhamma, which is called Kathâvatthu. A similar punishment, a similar destruction of an opposite doctrine never occurred. 57. 58. After having promulgated the treatise called Kathâvatthu which belongs to the Abhidhamma, the presiding Thera, in order to purify his own doctrine and (to establish) the Faith for a long time, selected one thousand Arahats, choosing the best ones, and

held a Council. 59. In the monastery of the Asokârâma which had been built by king Dhammâsoka, this third convocation was finished in the space of nine months.

Here ends the Council of the true Faith which lasted nine months.

VIII.

1. Far-seeing Moggaliputta who perceived by his supernatural vision the propagation of the Faith in the future in the neighbouring countries, — 2. sent Majjhantika and other Theras, each with four companions, for the sake of establishing the Faith in foreign countries (and) for the enlightenment of men. 3. „Preach ye together with your brethren (?) powerfully the most excellent religion to the foreign countries, out of compassion for created beings.“

4. The great sage Majjhantika went to the country of the Gandhâras; there he appeased an enraged Nâga and released many people from the fetters (of sin). 5. Mahâdeva who possessed the great (magical) powers, went to the realm of Mahisa; urging (the people) by (the description of) the suffering in hell, he released many people from their fetters. 6. Then another (Thera), Rakkhita, skilled in magical transformations, rising into the air, preached the Anamataggiya discourse[1]). 7. The wise Thera called Yonakadhammarakkhita converted the Aparantaka country by preaching the Aggikkhandhopama Sutta. 8. The Thera Mahâdhammarakkhita who possessed the great (magical) powers, converted Mahâraṭṭha by preaching the Nâradakassapajâtaka. 9. The Thera Mahârakkhita who possessed the great magical powers, converted the Yavana region by preaching the Kâlakârâma Suttanta. 10. The Thera who originated from the Kassapa tribe, Majjhima, Durabhisâra, Sahadeva, Mûlakadeva, converted the multitude of Yakkhas in the Himavat. 11. They preached there the Suttanta called Dhammacakkappavattana. 12. Sona and

1) The country converted by this Thera is called by Buddhaghosa Vanavâsa.

Uttara who possessed the great magical powers, went to Suvaṇṇabhûmi; there they conquered the multitudes of Pisâcas and released many people from their fetters. 13. Mahinda, going with four companions to the most excellent island of Lañkâ, firmly established (there) the Faith and released many people from their fetters.

IX.

1. The island of Lañkâ was called Sîhala after the Lion (sîha); listen ye to the narration of the origin of the island which I (am going to) tell.

2. The daughter of the Vañga king cohabited in the forest with a lion dwelling in the wilderness, and in consequence gave birth to two children. 3. Sîhabâhu and Sîvalî were beautiful youths; the name of their mother was Susimâ, and their father was called the Lion. 4. When their sixteenth year had elapsed, (Sîhabâhu) departed from his cave, and then built a most excellent town called Sîhapura. 5. The son of the Lion, a powerful king, ruled over a great kingdom, in Lâḷaraṭṭha, in the most excellent town of Sîhapura. 6. Thirty-two brothers were the sons of Sîhabâhu; Vijaya and Sumitta were the eldest among them, beautiful princes. 7. Prince Vijaya was daring and uneducated; he committed most wicked and fearful deeds, plundering the people. 8. The people from the country and the merchants assembled; they went to the king and complained against the bad conduct of Vijaya. 9. The king, having heard their speech, full of anger, gave this order to the ministers: „Remove ye that boy. 10. Let them remove from the country all those attendants, his wives, children, relations, maid-servants, man-servants, and hired workmen.“ 11. He was then removed, and his relations were separated from him; so they went on board ship, and (the ship) sailed away on the sea. 12. „May they drift whereever they like; they shall not show their faces again nor shall they ever come back to dwell in our kingdom and country.“ 13. The ship in which the children had

embarked was helplessly driven to an island, the name of which was then called Naggadîpa. 14. The ship in which the wives had embarked was helplessly driven to an island, the name of which was then called Mahilâraṭṭha. 15. The ship in which the men had embarked went, sailing on the sea, losing her way and her bearings, to the port of Suppâra. 16. The people of Suppâra then invited those seven hundred men to disembark, and offered them lavish hospitality and honours. 17. During this hospitable reception Vijaya and all his followers unnoticed (?) committed barbarous deeds. 18. They made themselves guilty of drinking, theft, adultery, falsehood, and slander, of an immoral, most dreadful, bad conduct. 19. (The people) indignant at such cruel, savage, terrible and most dreadful deeds being committed against themselves, consulted together: „Let us quickly kill those rascals."

20. There is an island (formerly) called Ojadîpa, Varadîpa, or Maṇḍadîpa, the (recent) name of which is Lañkâdîpa, and which is (besides) known by the name of Tambapaṇṇi. 21. 22. At the time, when Sambuddha, highest of men, attained Parinibbâna, that son of Sîhabâhu, the prince called Vijaya, having left the land called Jambudîpa, landed on Lañkâdîpa. It had been foretold by the most excellent Buddha, that that prince one day would be (its) king. 23. The Teacher at that time had addressed Sakka, the chief of gods: „Do not neglect, Kosiya, the care of Lañkâdîpa." 24. Sujampati the king of gods, having heard the Sambuddha's command, committed to Uppalavaṇṇa the business of guarding the island. 25. Having heard the command of Sakka that powerful Devaputta with his attendant demons kept guard over the island.

26. Vijaya, having stopped three months at Bhârukaccha and exasperated the inhabitants, went again on board his ship. 27. That crowd of men having gone on board their ship, sailing over the sea, were driven away by the violence of the wind, and lost their bearings. 28. They came to Lañkâdîpa, where they disembarked and went on shore. Standing on dry ground, being ex-

hausted by great hunger, thirst and fatigue, they were unable (?) to walk on foot. 29. They crawled about on the ground with both hands and knees; afterwards, when they rose and stood upright, they saw that their hands were resplendent (copper-coloured). 30. The red-coloured dust of the ground covered their arms and hands; hence the name of that place was called Tambapaṇṇi (copper-palmed). 31. Tambapaṇṇi was the first town in the most excellent Laṅkâdîpa; there Vijaya resided and governed his kingdom. 32. Vijaya and Vijita together with Anurâdhanakkhatta, Accutagâmi, and Upatissa are those who came first to this country. 33. Many people, crowds of men and women, came together; (hence each) prince founded a town in the different parts. 34. The town of Tambapaṇṇi surrounded by suburbs was built by Vijaya in the south on the most lovely bank of the river. 35. Vijita founded Vijita(pura), the same founded Uruvela. The minister who was called after the asterism (Anurâdhâ) founded Anurâdhapura. 36. He who was called Accutagâmi then founded Ujjenî, Upatissa founded Upatissanagara which had well arranged markets, which was prosperous, opulent, large, charming, and lovely. 37. The king called Vijaya by name was the first ruler who reigned in Tambapaṇṇi over the delightful island of Laṅkâ. 38. When seven years (of his reign) had passed, the land was crowded with people. That prince reigned thirty-eight years.

39. In the ninth month after (Gotama) had become Buddha, the host of Yakkhas was destroyed; in the fifth year after his attaining Buddhaship the Jina conquered the Nâgas; in the eighth year after his attaining Buddhaship he completed the Samâpatti meditations (in Laṅkâ). 40. On these three occasions the Tathâgata came hither. In the last year of the Buddha Vijaya came hither. 41. The Sambuddha, the most excellent of men, made (the island fit for) the residence of men; the Sambuddha (afterwards) reached complete Nibbâna by the entire annihilation of the substrata of existence.

42. Prince (Vijaya) reigned thirty-eight years after the Parinibbâna of the Sambuddha, the light-giving king of Truth. 43. He despatched a messenger to Sîhapura to the (prince) called Sumitta, (with this message): „Come one (of you) quickly to us, to the most excellent island of Lañkâ; — 44. there is nobody to govern this kingdom after my death. I hand over to you this island which I have acquired by my exertions.“

X.[1])

1. The daughter of the Sakka prince Paṇḍu, the princess called Kaccânâ, came over hither from Jambudîpa in order to preserve the dynasty. 2. She was crowned as the queen-consort of Paṇḍuvâsa; from this marriage eleven children were born: 3. Abhaya, Tissa, and Utti, Tissa, and Asela the fifth, Vibhâta, Râma, and Siva, Matta together with Mattakala. 4. The youngest of them was a daughter known by the name of Cittâ; because she fascinated the hearts of the men who saw her, she was called Ummâdacittâ (fascinating Cittâ).

5. (Paṇḍuvâsa) arrived in Upatissagâma in the same year in which he was crowned. This king reigned full thirty years.

6. There were seven Sâkiya princes, the grand-children of Amitodana, born in the family of the Lord of the world: Râma, Tissa, and Anurâdha, Mahâli, Dîghâvu, Rohana, Gâmanî the seventh of them.

7. The son of Paṇḍuvâsa, prince Abhaya by name, reigned immediately (after his father) twenty years. 8. The wise son of Dîghâvu, the clever Gâmanî, who attended Paṇḍuvâsa, cohabited with the princess Cittâ. 9. In con-

1) This chapter belongs to the most fragmentary parts of the whole work. First is related the marriage of Paṇḍuvâsa and Kaccânâ (vv. 1—4). After a stanza referring to the length of Paṇḍuvâsa's reign (v. 5), the names of Kaccânâ's brothers are given who came over to Ceylon (see Mahâvaṃsa, p. 56). The following verses contain a short abstract of what is related at length in the Mahâvaṃsa, pp. 57 et seq.

sequence of that intercourse the prince called Paṇḍuka was born. Saving his life (from the persecutions of his uncles), (Paṇḍuka) resided in Dovârikamaṇḍala.

XI.

1. Abhaya's twentieth year having elapsed, Pakuṇḍa had completed his twentieth year. Pakuṇḍaka was crowned when the thirty-seventh year from his birth had elapsed. 2. After Abhaya's twentieth year Pakuṇḍaka lived as a robber; seventeen years later he put to death seven of his maternal uncles, and received the royal coronation in the town of Anurâdhapura. 3. When ten years (of his reign) had elapsed and sixty years (of it) were still to follow, he fixed the boundaries of the villages and completely tranquillized (the country). 4. Enjoying sovereignty both over men and Yakkhas, Pakuṇḍa reigned during full seventy years. 5. The son of Pakuṇḍa was the prince called Muṭasîva; this king reigned sixty years over Tambapaṇṇi.

6. 7. There were then ten brothers, the sons of Muṭasîva: Abhaya, Tissa, and Nâga, Utti together with Mattâbhaya, Mitta, Siva, and Asela, Tissa, and Kira completing the number of ten, and princess Anulâ and Sîvalâ, the daughters of Muṭasîva. 8. When eight years of Ajâtasattu had elapsed, Vijaya came hither; after the fourteenth year of Udaya Vijaya expired. After the sixteenth year of Udaya they crowned Paṇḍuvâsa. 9. In the interval between the two kings Vijaya and Paṇḍuvâsa, Tambapaṇṇi was without a king during one year. 10. In the twenty-first year of Nâgadâsa, Paṇḍuvâsa died, and they crowned Abhaya in the twenty-first year of Nâgadâsa.

11. ... seventeen years [1]); twenty-four ...

12. In the fourteenth year of Candagutta the king called Pakuṇḍaka died; in the fourteenth year of Canda-

1) The first words of this fragment seem to refer to the interreign after Abhaya's death, which lasted seventeen years. The number of twenty-four I cannot explain.

gutta they crowned Muṭasîva. 13. Seventeen years had elapsed after the coronation of Asoka, then Muṭasîva died.

14. When seventeen years of that king (that is, Asoka) and six months of the next year had elapsed, in the second month of the winter season, under the most auspicious Nakkhatta of Asâḷhâ, Devânampiya was installed in the kingdom of Tambapaṇṇi. 15. At the foot of the Châta mountain three bamboo poles were to be found. (The first was) white like silver; its creeper shone like gold. 16. 17. There was also (the second), the flower pole, (whereon most beautiful,) delightful (figures) like the shapes of flowers (presented themselves), dark blue, yellow, red, pure white, and black; and so also (the third), the bird-pole on which birds (appeared), each with its natural colours, and also quadrupeds. 18. The eight descriptions of pearls (also presented themselves), viz. the horse pearl, the elephant pearl, the chariot pearl, the myrobalan pearl, the bracelet pearl, the signet pearl, the Kakubha pearl, the Sadisa (Pâkatika?) pearl. 19. When Devânampiya had succeeded to the throne, (the people,) moved by the splendour of his coronation, brought the three kinds of gems from the Malaya country, the three bamboo poles from the foot of the Châta hill, and the eight kinds of pearls from the sea-shore. 20. Great crowds brought in the space of seven days, in consequence of Devânampiya's merit, the gems which were produced in Malaya and which were worthy of a king. 21. When the king saw these costly, precious treasures, the unequalled, incomparable, wonderful, rare treasures, — 22. 23. he spoke with a heart full of joy: „I am high-born, noble, the chief of men; such is the reward of my righteous deeds; look at the treasures I have gained, which are worth many lacs and are produced in consequence of my merit. Who is worthy to receive the donation of these treasures, — 24. my mother or my father, a brother, relations, friends, or companions?“ Thus meditating the king remembered prince Asoka. 25. Devânampiyatissa and Dhammâsoka, the master of men, were both intimate friends, united by faithful

affection, though they never had seen each other. 26. „I have a dear ally, the ruler of Jambudîpa, the righteous Asokadhamma, a friend dear as my life. 27. He is worthy to receive from me the gift of these treasures, and I also am worthy to present unto him the treasure of these most precious ornaments (?). 28. Arise, my dear (?)[1]), quickly take these treasures, go to Jambudîpa, to the city called Puppha(pura), and present these most precious treasures to Asoka, my ally."

29. Mahâariṭṭha, Sâla, the Brâhmaṇa Parantapabbata, the astrologer Puttatissa, these four men were the messengers despatched by Devânampiya. 30. Devânampiya sent the three resplendent gems, the eight excellent pearls, and the three (bamboo poles which had the size of) chariot poles, besides a collection of the most precious chanks, together with many valuable objects. 31. The king sent his minister Sâla and his commander-in-chief Ariṭṭha, Parantapabbata, and his astrologer Puttatissa, who were delighted (?) (with this service).

32. (Asoka in return sent) a royal parasol, a ... of Sâra wood (?), a diadem, ear ornaments, water from the Ganges, and an (anointing) vase, a chank trumpet, and a palanquin, — 33. a right hand chank, a virgin, all that being worthy (?) of a royal coronation; a suit (a koṭi?) of clothes which are (cleansed by being passed through the fire) without being washed[2]), costly towels, — 34. most precious yellow sandal wood, and measures of rouge, yellow, and emblic myrobalan; and therewith he sent this message: 35. „The Buddha is the best among those who are worthy of presents, the Faith is the best of all things which refer to the extinction of the passions, and the Saṃgha is the best field of merit: these are the three best objects in the world of men and Devas. 36. To this (triad) I, the prince, pay my reverence for the sake of the highest bliss."

1) The king addresses his nephew Ariṭṭha; see the Mahâvaṃsa, p. 69.

2) I have adopted Turnour's translation of „adhovimaṃ" (Mahâvaṃsa, p. 70).

37. Those four messengers having sojourned five months (in Pâṭaliputta, departed,) taking away the presents sent by Asokadhamma, — 38. and arrived in this island from Jambudîpa on the twelfth day of the increasing moon in the month of Vesâkha. The requisites for the coronation having been sent by Asokadhamma, — 39. they celebrated a second coronation of king Devânampiya. This second coronation took place on the full moon day of the month of Vesâkha; — 40. one month after that day, on the full moon day of the month of Jeṭṭha, Mahinda arrived in this island from Jambudîpa together with his six companions.

Here ends the description of the things for the royal coronation.

XII.

1. The (monarch) called Asoka sent (to Devânampiya) a chowrie, a turban, a sword, a royal parasol, slippers, a diadem, a ... of Sâra wood, an (anointing) vase, a right hand chank, — 2. a palanquin, a conch trumpet, water from the Ganges, a koṭi of clothes which are (cleansed by being passed through the fire) without being washed, a golden vessel and spoon, costly towels, — 3. a man's load of water from the Anotatta lake, most precious yellow sandal wood, a measure of rouge, eye collyrium brought by the Nâgas, — 4. yellow and emblic myrobalan, costly Amata drugs, one hundred and sixty cart loads of fragrant hill paddy which had been brought by parrots; (all these things being) the rewards for his meritorious actions. 5. (Besides he sent the following message:) „I have taken my refuge in the Buddha, the Dhamma, and the Saṃgha; I have avowed myself a lay pupil of the Doctrine of the Sakyaputta. 6. Imbue your mind also with the faith in this triad, in the highest religion of the Jina, take your refuge in the Teacher.“ 7. Doing honour (to Devânampiyatissa by) this (commission), Asoka the illustrious despatched the messengers to Devânampiya.

As soon as the messengers had departed, — 8. many Theras who possessed the great (magical) powers addressed Mahinda, in the most excellent Asokârâma, out of compassion for the country of Lankâ, (as follows:) 9. „The time has come to establish the Faith in the island of Lankâ; go, most virtuous one, convert the island of Lankâ." 10. The wise and learned Mahinda, the enlightener of the island, having heard the speech of the Fraternity, consented together with his companions. 11. Adjusting his robe so as to cover one shoulder, raising his clasped hands, and saluting them with an inclination of the head, (he said:) „I go to the island of Lankâ." 12. The (prince) called Mahinda became then the chief of that number; Iṭṭhiya and the Thera Uttiya, Bhaddasâla and Sambala, — 13. and the novice Sumana who was possessed of the six (supernatural) faculties and of the great (magical) powers, those five great Theras being possessed of the (same) six (supernatural) faculties and great (magical) powers, departing from the Asokârâma went forth together with their retinue. 14. Wandering from place to place they reached Vedissagiri. They sojourned as long as they liked in the monastery of Vedissagiri. 15. Thera (Mahinda), having instructed his mother (in the doctrine of) the refuges, the moral precepts, and the Uposatha ceremonies, made the inhabitants of the island firm in the true faith and in the religion.

16. (Once) in the evening, Thera Mahinda, the great teacher, retiring into solitude, reflected whether the time would be favourable or unfavourable (for the conversion of Lankâ). 17. Perceiving the thought of the Thera, Sakka the chief of gods appeared to the Thera, and thus addressed him face to face: 18. „The time has come to thee, great hero, to convert Lankâdîpa; go quickly to the best of islands out of compassion for created beings. 19. Go to the most excellent Lankâdîpa, preach the Dhamma to created beings; proclaim the four Truths, release men from the fetters (of sin); — 20. make illustrious the doctrine of the supreme Buddha in Lankâdîpa. Thy (advent)

has been foretold by the Chief (of the Faith); the fraternity of Bhikkhus has elected thee, — 21. and I shall do service to thee at thy arrival in Laṅkâdîpa and perform all that is necessary; it is time for thee to depart.“ 22. Having heard the speech of Sakka, Mahinda, the enlightener of the island, reflected (thus): „Bhagavat has rightly prophesied about me, the fraternity of Bhikkhus has elected me, — 23. and Sakka has exhorted me; I shall establish the Faith; I will go to Tambapaṇṇi; subtle is the people of Tambapaṇṇi, — 24. (yet) they have not heard of the well proclaimed path which leads to the destruction of all suffering. I shall proclaim it to them; I shall go to the island of Laṅkâ.“ 25. Mahinda, the son of Asoka, who well knew the time and the season, having resolved to go to Laṅkâ, told his companions (to come). Mahinda was the chief of that number; there were (then) his four fellow-pupils, — 26. the novice Sumana, and the lay-disciple Bhaṇḍuka. To these six men who were endowed with the six (supernatural) faculties, (Mahinda) who possessed the great (magical) powers, thus made known (his intention): 27. „Let us go now to the extensive, most excellent island of Laṅkâ, let us convert many people and establish the Faith.“ 28. Expressing their assent (by exclaiming:) „Be it so“, they all were joyful. (They added:) „It is time, venerable sir, let us go to the mountain called Missaka; the king (Devânampiyatissa) is just leaving the town in order to hunt.“

29. Sakka, the chief of the gods, was delighted and addressed Thera Mahinda who had retired into solitude, with the following speech: 30. „Venerable sir, Bhagavat has given this prediction about thee: ‚In future times the Bhikkhu Mahinda will convert the island, he will propagate the religion of the Jina, he will set on foot there the kingdom of Righteousness, he will deliver created beings from great pain, and will establish them on firm ground, he will act for the welfare of many people, for the joy of many people, out of compassion for the world, for the good, for the welfare, and for the joy of gods and men.‘

31. Thus Bhagavat has indicated thee, and now, at the present time, the Thera and the Bhikkhus have charged thee with the conversion of the island. It is time, great hero, to convert the island; the hour has come, great hero, to convert the island; upon thee this task has devolved; bear this burden, convert Tambapaṇṇi, propagate the religion of the Jina. I am thy obedient pupil who gets up before thee and walks behind thee.“ 32. (Mahinda replied:) „I accept what Bhagavat, our Teacher, has said; I will save Tambapaṇṇi, I will show the light (to the island) and cause the splendour of the Jina to increase. (Tambapaṇṇi) is covered and enclosed by the overclouding darkness of ignorance and of (worldly) existence; it is ruined by envy and selfishness; it cannot rise from the delusions which are produced by the fault of idleness; it has entered on a wrong way and goes far astray from the true path; it is exhausted; high born people have become (as it were) people covered with sores, and have become (feeble like) Muñja or Babbaja grass. Tambapaṇṇi has entirely been subdued by obstacles and passions in consequence of the obscurity of error and of the darkness of ignorance and of (worldly) existence; it is covered, pervaded, veiled, overshadowed, and girt round with that great darkness, the obscurity of error. 33. I shall destroy the darkness of error and throw light on all Tambapaṇṇi, I shall cause to shine the religion of the Jina.“

Being thus exhorted by Vâsavinda, the chief of gods, by such a speech, he rose up from his solitude, and having attained to the fullness of resolve, he thus asked for the assent of the fraternity of Bhikkhus: 34. „Let us go to Tambapaṇṇi; the people of Tambapaṇṇi are subtle; (yet) they have not heard of the well proclaimed path which leads to the destruction of all suffering. I shall proclaim it to them, I shall go to the island of Lañkâ.“

35. Having resided thirty days on the delightful hill of Vedissa, (they reflected thus:) „It is now time to start; let us go to the best of islands.“ 36. They flew through the air from Jambudîpa, as the king of swans flies in the

air. Having thus risen, the Theras alighted on the best of mountains (Missaka). 37. To the east of the most excellent town (Anurâdhapura), on the cloud-like mountain they stationed themselves, on the top of Missaka, as swans (alight) on the summit of a hill. 38. The (Thera) called Mahinda was then the chief of that fraternity; Iṭṭhiya, Thera Uttiya, Bhaddasâla, and Sambala, — 39. the novice Sumana, and the lay-pupil Bhaṇḍuka, all these possessing the great (magical) powers, were the converters of Tambapaṇṇi. 40. The Thera, rising into the air as the king of swans rises to the sky, stationed himself to the east of the most excellent town on the cloud-like mountain, — 41. 42. on the top of Missaka, as swans (alight) on the summit of a hill. At that time Devânampiyatissa, the son of Muṭasîva, was king and ruler of Tambapaṇṇi. The eighteenth year had elapsed since the coronation of Asoka, — 43. and full seven months since the coronation of Tissa, when Mahinda, twelve years (after his Upasampadâ ordination), arrived in this island from Jambudîpa. 44. In the last month of summer, on the full moon day of the month Jeṭṭha, under the asterisms Anurâdhâ and Jeṭṭha, Mahinda at the head of his companions arrived on mount Missaka. 45. The king, going a hunting, (also) came to mount Missaka. A god who had assumed the form of an elk appeared to the king. 46. The king, seeing the elk, quickly rushed on him and running behind him he came to a place enclosed by hills. 47. There the Yakkha disappeared near the Thera; seeing the Thera sitting there, the king was frightened. 48. (The Thera reflected:) „As the king is alone, he shall see also me alone lest he should be frightened; when his troops have come up, then he may see the Bhikkhus (also).“ 49. There (Mahinda) saw the prince, the protector of the earth, who appeared like a wicked person, going to hunt; he called him by the name of that prince: „Come hither, Tissa“, thus he then addressed him. 50. (The king thought thus:) „Who is that solitary, bald-headed man without companion, wearing a yellow garment and wrapped in a mantle, who addresses me in the language of non-human beings?" 51. (Mahinda replied:) „I whom you ask, o prince, o protector of the earth, am a Samaṇa belonging to the world of men. We are Samaṇas, great king, pupils of the king of Truth; out of compassion towards thee we have repaired hither from Jambudîpa." 52. The king laid aside his weapons and seated himself by the side (of Mahinda); having seated himself, the king exchanged greetings with words full of deep meaning. 53. Having heard the speech of the Thera, he laid aside his weapons; then he approached the Thera, exchanged greetings with him, and sat down. 54. Gradually the ministers and the troops also arrived; fourty thousand men in number they surrounded (the king and the Theras). 55. When the troops had come up, the king perceived the (other) seated Theras (and asked:) „Are there many other Bhikkhus, pupils of the universal Buddha?" 56. „There are many disciples of Buddha, versed in the threefold science, possessed of the (magical) powers, well acquainted with the exposition of the qualities of mind, who have subdued their passions and reached Arahatship."

57. After having ascertained by means of the Amba parable that this victorious king was a clever person, (Mahinda) preached to him the most excellent Hatthipada Sutta. 58. When they had heard that most excellent (portion of the) Doctrine, these forty thousand men took their refuge (with Buddha), like a wise man in whose mind faith has arisen. 59. Then the king, glad, highly delighted and joyful, addressed the fraternity of Bhikkhus: „Let us proceed to the town, my capital." 60. Quickly (Mahinda) converted the pious, learned and wise king called Devânam(piya) together with his army. 61. Hearing what the kind said, Mahinda replied: „Go you, great king; we shall stay here." 62. When he had sent away the king, Mahinda, the enlightener of the island, addressed the fraternity of Bhikkhus: „Let us confer the Pabbajjâ ordination on Bhaṇḍuka." 63. Having heard what the Thera said, they all quickly turning their thoughts (to-

wards that object) examined the village boundary and conferred the Pabbajjâ ordination on Bhaṇḍuka. At the same time he received the Upasampadâ ordination and attained Arahatship.

64. The Thera standing on the top of the mountain said to the charioteer[1]): „Nay, a chariot is not suitable (to us); the Tathâgata has rejected (its use).“ 65. Having sent away the charioteer, the Theras who had subdued their senses and possessed the great (magical) powers, started throught the air, as the king of swans (rises) to the sky. Descending from the sky, they alighted on the ground. 66. When the charioteer saw them who put on their under garments and dressed themselves in their robes, he joyfully went to tell the king. 67. When the king had (first) despatched the charioteer, he had thus addressed his ministers: „Erect a pavilion in the town within the precincts of the palace. 68. The princes and princesses, the queens, and the women of the harem who desire to meet them, may see the Theras who have arrived.“ 69. The high-born ministers, after having heard the speech of the king, constructed in the middle of the precincts of the palace a pavilion canopied with cloth. 70. A canopy was spread, a clean, white and spotless cloth; it was decorated with flags and shells, and adorned with white strips of cotton. 71. White sand was scattered, well mixed with white flowers; (such was) the white, decorated hall, similar to the snowy regions (of the skies). 72. Having decorated the hall with entirely white cloth and having made the floor level, they spoke to the king: 73. „The well constructed, beautiful hall, great king, is completed; choose now, Sire, seats which are suitable for ascetics.“ 74. At that moment the charioteer arrived announcing to the king: „A chariot, Sire, is not suitable for the Bhikkhu fraternity to sit down (therein). 75. O wonderful, Sire! all the Theras who possess the great (magical) powers, first remained behind me after having sent me away, (but now)

1) The king had sent his chariot the next morning for bringing the Theras to the town; see Mahâv., p. 81.

they have arrived before me. 76. A high seat and a great seat are not suitable for the Bhikkhus; order a carpet (for them); the Theras approach.“ 77. The king, delighted at hearing the speech of the charioteer, went forth to meet the Theras, and having saluted, he exchanged greetings (with them). 78. Taking the alms-bowls of the Theras and honouring them with perfumed garlands, the prince together with the Theras arrived at the gate of the royal palace. 79. The Thera, having entered the hall in the interior appartments of the king, saw the floor strewn (as above described) and the seat covered with cloth. 80. They sat down on the seats prepared for them which were covered with cloth. When they had seated themselves, the king gave them water, rice-gruel and food, — 81. and served to them with his own hands a most excellent meal. When the Thera had finished his meal and removed his hand from the bowl, — 82. (the king) addressed queen Anulâ together with the women of the interior appartments: „You know the opportunity, queen; it is time to pay your respects to them (the Theras).“ 83. Queen Anulâ, surrounded by five hundred girls, bowed to the Theras and honoured them to her heart's content. 84. Having approached the Theras and saluted them, she sat down. (Mahinda) preached to them the Dhamma; the great teacher exposed the fearful Peta stories, — 85. 86. the Vimâna stories, the Saccasaṃyutta. When they had heard that most excellent (portion of the) Doctrine, princess Anulâ and her five hundred attendants, like a wise man (?) in whose mind faith has arisen, attained the reward of Sotâpatti; this was the first case of the attainment (of a stage of sanctification which occurred in Laṅkâ).

XIII.

1. The whole crowd, the multitude of people who had not seen the Theras before, assembled at the gate of the royal palace and set up a great shout. 2. The king hearing the great noise . . . (asked:) „For what reason have

all these numerous people, has this great crowd assembled?" 3. (The ministers said:) „This great crowd, Sire, has assembled for seeing the Fraternity; as they did not obtain a sight (of them), they set up that great shout." 4. (The king replied:) „The palace is much too small for this multitude to place themselves therein; the elephant stables are not too small; (there) these crowds may see the Thera." 5. When (Mahinda) had finished his meal and gladdened (the king by preaching the Dhamma), he rose from his seat, left the royal palace, and went to the elephant stables. 6. In the elephant stables they prepared a magnificent couch; on that excellent couch Mahinda, the enlightener of the island, sat down. 7. Seated on that most excellent couch Mahinda, the chief of (that) company (of Bhikkhus), then preached the most excellent Devadûta Sutta. 8. Having heard that Devadûta discourse (which treats of) the most fearful (consequences of) former deeds, they were frightened and seized by great emotion, being terrified by the fear of hell. 9. When he saw that the people were oppressed by fear, he proclaimed the four Truths; at the end (of his discourse) one thousand men attained (sanctification); this was the second case of the attainment (of sanctification which occurred in Lañkâ).

10. Leaving the elephant stables (he went forth), followed by a great crowd, delighting many people, as Buddha had done in Râjagaha. 11. The crowd left the town by the southern gate; there was a pleasure garden called Mahânandana, to the south of the town. 12. In (this) royal pleasure garden they prepared a magnificent couch; there the Thera sat down and preached the most excellent Dhamma. 13. There he preached the most excellent Bâlapaṇḍita Suttanta. At that time one thousand created beings attained sanctification through the Dhamma. 14. 15. A great crowd then gathered in the Nandana pleasure garden; noble women and maidens, the daughters-in-law and the daughters of noble families crowded together in order to see the Thera. While he exchanged greetings with them, night had fallen. 16. (The king there-

fore addressed Mahinda:) „The Theras may pass the night here in the Mahânandana garden; it is too late for going hence to the distant dwelling in the mountains.“ 17. (Mahinda replied:) „The town which is filled with so many people, is too close by; in the night there will be a great noise; nay, let us go to that mountain which is like the palace of Sakka and well fitting for a retired existence.“ 18. (Tissa answered:) „There is a solitary garden of mine, the Mahâmeghavana, suitable for going and coming, not too far and not too near, — 19. easily accessible for people who want (to see you), by day not exposed to much noise, at night there is no noise at all. 20. It is well fitted for a retired existence, and suits ascetic people; it is endowed with prospects and shadow, it is beautiful, and produces flowers and fruits, — 21. it is well enclosed by a wall and well protected by towers at the gates. There is a well arranged royal gate in my delightful garden, — 22. a well constructed lotus-pond covered with white and blue lotuses, cold water in suitable reservoirs, which is sweetly scented by flowers. 23. So delightful is my garden, appropriate for (you) and the fraternity of Bhikkhus. There, o Thera, reside; have compassion on me.“ 24. Hearing what the king said, Thera Mahinda with his companions, surrounded by the host of ministers, proceeded then to the Meghavana garden. 25. Being invited by the chief of men, Thera Mahinda, the great teacher, entered the suitable Mahâmeghavana garden. In that garden, in the royal pavilion, the Thera, the great teacher, passed the night.

26. On the second day the king again visited the Theras. Having bowed to them, he spoke thus to the Theras: 27. „Have you had a good night's rest? do you find this residence comfortable?“ (The Theras replied:) „The dwelling is solitary, well fitting the season, agreeable to lie in for men, — 28. convenient for a retired existence and desirable.“ The king, delighted by that speech, rejoicing and excited, — 29. he the ruler of the earth, took a golden vessel and dedicated the garden (to the Frater-

nity). Raising his clasped hands, he pronounced the following words: 30. „Here, venerable Sir, I give up the beautiful Mahâmeghavana garden to the Fraternity of the four quarters of the world; accept it.“ 31. Mahinda, the enlightener of the island, hearing what the chief of men said, accepted the garden for the sake of the construction of a monastery for the Fraternity. 32. At the moment when the Mahâmeghavana garden was given and accepted, the earth began to quake, and again and again thunder (was heard). 33. The chief of men called Tissa bestowed it on the Fraternity; they turned the Mahâmeghavana garden into (a monastery called) the Tissârâma. 34. The Mahâmeghavana was the first Ârâma, worthy of the Religion, which Devânampiya bestowed on the Fraternity. 35. Then the earth quaked, a horror-exciting portent. All people and the king, being terrified, asked the Theras (about the reason of that earth-quake). 36. „This is the first monastery in the most excellent island of Laṅkâ; the reason of this first earth-quake is that the Faith has been established here.“ 37. Witnessing that astonishing, terrifying miracle, they all waved their garments, as nothing of the kind had been experienced in the town. 38. Thence the rejoicing king in whose mind wisdom had arisen, raising his clasped hands, presented many flowers to Mahinda, the enlightener of the island. 39. The Thera accepted the flowers and threw them down in one place; then the earth again quaked; this was the second earth-quake. 40. Witnessing this miracle also, the royal retinue together with the people of the kingdom shouted; this was the second earth-quake. 41. The delighted king who rejoiced still more, (then asked:) „Satisfy my desire (to learn the reason of) this second earth-quake.“ 42. „The Fraternity will (here) perform its business which is irreproachable and worthy of the Faith. At this very spot, o great king, will be the consecrated enclosure.“ 43. The king, still more delighted, presented flowers to the Thera; the Thera accepted the flowers and threw them down on another spot; then the earth quaked again; this was the third earth-quake. 44. (The king asked:) „What is the reason, o great hero, of this third earth-quake? Satisfy all my wishes, tell me, you are well experienced.“ 45. „On this spot will be the bath-house with a tank; here the Bhikkhus always will fill the bath.“ 46. Devânampiya, filled with high joy and delight, presented full-blown jasmine flowers to the Thera. 47. The Thera accepted the flowers and threw them down on another spot. Then the earth quaked again. This was the fourth earth-quake. 48. Witnessing that miracle, the great crowds who had assembled, raising their clasped hands, paid reverence to (the Thera) who possessed the great (magical) powers. 49. The king, glad and delighted, quickly asked: „What is the reason, o great hero, of this fourth earth-quake?“ 50. „The descendant of the Sakyas, the great hero, was enlightened regarding the whole Truth near the Assattha tree; (there) he became the highest Buddha. That tree will be established on this very spot in this most excellent island.“ 51. Hearing that, the king, glad, joyful, and excited, presented most excellent jasmine flowers to the Thera. 52. The Thera accepted the flowers and threw them down on the ground; at that moment also the earth quaked; this was the fifth earth-quake. 53. Witnessing that miracle also, the royal retinue together with the people of the kingdom shouted and waved their garments. 54. (The king asked:) „What is the reason, o great sage, of the fifth earth-quake? Tell me this matter, if that is consistent (?) with your pleasure and will.“ 55. „Each fortnight they will here recite the Pâtimokkha; on this very spot the Uposatha hall will stand.“ 56. (The king) presented beautiful flowers to the Thera also in another place; the Thera accepted the flowers and threw them down on that spot. Then the earth quaked again; this was the sixth earth-quake. 57. Witnessing this miracle also, the crowds who had assembled, joyfully thus addressed each other: „Here a Vihâra will stand.“ 58. The king who was still more delighted, said to the Theras: „What is the reason, o great Sage, of the sixth earth-quake?“ 59. „As long as in future times the alms due to the Fraternity (will be distributed), the assembled Fraternities of Bhikkhus will receive them, o great king, on this very spot." 60. Hearing the Thera's speech, the delighted king presented most beautiful flowers to the Thera. 61. The Thera accepted the flowers and scattered them on another spot; then the earth quaked again; this was the seventh earth-quake. 62. Witnessing this miracle, the whole royal retinue and the people of the kingdom waved their garments, when the ground of the earth quaked. 63. (The king asked:) „What is the reason, o great sage, of the seventh earth-quake? Explain it, o great sage, satisfy the desire of the multitude." 64. (Mahinda replied:) „As long as learned people will reside in this monastery, the refectory and the dinner hall will be on this spot."

XIV.

1. Having heard the speech of the Thera, the king was still more delighted. Not accepting the Campaka flowers (offerred to him by the gardener), he presented them to the Thera. 2. The Thera threw down the Campaka flowers on the ground; then the earth quaked again; this was the eighth earth-quake. 3. Witnessing this miracle, the royal retinue and the people of the kingdom shouted and waved their garments. 4. (The king asked:) „What is the reason, o great hero, of the eighth earthquake? Explain it, o great sage, we listen to your speech?" 5. 6. „The relics of Tathâgata's body consist of eight Doṇa-measures, men possessed of magical power will convey hither one Doṇa, o great king, and deposit it at this very spot, and erect (here) a resplendent Thûpa which will be the means whereby hearts will be touched and many people will be converted." 7. The whole crowd that had assembled, the royal retinue and the people of the kingdom shouted at the quaking of the great earth.

8. (The Thera) resided (during the next night) in the Tissârâma, and when the night had passed, he put on

his under garment and wrapped himself in his robe; — 9. then he took his alms-bowl and entered the town, the capital. Going about in quest of alms he came to the gate of the palace. 10. He entered the royal palace and sat down on a seat; there he took his meal and cleansed the bowl with his hand. 11. 12. Having finished his meal and gladdened (the king by preaching the Dhamma), he left the palace and the town by the southern gate. He then preached in the Nandana garden the most excellent Aggikkhandha Suttanta. There one thousand men attained sanctification. 13. Having preached the true Faith and having delivered many created beings (from their sinful condition), the Thera rose from his seat and resided again (during the next night) in the Tissârâma. 14. Having resided there during the night, when the night had passed, he put on his under garment and wrapped himself in his robe; — 15. then he took his alms-bowl and entered the town, the capital. Going about in quest of alms he came to the gate of the palace. 16. He entered the royal palace and sat down on a seat; there he took his meal and cleansed his bowl with his hand. 17. 18. Having finished his meal and gladdened (the king by preaching the Dhamma), he left the town, the capital. When he had rested at noon in the most excellent Nandana garden, he preached there the beautiful Suttanta of the Âsivisa parable. At the end (of this sermon) one thousand men attained sanctification; (this was) the fifth case of the attainment of sanctification (which occurred in Lankâ). 19. Having preached the true Faith and awakened created beings, he rose from his seat and went to the Tissârâma.

20. The king was greatly delighted at the eightfold (?) earth-quake; glad, rejoicing and satisfied the king thus addressed the Theras: 21. „The monastery has been firmly established, an excellent resting-place for the Fraternity. (Your) Abhiññâpâdaka meditation, venerable Sir, (has caused) this great earth-quake.“ 22. (The Thera replied:) „By this alone, o king, the rest-house for the Fraternity has not yet been firmly established; the Tathâgata

has instituted (the ceremony) called the determination of boundaries. 23. 24. Having defined on all sides by the eight classes of landmarks the boundaries within which all Bhikkhus are considered as one section, and (having decreed about) not parting with the three robes[1]), all the sections (of the Fraternity) assemble and vote on their affairs. A place enclosed by boundaries which have been fixed in that way, is called one community. (Then) the monastery is well established, and the rest-house duly founded." 25. (The king answered:) „My sons and wives together with my ministers and my retinue, all have become your lay pupils and have taken for all their life their refuge (in the Faith). 26. I ask you, great hero, do what I say; let the whole multitude (of the town's-people) reside on the ground included by the boundaries. 27. Here always they will find a defence through the protecting power (?) of charity and compassion." (Mahinda said:) „Determine you the limits, o king, as you like; — 28. the limit being given, the Fraternity will settle the boundaries." Mahâpaduma and Kuñjara, the two state-elephants, — 29. were first harnessed to a golden plough in Koṭṭhamâlaka. The great army consisting of four hosts (proceeded), and together with the Theras the king, — 30. the destroyer of his enemies, made a furrow with the golden plough. (During this progress there were seen) adorned full vases, beautiful flags of different colours, — 31. triumphal arches decorated with various flowers and flags, garlands (?), and many burning lights (?). (Thus the king) ploughed with the golden plough. 32. For the sake of the conversion of many people, the prince together with the Theras, turning his right hand towards the city, walked around it and came to the bank of the river. 33. Drawing (?) the furrow which indicated the line of the great boundary, on the ground with the golden plough, he then (?) arrived (again) at Koṭṭhamâlaka. 34. The two ends of the furrow having been united in the presence of

1) See the rules about the definition of boundaries and about the „ticîvarena avippavâsa", Mahâvagga, II, 6—12.

a great crowd, the earth quaked; this was the first earthquake. 35. Witnessing that miracle, the whole royal retinue together with the people of the kingdom joyfully said to each other: „There will be a monastery within the boundary." 36. The ruler Devânampiya indicated to the Theras how far they had fixed the marks of the boundary line, of the enclosure, (and spoke thus:) 37. 38. „As the preparatory ceremonies for fixing the boundary and the enclosure have been performed, may the Thera now out of compassion for me settle the limits, in order to establish firmly the Vihâra which will be suitable for the fraternity of Bhikkhus." Having heard what the king said, Mahinda, the enlightener of the island, — 39. thus addressed the fraternity of Bhikkhus: „O Bhikkhus, let us fix the boundary." Under the constellation of Uttarâsâḷhâ the whole Fraternity assembled. 40. Having determined the extent of the sacred enclosure, (Mahinda) who was gifted with (supernatural) vision, fixed the boundary within which the Bhikkhus were to be considered as one section. Having firmly established the most excellent Tissârâma monastery, — 41. he resided (during the next night) in the Tissârâma, and when the night had passed, he put on his under garment and wrapped himself in his robe; — 42. then he took his alms-bowl and entered the town, the capital. Going about in quest of alms, he came to the gate of the palace. 43. He entered the royal palace and sat down on a seat; there he took his meal and cleansed the bowl with his hand. 44. Having finished his meal and gladdened the king (by preaching the Dhamma), he left the town, the capital. When he had rested at noon in the Nandana pleasure garden, — 45. he then preached the Âsivisûpama Suttanta, the Anamataggiya Sutta, and the incomparable Cariya Piṭaka; — 46. he also repeatedly propounded the Gomayapiṇḍaovâda and the Dhammacakkappavattana in that same place, in the Mahânandana garden. 47. 48. These Suttantas he preached during (those) seven days, and (in this time) Thera Mahinda, the enlightener of the island, delivered eight thousand and five hundred people from the fetters (of sin). Having resided in the Tissârâma together with his companions something less then a month, — 49. he thus addressed all the townsmen on the full-moon day of Âsâḷha, when the time of Vassa had approached: „The time of Vassa is near.“

Here ends the acceptance of the Mahâvihâra.

50. Having arranged his sleeping-place, Mahinda, the enlightener of the island, took his alms-bowl and his robe, and left the Tissârâma. 51. He put on his under garment and wrapped himself in his robe; then he took his alms-bowl and entered the town, the capital. 52. Going about in quest of alms, he came to the gate of the palace. He entered the royal palace, and (there the Theras) sat down on the becoming seats. 53. There (Mahinda) took his meal and cleansed the bowl with his hand; (then) he preached the Mahâsamaya Suttanta in order to exhort (the king). 54. Having exhorted the king, Mahinda, the enlightener of the island, rose from his seat and departed without taking leave. 55. The great teacher left the town by the eastern gate, and sending back all people he proceeded to the (Missaka) mountain. 56. The ministers were filled with anxiousness, and announced to the king: „All the great Theras, Sire, have gone to the Missaka mountain.“ 57. The king, frightened at this news, ordered the horses quickly to be put to the chariot. The prince taking the queens with him, quickly ascended the chariot. 58. Thera Mahinda together with his companions had proceeded to the foot of the mountain. There was a lake called Nâgacatukka, situated amidst the rocks; after bathing at that place and drinking (the water of that lake), he ascended the summit of the mountain. 59. The prince who profusely perspired in consequence of his great haste, saw from afar the Thera, standing on the summit of the mountain. 60. Leaving the queens in the chariot, the prince descended from the chariot, approached the Theras, saluted, and addressed them thus: 61. „Why, great hero, have you left the delightful kingdom, myself, and the

people, and retired to this mountain?" 62. (Mahinda replied:) „Here we shall spend, three full months, the Vassa which Tathâgata has allowed to begin earlier or later"[1]). 63. (The king replied:) „I do everything that is required for the comfort of the Bhikkhu fraternity; have compassion on me, and instruct me." 64. „The Bhikkhus have been permitted by Buddha to begin the Vassa in a village as well as in the forest, (provided they) dwell in a room with shut doors." 65. „I have understood what you have said, the whole sense with its reasons; this very day I shall erect a residence suitable for the Vassa." 66. The illustrious monarch who had reached the full perfection attainable by a layman, looked out (for a place), and dedicated (it) to the Theras, (saying:) „Reside here out of compassion; — 67. well, venerable Thera, take possession of these rock-cut cells (and of this) Ârâma. In order to establish firmly the Vihâra, fix the boundary, great Sage."

68. 69. The son of the king's sister, renowned by the name of Mahâriṭṭha, and also fifty-five illustrious noblemen approached the king, saluted him, and said: „We all desire to receive the Pabbajjâ ordination from that man endowed with highest wisdom; — 70. 71. we will embrace a life of holiness; give us your consent, Sire." Hearing what they all had said, the delighted king, the ruler of the earth, approached the Theras, and thus addressed (Mahinda): „(There are) fifty-five chiefs with Mahâariṭṭha at their head; confer on them personally the Pabbajjâ ordination, great hero; I give my consent." 72. Hearing the king's speech, Mahinda, the enlightener of the island, thus addressed the Bhikkhu fraternity: „Let us fix the boundary, o Bhikkhus." 73. (The Theras), in order to establish firmly the Vihâra, consecrated the boundary within which all Bhikkhus were to be considered as one section, and the enclosure (?), and proclaimed the decree about not parting with the three robes. 74. Having fixed the

1) See Mahâvagga, III, 2, 2.

inner and the outer boundary at the Tumba enclosure, Mahinda, the enlightener of the island, proclaimed the (extent of) the great boundary. 75. The (Thera) who was gifted with (supernatural) vision, consecrated the whole enclosure and the boundary, and firmly established the second monastery which was situated on the Tissapabbata. 76. After having consecrated the boundary on the mountain precisely on the full-moon day of the month Âsâḷha, on the Uposatha day, under the constellation of Uttarâsâḷhâ, — 77. he conferred the Pabbajjâ ordination on Mahâriṭṭha who was the first person (who received it) in this second enclosure; at the same time he conferred the Upasampadâ ordination on this prince who belonged to the royal family of Tambapaṇṇi. 78. At the same time (those) fifty-five (other noblemen received) the Pabbajjâ and Upasampadâ ordinations.

In the first Ârâma thirty-two consecrated enclosures were established; — 79. thirty-two in the second Ârâma, in the monastery of the Tissa mountain. The other small Ârâmas contained one enclosure each. 80. The Ârâma and the monastery being founded on that most excellent mountain, sixty-two persons, who were all Arahats, entered on the Vassa residence; this was the first time (that this event occurred in Lañkâ).

Here ends the acceptance of the Cetiya mountain.

XV.

1. (Mahinda said to the king:) „In the first month of the summer, on the full moon, on the Uposathâ day, we have come hither from Jambudîpa; we have dwelt on this most excellent mountain. 2. During five months we have not left the Tissârâma nor the mountain; now we will go to Jambudîpa; permit it, o lord of charioteers.“ 3. (The king replied:) „We serve you with food and drink, with clothes and dwelling-places; the whole people has taken refuge (in the Faith); what causes you dissatisfaction?“ 4. (Mahinda said: „We have no object here

to which we may pay respect by) salutations and by rising from our seats, or by raising our clasped hands, and by respectful contemplation. For a long time, o great king, we have not seen the Sambuddha, the highest among men.“ 5. (The king answered:) „Verily I have understood you, venerable sir; I will erect a most excellent Thûpa; find you out a suitable place (?); I will build a Thûpa in honour of the Teacher.“

6. (Mahinda gave the following order to Sumana:) „Go, chief Sumana; repair to Pâṭaliputta, and address thus the righteous king Asoka: 7. „Your ally, great king, has been converted to the faith of Buddha; grant to him (some of) the most excellent relics; he is going to erect a Thûpa in honour of the Teacher.“ 8. Learned (Sumana) who was versed in the scriptures, a powerful, eloquent speaker, who had reached the perfect possession of (magical) power, who was firm and well grounded (in the Faith), — 9. took his alms-bowl and his robe, and instantly departed from the mountain. According to the truth he thus addressed king Dhammâsoka: 10. „Hear, great king, the message which my teacher sends you. Your ally, great king, has been converted to the faith of Buddha; grant to him (some of) the most excellent relics; he is going to erect a Thûpa in honour of the Teacher.“ 11. Having heard this speech, the rejoicing and excited king filled the alms-bowl with relics, (saying:) „Quickly depart, pious man.“ 12. The powerful, eloquent speaker then took the relics, rose into the air and repaired to Kosiya (Indra). 13. The eloquent man having approached Kosiya thus addressed him: „Hear, great king, the message which my teacher sends you. 14. King Devânampiya has been converted to the faith of Buddha; grant to him a most excellent relic; he is going to erect a splendid Thûpa.“ 15. Having heard his speech, Kosiya rejoicing gave him the right collar-bone (of Buddha, saying:) „Quickly depart, pious man.“ 16. The novice Sumana, leaving Kosiya and taking away the right collar-bone, descended on the most excellent mountain (Missaka). 17. The

wise man who was filled with modesty, fear of sin, and reverence, despatched by the king of Theras, placed himself on the most excellent mountain. 18. The king together with his brothers, at the head of a great army, and accompanied by the most excellent Bhikkhu fraternity, then went to meet the relics of the highest Buddha. 19. 20. On the day of the full moon of the month Kattika, on the day of the Câtumâsa festival, the great hero arrived. (The dish with the relics) was placed on the frontal globe of the (state) elephant. 21. (The elephant) roared, like a struck gong; at that moment the earth quaked, when the Sage in the neighbourhood (of the mountain) approached. 22. The sound of the chanks and the roll of the drums mixed with the boom of the kettle-drums (was heard). The prince escorting (the relic) paid reverence to the highest of men. 23. The noble elephant turning westward proceeded together with the foot soldiers; he then entered the town by the eastern gate. 24. Men and women (there) offered various perfumes and garlands. The most excellent elephant leaving (the town) by the southern gate, — 25. proceeded to the very spot which teacher Kakusandha, Konâgamana and Kassapa, the old Sages, formerly had visited. 26. When the most excellent elephant had proceeded to that hill, the chief of men (there) deposited the relics of Sakyaputta. 27. At the moment when the relics were placed (there), the gods expressed their delight, and the earth began to quake in an astonishing, terrifying manner. 28. (The king) with his brothers, gladdening the ministers and the people of the kingdom (by his order), caused the bricks for the Thûpa to be manufactured.

29. The noblemen paid singly their reverence to the most excellent Thûpa; the highly precious relics which shone like a light, were covered with excellent gems. 30. (There were) white (?) canopies, separate canopies, covers (?), various (?) canopies, suitable ornaments, beautiful chowries. 31. Near the Thûpa a brilliancy spread in all directions over the four quarters from the lamps, like

the brilliancy of the rising sun. 32. Cloths brilliant with various colours were spread (?), and above (the Cetiya?) shone like (?) the cloudless sky. 33. A canopy covered with gold, which was encircled by (ornaments) made of gems and by most precious crystal, and adorned by gold sand . . . .

(Mahinda related to the king the story of the relics of the three former Buddhas:) 34. „Here Sambuddha Kakusandha, chief of men, surrounded by forty thousand (Bhikkhus who were holy) like (himself), looked (over this island). 35. The Buddha, gifted by (supernatural) vision, moved by compassion, looked on created beings, and on the suffering men in Ojadîpa, Abhayapura. 36. In Ojadîpa (he looked) with the power of the rays of his Bodhi on many created beings, on a great multitude that was to attain (supreme) knowledge, as the sun (awakens) the lotuses. 37. Accompanied by forty thousand Bhikkhus he repaired to Ojadîpa, resembling the rising sun. 38. (The Buddha's name was) Kakusandha, (that of the chief Thera) Mahâdeva, the mountain (was called) Devakûṭa; (there reigned in the island of) Ojadîpa, (in the town of) Abhayapura, a prince named Abhaya. 39. The well constructed town which was worth seeing, delightful, and pleasant, was situated near the Kadambaka river. 40. (At that time there raged in the island) a fearful epidemic fever called Puṇṇakanaraka; the people were in a state of affliction like fishes in a net. 41. In consequence of the power of the Buddha the fever ceased. When (the Buddha) had preached the Truth which delivers from death, and had established the Faith of the Jina, — 42. eighty-four thousand men attained sanctification. At that time the monastery was the Paṭiyârâma, and (the Cetiya was) the Dhammakarakacetiya (Cetiya where the drinking vessel of the Buddha is preserved). 43. Mahâdeva accompanied by one thousand Bhikkhus, remained (there), and the Jina, the highest being, himself departed from that place.

44. Here Sambuddha Konâgamana, the great Sage, accompanied by thirty thousand Bhikkhus, looked (over the island). 45. The Sambuddha gifted with (supernatural) vision, diffused his compassion through ten thousand worlds; the great hero looked on the suffering people of Varadîpa. 46. In Varadîpa (he looked) with the power of the rays of his Bodhi on many created beings, on a great multitude that was to attain (supreme) knowledge, as the sun (awakens) the lotuses. 47. Accompanied by thirty thousand Bhikkhus the Sambuddha repaired to Varadîpa, resembling the rising sun. 48. (The Buddha's name was) Konâgamana, (that of the chief Thera) Mahâsumana, the mountain (was called) Sumanakûṭa; (there reigned in the island of) Varadîpa, (in the town of) Vaḍḍhamâna, a prince named Samiddha. 49. 50. At that time the island suffered from a drought; there was a famine ... When the created beings were afflicted by the famine like fishes in shallow water, abundant rain fell, when the Omniscient had arrived; the country became prosperous; he brought consolation to many people. 51. To the north of the town which was situated near the Tissatalâka, there was the Uttarârâma monastery; (the Cetiya at that time was) the Kâyabandhanacetiya (Cetiya where the girdle of the Buddha is preserved). 52. Eighty-four thousand men attained sanctification. When the Truth which delivers from death, had been preached, — 53. Mahâsumana, similar to the rising sun, accompanied by one thousand Bhikkhus, remained (there), and the great hero himself, the highest being, departed.

54. Here Sambuddha Kassapa, the ruler of the world, accompanied by twenty thousand Bhikkhus, looked (over the island). 55. Omniscient Kassapa looked down on the world of men and gods, and discerned by the pure vision of the Buddhas the beings who were to attain (supreme) knowledge. 56. Omniscient Kassapa, the receiver of offerings, diffusing (the rays of) his high compassion, perceived the furious contest (between king Jayanta and his brother Samiddha), — 57. and by the power of the rays

of his Bodhi, as the sun (awakens) the lotuses, he saw many beings in the island of Maṇḍadîpa who were to attain (supreme) knowledge. 58. „I shall go to Maṇḍadîpa and cause the Religion to shine there; I shall produce there high splendour like that of the moon in the darkness (of the night)“. 59. Surrounded by multitudes of Bhikkhus the Jina proceeded through the air; resembling the rising sun he repaired to Maṇḍadîpa. 60. (The Buddha's name was) Kassapa, (that of the chief Thera) Sabbananda, the mountain (was called) Subhakûṭa, the name of the town was Visâla, that of the prince was Jayanta. 61. To the east of the town which was situated near the Khema tank, there was the Pâcînârâma monastery; (the Cetiya at that time was) the Dakasâṭika Cetiya (Cetiya where the rain-cloak of the Buddha is preserved). 62. The Sambuddha, after having comforted and reconciled the (two) brothers, preached the Truth which delivers from death, and established the Faith. 63. When the Truth which delivers from death, had been preached, and the doctrine of the Jina had been established, eighty-four thousand men attained sanctification. 64. Glorious Sabbananda, surrounded by one thousand Bhikkhus, remained in Maṇḍadîpa; the ruler of the world departed.

65. Here (also stood) the Sambuddha who has appeared in the world (in the present age), the ruler of the world. „Out of compassion for the living I will save created beings.“ 66. The Sambuddha, the chief of the world, the highest among men, looked on the great armies of Nâgas which had assembled, ready for a battle. 67. The Serpents emitted smoke and flames, they raged, they spread great horror, they were destroying the great island. 68. (The Buddha) went alone (to the island:) „I shall go to the most excellent island; I shall pacify the two Serpents, the uncle and the nephew.“ 69. This Sambuddha was called Gotama; (it was) on the mountain called Cetiya(pabbata); there reigned in the delightful town called Anurâdhapura a prince named Tissa. 70. In Kusinârâ, in the Upavattana of the Mallas, the holy Sam-

buddha reached complete Nibbâna by the destruction of the substrata (of existence). 71. (He at that time foretold:) „Two hundred and thirty-six years will elapse; then (a Thera) called Mahinda by name will cause the splendour of the Religion to shine (in Lañkâ). 72. In the south of the town, at a delightful place (will be) a beautiful Ârâma called the Thûpârâma. 73. At that time the island (will be known) by the name of Tambapaṇṇi; they will deposit a relic of my body in that most excellent island."

---

74. The queen called Anulâ was a believer in the Buddha, the Dhamma, and the Fraternity; she confessed the true doctrine, and put away the desire of existence. (She expressed to the king her desire of being admitted into the Order.) 75. Having heard what the queen said, the king addressed the Thera thus: („Queen Anulâ) believes in the Buddha, the Dhamma, and the Fraternity; she confesses the true doctrine, — 76. and puts away the desire of existence. Confer the Pabbajjâ ordination on Anulâ." (Mahinda replied:) „It is not permitted to Bhikkhus, o great king, to confer the Pabbajjâ ordination on women; — 77. my sister Saṃghamittâ, o king, shall come hither. She will confer the Pabbajjâ ordination on Anulâ and will release her from all fetters. 78. Wise Saṃghamittâ and clever Uttarâ, Hemâ and Mâsagallâ, Aggimittâ, chary of speech, Tappâ and Pabbatacchinnâ, Mallâ and Dhammadâsiyâ, — 79. these Bhikkhunîs who are free from desire and firm, whose thoughts and wishes are pure, who are firmly established in the true Dhamma and Vinaya, — 80. who have subdued their passions, who have their senses under control and have attained (perfection), who possess the three-fold science and know well the (magical) powers, who are well grounded in the highest bliss, will also come hither.

81. (Devânampiya) sat down, surrounded by his ministers, and deliberated (about inviting princess Saṃghamittâ). Having sat down in order to hold a council (about

this matter), he thus addressed the ministers ... 82. Prince Ariṭṭha, having heard what the king said, — 83. and having heard the speech of the Thera and received his commission, respectfully saluted his uncle (?) and departed in the northern direction.

84. 85. Having established their residence in a certain quarter of the town, the noble ladies, five hundred virgins, queen Anulâ at their head, all high-born and illustrious, having undertaken to observe the ten moral precepts, all this multitude late and early surrounded Anulâ.

86. (Ariṭṭha) having proceeded to a sea-port went on board a great ship; when he had crossed the sea and reached the shore he stood (on dry ground). 87. The powerful minister (then) crossed the Viñjha range; having arrived at Pâṭaliputta, he presented himself to the king. 88. (Ariṭṭha thus addressed Asoka:) „Your son, Sire, your offspring, o great king Piyadassana, Thera Mahinda has sent me in your presence. 89. King Devânampiya, your ally, o Piyadassana, who is converted to Buddha, has sent me in your presence.“ 90. (Then) the great Sage (went to Saṃghamittâ and) communicated to her the message of her brother: „The royal virgins, o Saṃghamittâ, and princess Anulâ, — 91. all look to you for the Pabbajjâ ordination.“ Wise Saṃghamittâ, when she had heard the message of her brother, — 92. quickly went to the king and thus addressed him: „Give your consent, great king; I shall go to the island of Laṅkâ; — 93. the great Sage has communicated to me the message of my brother.“ (Asoka replied:) „Your sister's son Sumana and my son, your elder brother, — 94. being gone, prevent, dear, that you, my daughter, should go also.“ (Saṃghamittâ replied:) „Weighty, o great king, is my brother's command. 95. The royal virgins, o great king, and princess Anulâ, they all look to me for their Pabbajjâ ordination.“

XVI.

1. The prince (Asoka) fitted out a great army consisting of four parts, and then went forth, taking with

him a branch of the Bo tree of the Tathâgata. 2. Having passed through three kingdoms and the Viñjha range, having passed through the great forest, the prince came to the ocean. 3. The great four-fold army with the Bhikkhunî congregation at its head (?), proceeded to the great sea, carrying the excellent Bo tree. 4. When (the Bo branch) was carried to the sea, on high the musical instruments of the gods (were heard,) and below those of men, the instruments of men from all four quarters. 5. Prince Piyadassana bowing paid his reverence to the Bo tree, and spoke thus: 6. „Learned, possessed of (magical) power, virtuous, most firm ...“ 7. The prince then (when the Bo branch had been despatched) wept, shed tears, and looked (on the parting vessel). Then he returned and came to his residence.

8. The Nimmita Nâgas in the water, the Nimmita Devas in the heavens, the Nimmita Devas in the tree (itself), and (the Nâgas) of the Nâga world, — 9. they all surrounded the most excellent branch of the Bo tree which was carried away. The wild Pisâcas, the Bhûtas, Kumbhaṇḍas, and Rakkhasas, these non-human beings surrounded the branch of the Bo tree as it approached. 10. The Tâvatiṃsas and Yâmas and also the Tusita gods, the Nimmânarati gods and the Vasavatti gods — 11. (were) glad, joyful and delighted, when the Bo branch approached. And all the Tettiṃsa Devaputtas with Inda as their leader, — 12. 13. snapped their fingers and laughed when the Bo branch approached. The four (divine) Mahârâjas of the four quarters (of the horizon), Kuvera and Dhataraṭṭha, Virûpakkha and Virûḷhaka, surrounded the Sambodhi tree which was carried to the island of Lañkâ. 14. Mahâmukhas and kettle-drums, Divillas (?), leather-covered drums, and tabors (resounded); the gods joyfully shouted „Sâdhu“ when the Bo branch approached. 15. Pâricchattaka flowers, celestial Mandârava flowers, and celestial sandal powder rained through the air, and the gods did homage to the Bo branch when it approached. 16. The gods offered on the ocean to the Bo tree of the Teacher

Campaka flowers, Salla, Nimba, Nâga, Punnâga, Ketaka flowers. 17. The Nâga kings, the Nâga princesses, the young Nâgas, great crowds, left their residence and showed honour to the excellent Bo branch. 18. The Nâgas, dressed in garments of various colours and wearing ornaments of various colours, joyfully sported around the great Bodhi on the ocean (shouting:) „Hail to us.“ 19. 20. The Nâgas offered to the Bo branch on the glittering ocean red, white and blue lotuses of various kinds, Atimutta of honey-sweet scent, Takkârika and Kovilâra flowers, trumpet flowers, and quantities of Bimbajâla flowers, Asoka and Sâla flowers mixed with Piyañgu. 21. The delighted Nâga virgins, the joyful Nâga kings, (all the) Nâgas joyfully sported around the Bo branch which was carried along, (shouting:) „Hail to us.“ 22. There the ground consisted of gems, and was covered with pearls and crystals; there were gardens and tanks adorned with various flowers. 23. Having remained there seven days, (the Nâgas) together with gods and men paid honour to the excellent Bo branch on its departure from their residence. 24. The Nâga virgins and the gods, surrounding the Sambodhi branch, (offered) strings of garlands and flower wreaths, and waved their garments. 25. The gods sported around the Bodhi which was carried along, (shouting:) „Hail.“ Pâricchattaka flowers, celestial Mandârava flowers, and celestial sandal power rained through the air. 26. The Nâgas, Yakkhas, and Bhûtas, together with gods and men, surrounded the Sambodhi branch which was carried along on the ocean. 27. There, surrounding the Bo branch, they danced, sung, played (instruments), laughed, and snapped the fingers of both hands. 28. The Nâgas, Yakkhas, and Bhûtas, together with gods and men, when the most excellent Bodhi was carried along, exclaimed: „Oh auspicious event, hail.“ 29. Beautiful Nâgas of brilliantly blue colour, holding flags, praised the most excellent Bodhi which was being established in the island of Lañkâ.

30. Great crowds, the prince with the queens, left the delightful (town of) Anurâdhapura, and went to meet

the Sambodhi tree. 31. The prince together with his sons surrounded the Sambodhi tree; they offered scented garlands and most excellent perfumes (?). 32. The streets were well swept and offerings were prepared. When the Bodhi was established, the earth quaked.

33. The king appointed eight (persons of each class?) and the chiefs of each of eight warrior clans (?) to be Bodhi gards (?), for the custody of the most excellent Bodhi. 34. He fitted them out with great state, and bestowed on them beautiful ornaments of every description; out of reverence for the Bo branch he ordered sixteen great lines to be traced on the ground (?)[1]. 35. Then he caused also pure white sand (?) to be scattered on that spot where the great lines had been drawn. He appointed one thousand families ... 36. He bestowed on them golden drums for the performance of the rites of royal coronations and other festivals. He gave (to them) one province and erected (for them) the Candagutta (palace?) — 37. (and) the Devagutta palace, (and) duly (bestowed on them) land donations (?); to other families he gave the revenue of villages.

38. The five hundred high-born, illustrious virgins of the royal court who were free from passion and steadfast, all received the Pabbajjâ ordination. 39. The five hundred virgins who surrounded Anulâ, who were free from passion and steadfast, all received the Pabbajjâ ordination. 40. Prince Ariṭṭha, released from the chain of fear, received the Pabbajjâ ordination according to the doctrine of the Jina, together with five hundred companions. All these persons attained Arahatship and full perfection in the doctrine of the Jina. 41. In the first month of the winter season, when the tree was full of blossoms, the great Bo branch was brought (hither) and established in Tambapaṇṇi.

1) If my translation of this very corrupted passage is correct, the sixteen lines mentioned here may stand in some connexion with the sixteen lines drawn on the ground by Mâra near the Bo tree at Uruvela (Jâtaka, I, p. 78).

XVII.

1. 2. The excellent island of Lankâ is thirty-two yojanas long, eighteen yojanas broad, its circuit is one hundred yojanas; it is surrounded by the sea, and one great mine of treasures. It possesses rivers and lakes, mountains and forests. 3. The island, the capital, the king, the affliction (which vexed the island), the relics, the Thûpa, the lake, the mountain, the garden, the Bodhi tree, the (chief) Bhikkhunî, — 4. the (chief) Bhikkhu, and the most excellent Buddha: these are the thirteen subjects (to be treated in the following exposition). Listen to my enumeration of the four names of each of these subjects (in the time of the four last Buddhas).

5. (The island) was called Ojadîpa, Varadîpa, Maṇḍadîpa, and the excellent Lankâdîpa or Tambapaṇṇi. 6. Abhayapura, Vaḍḍhamâna, Visâla, Anurâdhapura are the four names of the capital at (the time of) the teaching of the four Buddhas. 7. Abhaya, Samiddha, the ruler of men Jayanta, and Devânampiyatissa are the four kings. 8. The fever, the drought, the contest (of the two kings), and (the island's) being inhabited by the Yakkhas, these are the four afflictions which the four Buddhas have removed. 9. The relic of holy Kakusandha was the drinking vessel, the relic of Buddha Konâgamana the girdle, — 10. the relic of Sambuddha Kassapa the rain-cloak; of glorious Gotama there is a Doṇa of corporeal relics. 11. In Abhayapura was the Paṭiyârâma, in Vaḍḍhamânapura the Uttarârâma, in Visâla the Pâcînârâma, in Anurâdhapura the Thûpârâma which is situated in the southern direction: (there) the four Thûpas at (the time of) the teaching of the four Buddhas (were situated). 12. 13. The town of Abhayapura was situated near the Kadambaka (lake), the town of Vaḍḍhamâna near the Tissa lake, the town of Visâlapura near the Khema lake; Anurâdhapura ....; the indication of the four directions (?) is as above. 14. The four names of the mountain are Devakûṭa, Sumanakûṭa, and Subhakûṭa; now it is called Silâkûṭa. 15. The fam-

ous (?) garden (which was called in the four periods respectively) Mahâtittha, Mahânâma, Sâgara, and Mahâmeghavana, a path worthy of Saints, was the first resting place of the four chiefs of the world. 16. The Bodhi tree of holy Kakusandha was the most excellent Sirîsa; Rucânandâ who possessed the great (magical) faculties, took its southern branch and planted it in Ojadîpa, in the Mahâtittha garden. 17. The Bodhi tree of holy Konâgamana was the most excellent Udumbara; Kanakadattâ who possessed the great (magical) faculties, took its southern branch — 18. and planted it in Varadîpa, in the Mahânâma garden. The Bodhi tree of holy Kassapa was the most excellent Nigrodha; — 19. (the Therî) called Sudhammâ who possessed the great (magical) faculties, took its southern branch and planted the sacred tree in the garden called Sâgara. 20. The Bodhi tree of holy Gotama was the most excellent Assattha; Saṃghamittâ who possessed the great (magical) faculties, took its southern branch — 21. and planted it in the island of Lañkâ, in the delightful Mahâmeghavana. Rucânandâ, Kanakadattâ, Sudhammâ who possessed the great (magical) powers, — 22. and learned, wise Saṃghamittâ who was endowed with the six (supernatural) faculties, these were the four Bhikkhunîs who brought each a Bo branch (to this island). 23. The Sirîsa Bo tree (was planted) in the Mahâtittha garden, the Udumbara in the Mahânâma, the Nigrodha in the Mahâsâgara garden; so the Assattha was planted in the Mahâmeghavana. 24. On a mountain, in those four gardens, the four Bo trees have been planted; on a mountain was the delightful resting-place (of the four Buddhas), when the four Buddhas proclaimed their doctrine. 25. Mahâdeva who possessed the six (supernatural) faculties, Sumana versed in the analytical knowledge, Sabbananda possessing the great (magical) powers, and learned Mahinda, these highly wise Theras were the converters of Tambapaṇṇi.

26. Kakusandha, the highest in the whole world, who was endowed with the five kinds of (supernatural) vision, looking on the whole world, saw the excellent Ojadîpa.

27. There raged then an epidemic fever called Puṇṇakanaraka; at that time there raged an epidemic fever among the people. 28. Many people, attacked by this sickness, became distressed and disconsolate like fish which lie lost on the bank (of a river). 29. 30. Vexed by fear they were unable to regain happiness and tranquillity of mind. Kakusandha, the chief of the world, when he saw the afflicted beings who were being destroyed by the bonds of sickness, came hither from Jambudîpa together with forty thousand companions, for the sake of subduing the disease. 31. Forty thousand (Saints) who possessed the six (supernatural) faculties and the great (magical) powers, surrounded the Sambuddha, as the stars in the sky surround the moon. 32. Kakusandha, the illuminator of the world, established himself with his pupils on the Devakûṭa mountain, shining in splendour like a god. 33. When he stood resplendent in Ojadîpa on the Devakûṭa mountain, all people believed him to be a god. They did not understand that he was the Tathâgata. 34. (When they saw him) who arose with the rising dawn, on the day of the full moon, on the Uposatha day, and who illumined that mountain with its forests as if it were burning, — 35. when they saw the burning mountain which diffused light through the four quarters, all the people of Abhayapura with the king were joyful and delighted. 36. Buddha Kakusandha, the ruler of the world, formed the following resolution: „May all people, all men who live in Ojadîpa, see me.“ 37. 38. The Devakûṭa mountain was honoured among Rishis and liked by men; to that place went the hosts of people (who had been afflicted) by the distress of that fever, all the citizens together with the king, leaving the town, the capital, and there they paid homage to Kakusandha, the highest among men. 39. The royal retinue together with the people of the kingdom, a great crowd, arrived respectfully saluting the Sambuddha whom they believed to be a god. 40. 41. All this multitude approached the most excellent Buddha, the highest among men. (The king thus addressed him:) „Consent, o Bhaga-

vat, to dine to-day together with the Bhikkhu fraternity (in my palace); let us go to the town, to the capital.“ The Sambuddha agreed to the request of the king by remaining silent. 42. Having understood his consent, the royal retinue and the people of the kingdom, paying great honour and respect (to the Buddha), then returned to the town. 43. (The king thus reflected:) „This fraternity of Bhikkhus is numerous, the crowd of the people is great; there is no place prepared for its reception in this narrow town, in my capital. 44. I possess a great pleasure garden, the delightful garden of Mahâtittha which is not too narrow nor too distant, which will be convenient for the ascetics — 45. and will be suitable for a retired existence and for the Tathâgata. There I will bestow presents on the Buddha and on the Bhikkhu fraternity. 46. 47. May all people obtain the sight of the Buddha and of the Fraternity.“ Omniscient Kakusandha, followed by forty thousand Bhikkhus, arrived at the Mahâtittha garden. When the highest among men had entered the Mahâtittha garden, — 48. the creepers and trees (were covered?) with flowers out of season. The king took a golden water-pot, — 49. and dedicated (the garden) for the sake (of the welfare) of Lañkâ, by pouring water over the hand (of the Buddha, saying): „I give, o Lord, this garden to the Saṃgha and to the Buddha, its chief.“ It was a delightful resting-place, an appropriate residence for the Fraternity. 50. Kakusandha, the ruler of the world, accepted the garden. At that moment the earth quaked; this was the first resting-place (of the Saṃgha in Lañkâ). 51. The highest leader of the world stood there, causing the immovable earth to quake. (He then formed the following wish:) „Oh that Rucânandâ might take the Bo branch and come hither.“ 52. The Bhikkhunî who possessed the high (magical) powers, understanding the thought of holy Kakusandha, went to the great Sirîsa Bodhi, and standing at its foot (she thought:) 53. „The Buddha desires that the Bodhi tree shall grow in Ojadîpa.“ Thither she went in order to fetch the Bodhi tree, (the majesty of) which is beyond human reason (?). 54. (She then expressed the following resolution:) „May, with the consent of the most excellent Buddha, out of compassion for mankind, the southern branch sever itself through my magical power.“ 55. When Rucânandâ had pronounced this demand with clasped hands, the right branch severed itself (from the tree) and fixed itself in the vase. 56. Rucânandâ who possessed the high (magical) powers, took the Bo branch in the golden vase, and ordered five hundred Bhikkhunîs to surround it. 57. At that moment the earth quaked together with oceans and mountains; it was a grand sight, wonderful and astonishing. 58. Witnessing this, the royal retinue and the people of the kingdom delighted all raised their clasped hands and paid reverence to the excellent Bodhi branch. 59. All the gods were delighted; the Devas joyfully shouted when they perceived the most excellent Bodhi branch. 60. The four (divine) Mahârâjas, the glorious guardians of the world, all these gods kept guard over the Sirîsa Bodhi branch. 61. The Tâvatiṃsa gods, the Vasavatti gods, Yama, Sakka, Suyâma, Santusita, Sunimmita, all surrounded the most excellent Bo branch. 62. The delighted crowds of gods, raising their clasped hands, together with Rucânandâ, paid reverence to the most excellent Bo branch. 63. Rucânandâ who possessed the high (magical) powers, carrying the Sirîsa Bo branch, went to the excellent Ojadîpa, accompanied by the sisterhood of Bhikkhunîs. 64. The gods danced, laughed, and snapped the fingers of both hands, when the most excellent Sirîsa Bo branch was carried to the excellent Ojadîpa. 65. Rucânandâ who possessed the high (magical) powers, accompanied by a host of Devas, approached Kakusandha, carrying the Sirîsa Bo branch. 66. At that moment the great hero Kakusandha, the ruler of the world, repaired to the spot in the Mahâtittha garden destined for the reception of the Bo tree. 67. Rucânandâ herself did not plant the resplendent Bo branch; Kakusandha, perceiving that, himself stretched out his right hand. 68. Rucânandâ who possessed the high (magical) powers, placed the southern branch of the Bo tree in the Buddha's right hand, and respectfully saluted him. 69. Kakusandha, the chief of the world, the highest among men, took it and gave it to king Abhaya (saying:) „Plant it on this spot.“ 70. Abhaya, the increaser of the kingdom, planted it on the spot which Kakusandha, the leader of the world, had indicated. 71. When the Sirîsa Bo branch had been planted in that delightful place, the Buddha preached the Doctrine, the four Truths which soothe (the mind of men). 72. When he had finished, one hundred and forty thousand men and thirty koṭis of gods attained (sanctification).

73. The Bo tree of Kakusandha was a Sirîsa, that of Konâgamana an Udumbara, that of Kassapa a Nigrodha; (this is) the description of the three Bo trees. 74. The Bo tree of the incomparable Sakyaputta is the most excellent Assattha; taking it (hither) they planted it in the Meghavana garden.

75. 76. The children of Muṭasîva were ten [other] brothers, Abhaya, Tissa, and Nâga, Utti and also Mattâbhaya, Mitta, Sîva, and Asela, Tissa, and Kira; these were the brothers. Princess Anulâ and Sîvalî were the daughters of Muṭasîva.

77. How great is the number of years which elapsed between the time when Vijaya came over to the most excellent Lañkâdîpa, and the royal coronation of the son of Muṭasîva? 78. Devânampiya was crowned two hundred years and thirty-six years more after the Sambuddha attained Parinibbâna. 79. When Devânampiya was crowned, the royal (magical) powers came over him; the lord of Tambapaṇṇi diffused rays of pure splendour. 80. At that time the most excellent Lañkâdîpa was a storehouse of treasures. Produced by the pure splendour of Tissa many treasures came to light. 81. When the glad and excited king saw these treasures, he sent them as a present to Asokadhamma. 82. Asoka was delighted when he saw these presents. He sent in return to Devânampiya various treasures destined to be used at his coronation.

83—86. The (monarch) called Asoka sent a chowrie, a turban, a royal parasol, a sword, slippers, a diadem, a ... of Sâra wood, an (anointing) vase, a right hand chank, a palanquin, a conch trumpet, earrings, a koṭi of clothes which are (cleansed by being passed through the fire) without being washed, a golden vessel and spoon, costly towels, a man's load of water from the Anotatta lake, most precious yellow sandal wood, a measure of rouge, eye collyrium brought by the Nâgas, yellow and emblic myrobalan, costly Amata drugs, one hundred and sixty cart loads of fragrant hill paddy which had been brought by parrots; (all these things being) the rewards for his meritorious actions. 87. The requirements for his coronation as king of Lankâ having been sent by Asokadhamma, Tissa, the lord of Tambapaṇṇi, celebrated his second coronation. 88. When thirty nights had elapsed after the second coronation of Tissa, Mahinda together with his companions arrived on this island from Jambudîpa. 89. (King Devânampiya) erected the most excellent monastery called Tissârâma. He also planted the great Bo tree in the Mahâmeghavana garden. 90. He built the great, delightful Thûpa. Devânampiya erected a monastery on the Cetiya mountain; — 91. he constructed the Thûpârâma, the Tissârâma (Issarasamaṇa?) Vihâra, the Vessagiri (Vihâra), and the Colakatissa (Vihâra?). 92. Ârâmas too (where the minor Bo branches were planted) at the distance of a yojana from each other, were made by king Tissa. He gave the great donation (which is called) the most excellent Mahâpela. This prince reigned forty years.

93. Then (followed his) other four brothers, the sons of Muṭasîva. Prince Uttiya reigned ten years. 94. Eight years after the coronation (of Uttiya), the enlightener of the island attained Nibbâna. (The king) caused the funeral ceremonies to be performed to the east of the Tissârâma. 95. When the twelfth year (after his Upasampadâ) had been completed, Mahinda came hither; at the end of his sixtieth year he attained Nibbâna on the Cetiya mountain. 96. 97. When the enlightener of the island has at-

tained Nibbâna, king Uttiya, having ordered full vases, triumphal arches, garlands, and burning lamps to be prepared, erected a most excellent hearse which was worth seeing. (Thus) he paid reverence to the enlightener of the Island. 98. Both gods and men, Nâgas, Gandhabbas, and Dânavas, all were grieved and paid reverence to the enlightener of the Island. 99. When they had performed the ceremonies during seven days on the most excellent Cetiya mountain, some people spoke thus: „Let us go to the town, to the capital.“ 100. (Other people replied:) „There (in the town) is a great, fearful noise and uproar; let us here burn the enlightener of the island of Lañkâ.“ 101. When the king heard what the crowd said, (he answered:) „I will erect a great Thûpa to the east of the Tissârâma“. 102. Carrying Mahinda, the enlightener of the island, together with the funeral hearse, (the people) together with the king, entered the eastern gate of the town. 103. Marching through the centre of the town, they left it by the southern gate, and performed great ceremonies during seven days in the Mahâvihâra. 104. Both gods and men erected a funeral pile of odoriferous drugs and placed it in the royal garden, (saying:) „Let us burn the virtuous one.“ 105. They took Mahinda, the enlightener of the island, together with the funeral hearse, circumambulated the Vihâra, and caused (the people) to pay reverence to the most excellent Thûpa. 106. The great crowd, leaving the Ârâma by its eastern gate, performed the funeral ceremonies at a place close by it. 107. They all, weeping, raising their clasped hands, ascended the pile, and bowing they set the pile on fire. 108. The great teacher having thus been burnt entirely, they erected a most excellent Thûpa which contained his relics, and Ârâmas at the distance of one yojana from each other. 109. After the funeral ceremonies for Mahinda, the enlightener of the island, had been performed, that place first received the name of Isibhûmi.

XVIII.

1.[1]) At the present time there are other aged, middle-aged, and young (Bhikkhus), holders of the Vibhajja doctrine, preservers of the tradition of the Vinaya and of the Faith. 2. Learned and virtuous they illuminate this earth; by a conduct which conforms to the Dhutañga rules they shine in the island of Lañkâ. 3. Many followers of Sakyaputta are here who well understand the true religion and (its) history. Truly, for the sake of many people the possessor of (supernatural) vision has appeared in the world; the Jina has dispelled the darkness and shown the light. 4. They whose faith is well and firmly grounded on the Tathâgata, leave all wretched states of existence and are born again in heaven. 5. And those who penetrate the constituent members of Bodhi, the organs (of spiritual life), the (ten) powers, attention, right exertion, and the complete system of (magical) powers, — 6. the holy eightfold path which leads to the destruction of suffering, conquer the army of Death and are victorious in the world.

7. The younger twin-sister of queen Mâyâ, born from the same mother, kind like a mother, suckled Bhagavat. 8. (She was) called Mahâpajâpatî, known by the name of Gotamî, renowned, an original depositary (of the Faith), possessing the six (supernatural) faculties and the high (magical) powers. 9. The two chief female pupils were Khemâ and Uppalavaṇṇâ; (besides, there was) Paṭâcârâ, Dhammadinnâ, Sobhitâ, Isidâsikâ, — 10. Visâkhâ, Soṇâ, and Sabalâ, wise Saṃghadâsî, and Nandâ, a guardian of the Dhamma and well versed in the Vinaya. These (Bhikkhunîs) who well knew the Vinaya and the paths (of sanctification), (lived) in Jambudîpa.

---

1) The opening lines of this chapter were evidently intended to form the conclusion of a list of Theras which, however, is wanting in the Dîpavaṃsa or at least in the MSS. we possess. Vv. 1. 2 exactly correspond to v. 44 which ends the great list of Therîs. Buddhaghosa gives in the Introduction of the Samanta Pâsâdikâ a list of Theras which he says is composed by the Porâṇâ (comp. Introd., pp. 2—5). This list presents a close resemblance to the list of Therîs contained in this chapter.

11. The Therî Saṃghamittâ, and wise Uttarâ, Hemâ, and Pasâdapâlâ, and Aggimittâ, Dâsikâ, — 12. Pheggu, Pabbatâ, and Mattâ, Mallâ, and Dhammadâsiyâ, these young Bhikkhunîs (these eleven Bhikkhunîs?) came hither from Jambudîpa. 13. They taught the Vinaya Piṭaka in Anurâdhapura. They (also) taught the five Collections (of the Sutta Piṭaka) and the seven Treatises (of the Abhidhamma).

14. Saddhammanandî, and Somâ, and also Giriddhi, Dâsiyâ, and Dhammâ, a guardian of the Dhamma and well versed in the Vinaya, — 15. and Mahilâ who kept the Dhutaṅga precepts, and Sobhaṇâ, Dhammatâpasâ, highly wise Naramittâ who was well versed in the Vinaya, — 16. Sâtâ, versed in the exhortations of Therîs, Kâlî and Uttarâ, these Bhikkhunîs received the Upasampadâ ordination in the island of Laṅkâ.

17. 18. ... and renowned Sumanâ who well understood the true religion and (its) history, these Bhikkhunîs who were passionless and tranquil, the resolutions of whose minds were pure, who were firmly grounded in the true Faith and in the Vinaya, came together with twenty thousand Bhikkhunîs ..., honoured by illustrious, noble Abhaya. 19. They taught the Vinayapiṭaka in Anurâdhapura; they (also) taught the five Collections (of the Sutta Piṭaka) and the seven Treatises (of the Abhidhamma).

20. Renowned Mahilâ who well understood the true religion and (its) history, and Samantâ, the daughters of king Kâkavaṇṇa, — 21. and learned Girikâlî, the daughter of his Purohita, Dâsî and Kâlî, the daughters of a rogue, well versed in the whole of the sacred Scriptures (?), — 22. these Bhikkhunîs, well versed in the whole of the sacred Scriptures, unconquerable, the resolutions of whose minds were pure, who were firmly grounded in the true Faith and in the Vinaya, — 23. came from (?) Rohana together with twenty thousand Bhikkhunîs, honoured by illustrious king Abhaya. They taught the Vinayapiṭaka in Anurâdhapura.

24. Mahâdevî and Padumâ, illustrious Hemâsâ, Un-

nalâ, Añjalî, Sumâ, — 25. these Bhikkhunîs who possessed the six (supernatural) faculties and the great (magical) powers, came ... together with sixteen thousand Bhikkhunîs. 26. Honoured by illustrious king Tissa Devânampiya (?), they taught the Vinayapiṭaka in Anurâdhapura.

27. Mahâsoṇâ and Dattâ, wise Sîvalâ, zealous Rûpasobhinî, venerated Devamânusâ, — 28. Nâgâ and Nâgamittâ, Dhammaguttâ, and Dâsîyâ, and Samuddâ gifted with (supernatural) vision, who well understood the true Religion and (its) history, — 29. Sapattâ, Channâ, and Upâlî, excellent Revatâ, these were the highest among the Vinaya-studying Bhikkhunîs, the daughters of Somanadeva, — 30. Mâlâ and Khemâ and Tissâ, the highest among the preachers of the Dhamma, these taught the Vinaya first after the death of Abhaya (*or:* when the danger had disappeared?).

31. 32. Sîvalâ and Mahâruhâ who well understood the true Religion and (its) history, and had converted to the Faith many people in Jambudîpa, came hither from Jambudîpa together with twenty thousand Bhikkhunîs, invited by illustrious king Abhaya. 33. They taught the Vinayapiṭaka in Anurâdhapura; they (also) taught the five Collections (of the Suttapiṭaka) and the seven Treatises (of the Abhidhamma).

34. Sîvalâ together with queen Samuddanavâ, daughters of a king, wise Nâgapâlî, and clever Nâgamittâ, — 35. Mahilâ, a guardian of the Bhikkhunîs and well versed in the Vinaya, Nâgâ, and Nâgamittâ who well knew the true Religion and (its) history, these Bhikkhunîs then received the Upasampadâ ordination in the island of Lañkâ. 36. All these were high-born and renowned in the Doctrine, the most excellent ones among sixteen thousand Bhikkhunîs, acknowledged to be the leaders. 37. Honoured by Kuṭikaṇṇa (and by his son,) illustrious Abhaya, they taught the Vinayapiṭaka in Anurâdhapura.

38. Cûlanâgâ and Dhannâ, venerated Soṇâ, and renowned Saṇhâ who well knew the true Religion and (its) history, — 39. highly learned and wise Mahâtissâ, the

daughter of Gamika, Cûlasumanâ, Mahâsumanâ, and clever Mahâkâlî, — 40. illustrious Lakkhadhammâ, honoured and high-born, wise Dîpanayâ who was venerated in Rohana, — 41. renowned Samuddâ who well knew the true Religion and (its) history, holders of the Vibhajja doctrine and of the Vinaya, who both were ornaments of the Sisterhood, — 42. these and other Bhikkhunîs received the Upasampadâ ordination in the island of Lañkâ. (These Bhikkhunîs,) the resolutions of whose minds were pure, who were firmly grounded in the true Faith and in the Vinaya, — 43. learned, versed in the Tradition, free from evil passions, and illustrious, went out (attained Nibbâna) after having spread radiance, like fire-brands.

44. At the present time there are other aged, middle-aged, and young (Bhikkhunîs), holders of the Vibhajja doctrine and of the Vinaya, preservers of the tradition of the Faith. Learned and virtuous they illuminate this earth.

45. Prince Sîva reigned ten years; he established the Ârâma and the Vihâra of Nagarañgaṇa. 46. Prince Sûratissa reigned ten years; he constructed five hundred monasteries, a liberal, great, and meritorious deed. 47. Having conquered Sûratissa, the two Damila princes Sena and Gutta righteously reigned during twelve (twenty-two?) years. 48. Prince Asela, a son of Muṭasîva, put Sena and Gutta to death, and reigned ten years. 49. A prince, Elâra by name, having killed Asela, reigned righteously forty-four years. 50. Avoiding the four evil paths of lust, hatred, fear, and ignorance, this incomparable monarch reigned righteously. 51. (Once) no rain fell during a whole winter, summer, and the rainy season. (Then) continually the cloud rained, rain fell during seven times seven days. 52. There were three cases which the king decided[1]); (after that) rain fell only during the night and not in daytime. 53. A prince, Abhaya by name, the son of Kâkavaṇṇa, whom the ten warriors surrounded, whose elephant

1) In the Mahâvaṃsa (p. 128) an account of these three cases is given.

was Kaṇḍula, — 54. put thirty-two kings to death and alone continued the royal succession. This prince reigned twenty-four years.

End of the Mahâvâra.

XIX.

1.[1]) The king (Duṭṭhagâmani) built an exceedingly costly, quadrangular palace (the Lohapâsâda) of nine stories in height, at an expense of thirty koṭis. 2. (He also erected the Mahâthûpa, at the foundation of which the following materials were used:) chunnam work, great stones, clay, bricks, pure earth, a plate of iron, then marumba[2]), — 3. small gravel, eight layers (?) of stones, twelve (layers?) of crystal and silver. 4. After the prince had caused these foundations to be laid, the Fraternity of Bhikkhus was called together, and the circle (of the base) of the Cetiya was described. 5. Indagutta, Dhammasena, the great preacher Piyadassî, Buddha, Dhamma, and Saṃgha, wise Mittanna, —

1) This chapter is very confused and fragmentary. However by comparing the Mahâvaṃsa it is possible to ascertain what the single verses refer to. Verse 1 relates to the great palace called Lohapâsâda which was erected by king Duṭṭhagâmani (comp. Mahâv., p. 165, l. 2). Vv. 2—4 contain a description of the different preparatory works for the construction of the Mahâthûpa built by the same king. There is nothing, however, to indicate the transition of the narrative from the Lohapâsâda to the Mahâthûpa; perhaps v. 10 which would answer to this purpose, originally belonged to the place between vv. 1 and 2. — Vv. 5—9 refer to the Bhikkhus present at the solemn inauguratory ceremonies at the foundation of the Mahâthûpa (see Mahâvaṃsa, p. 171). — Vv. 11—17 refer to the acts of liberality performed by king Lajjitissa (Mah., p. 202), and to the history of his successors. — Vv. 18—20 give an account of the buildings erected by the seven great warriors of Abhaya Vaṭṭagâmani (Mah., p. 206). — Vv. 21—22 refer to Mahâcûli Mahâtissa, the successor of Vaṭṭagâmani (Mah., p. 208). The last verse relates to the death of Duṭṭhagâmani.

2) I cannot define the exact meaning of „marumba". Turnour translates this word by „incense" (Mah., p. 169), which is decidedly wrong. To me it seems to mean something like „gravel". In the explanation of the tenth Pâcittiya Rule, in the Sutta Vibhaṅga, I find the following passage which I give exactly according to the Paris MS. (*fonds Pâli* 6) which is written in Burmese characters: „pathavi nâma dve pathaviyo jâtâ ca pathavi ajâtâ ca pathavi. jâtâ nâma pathavi suddhapaṃsu suddhamattikâ appapâsâṇâ appasakkharâ appakathalâ a p p a m a r u m p â appavâlikâ . . .; ajâtâ nâma pathavi suddhapâsâṇâ suddhasakkharâ suddhakathalâ s u d d h a m a r u m p â suddhavâlikâ", etc.

6. Anattana, Mahâdeva, learned Dhammarakkhita, Uttara, and Cittagutta, and clever Indagutta, — 7. the great chief Suriyagutta of prompt wisdom, all these fourteen (Theras) came from Jambudîpa to this country (when the foundation of the Mahâthûpa was laid). 8. (Besides these there were present) Siddhattha, Mañgala, Sumana, Paduma, and also Sîvalî, Candagutta, and Suriyagutta, Indagutta, and Sâgara, Mittasena, Jayasena, and Acala, the twelfth of them. 9. (The person that held the circle by which the base of the Thûpa was described, and his parents, had the following auspicious names, viz.:) Suppatiṭṭhitabrahmâ, the son, Nandisena, the father, Sumanadevî, the mother, these three lay persons. 10. (The king constructed) the Mahâthûpa, the most excellent Mahâvihâra, expending twenty (twenty-four?) invaluable treasures.

11. (King Lajjitissa,) having heard the precepts for the conduct of itinerant Bhikkhus, which were propounded by the Fraternity, gave medicaments for the itinerant Bhikkhus, for the sake of their comfort, ... 12. Having heard the well-spoken speech of the Bhikkhunîs, which had been delivered at the ... time (at Harikâla?), the royal lord gave to the Bhikkhunîs whatever they desired. 13. He constructed the Silâthûpa, a Vihâra on the Cetiya mountain, and the most excellent assembly hall which is called Jalaka.

14. (By the next king, Vaṭṭagâmani, a monastery) was constructed at the place where the Nigaṇṭha Giri had dwelt. (From this circumstance,) the appellation and the name of Abhayagiri derived its origin. 15. The five kings Âlavatta (Pulahattha!), and Sâbhiya (Bâhiya!), Panaya, Palaya, and Dâṭhika reigned fourteen years and seven months. 16. Prince Abhaya (Vaṭṭagâmani), the son of Saddhâtissa, put the Damila Dâṭhika to death and became king. 17. He erected the Abhayagiri (monastery) between the Silâthûpa and the Cetiya. This prince reigned twelve years and five months. 18. The seven champions of Abhaya constructed five Ârâmas. Uttiya and Sâliya, Mûla, Tissa, and Pabbata, Deva, and Uttara, these were the seven

champions (of that king). 19. The (warrior) called Uttiya constructed the (monastery) called the Dakkhiṇavihâra, Sâliya the Sâliyârâma, Mûla the Mûlâsaya, — 20. Pabbata the Pabbatârâma, Tissa constructed the Tissârâma, Deva and Uttara constructed the Devâgâra.

21. The son of Kâkavaṇṇa, Mahâtissa, the ruler of the earth, made an agreement to work for wages in the paddy fields, and gave (the money) to the tranquil, thoughtful Thera Summa. 22. Having made an agreement for full three years' labour at a (sugar-) mill, he bestowed a great donation of a thousand koṭis on the Bhikkhus.

23. Wise, enlightened Abhaya Duṭṭhagâmani, after having performed meritorious deeds, entered after the dissolution of his (human) body, the body of a Tusita god.

XX.

1. The illustrious son of Kâkavaṇṇa, known by the name of Tissa, built the Mahâthûpa (and) a Vihâra. 2. He ordered the most excellent Kallakâlena monastery to be constructed; and many other Vihâras have been erected by Saddhâtissa. 3. The number of the highly precious divisions of the Dhamma is eighty-four thousand; he paid reverence to each single division of the Dhamma separately. 4. Illustrious Saddhâtissa constructed a beautiful palace with seven stories, and ordered it to be roofed with iron plates; — 5. 6. (hence) it first received the name Lohapâsâda (iron palace). He made a lump of glass (?). Around the most excellent Mahâthûpa he constructed a wall, decorated with figures of elephants, a beautiful enclosure; he (also) constructed a quadrangular tank (and gave it) for a certain time (to the Fraternity). 7. This prince reigned eighteen years. Having done many other meritorious deeds and distributed rich donations, this wise monarch after the dissolution of his (human) body entered the body of a Tusita god.

8. The son of Saddhâtissa, known by the name of Thûlathana, constructed a great Ârâma, the Alakandara monastery. This prince reigned one month and ten days.

9. The son of Saddhâtissa, known by the name of Ḷajjitissa, governed nine years and six months. 10. He constructed a ....[1]) at the most excellent Mahâthûpa and established the most delightful Kumbhila Ârâma. 11. He built the Dîghathûpa to the east of the Thûpârâma; in the most excellent Thûpârâma he constructed receptacles cased in stone.

12. After the death of Lajjitissa his younger brother named Khallâṭanâga reigned six years. 13. His commander-in-chief, Mahârattaka by name, put this Khallâṭaka to death and reigned one day, a wicked, ungrateful person. 14. The younger brother of the king, called Vaṭṭagâmani, killed that wicked general and reigned five months. 15. (After that time) the Damila Pulahattha reigned three years, and the general Bâhiya two years. 16. Having killed this (king), Panayamâra reigned seven years. Having killed this (king), Palayamâra reigned seven months. 17. Having killed this (king), a person Dâṭhiya by name reigned two years. These five sovereigns belonging to the Damila tribe governed fourteen years and seven months in the interval (between the two parts of Vaṭṭagâmani's reign). 18. Then the glorious, great king Vaṭṭagâmani came back and having put to death the Damila Dâṭhika, gained the sovereignty himself. 19. This king Abhaya Vaṭṭagâmani reigned twelve years and in the beginning (before the above-mentioned interruption) five months. 20. Before this time, the wise Bhikkhus had orally handed down the text of the three Piṭakas and also the Aṭṭhakathâ. 21. At this time, the Bhikkhus who perceived the decay of created beings, assembled and in order that the Religion might endure for a long time, they recorded (the above-mentioned texts) in written books.

22. After his (Vaṭṭagâmani's) death Mahâcûli Mahâtissa reigned fourteen years justly and righteously. 23. This king, full of faith, having done many meritorious deeds,

---

1) Probably this passage refers to the three „pupphayâna“ mentioned in the Mahâvaṃsa (p. 201, l. 14), though I do not know how to explain or to correct the word used here (tilañcanaṃ).

went to heaven after fourteen years. 24. The son of Vaṭṭagâmani, known by the name of Coranâga, reigned twelve years living like a robber. 25. The son of Mahâcûli, the prince known by the name of Tissa, reigned three years over the Island. 26. King Sîva cohabited with queen Anulâ; he ruled one year and two months. 27. A king from a foreign country, Vaṭuka by name, a Damila, governed one year and two months. 28. Then followed king Tissa, known by the surname „the wood-cutter"; he then ruled one year and one month. 29. (A person) called Niliya by name, known as the Damila king, ruled the kingdom and governed three months. 30. A woman, Anulâ, killed these excellent persons and governed four months over Tambapaṇṇi.

31. The son of Mahâcûli, called Kuṭikaṇṇatissa, constructed an Uposatha hall near the Cetiyapabbata monastery. 32. In front of the building he erected a beautiful stone Thûpa; there he planted a Bo branch and constructed a great structure (around the Bo branch?). 33. He built a bath ... for the Bhikkhunîs. He also made a fence round the Padumassara garden. 34. He caused a ditch to be dug for the protection of the town, and a wall to be constructed full seven yards (in height). 35. He (also) caused the ponds Khema and Dugga to be dug (which he gave) for a certain time (?) (to the Fraternity). He (also) caused the Setuppala well and the beautiful Vaṇṇaka dike (?) to be constructed. This prince reigned twenty-two years.

XXI.

1. Prince Abhaya, the son of Kuṭikaṇṇa, went to visit the Fraternity (?) in the beautiful Mahâthûpa. 2. The (Bhikkhus) who had subdued their passions and obtained self-control, who were spotless and pure of heart, recited (the Dhamma) in the relic room in honour (of the relics). 3. The king, when he heard them reading in the delightful relic room, walked round the Thûpa; but he could not see them at any of the four gates. 4. The royal ruler

of men, having paid in every way reverence to the most venerable recitation, thus thought: „Were do they read? 5. They do not recite at the four gates nor outside; surely the wise men read in the relic room. 6. I also desire to see the most excellent relic room, I will hear the recital and see the Bhikkhu fraternity.“ 7. Sakka, the king of gods, when he perceived the desire of the king, appeared in the relic room and thus addressed the Theras: 8. „The king, venerable sirs, desires to see the relic room.“ For the sake of the preservation of his faith they conducted him into the relic-room. 9. As the king beheld the relic-room, wisdom arose in his mind; he raised his clasped hands and worshipped the relics and made great offerings during seven days. 10. He seven times made most excellent offerings, prepared with honey. He seven times made priceless offerings of ghee (?), — 11. and (also) duly seven times other (?) offerings. Seven times he made offerings of lamps, repeating them, — 12. and seven times beautiful offerings of flowers. During seven days he made offerings of water full (of flowers), and during seven days offerings of (common) water. 13. He ordered a priceless net-work of corals to be made, covering the surface of the Mahâthûpa as if it were dressed in a garment. 14. He made strong pillars for placing lamps around the foot of the Thûpa, and got a tube filled with ghee; then he ordered the lights seven times to be lit. 15. He caused a tube (to be laid) around the foot of the Thûpa and to be filled with oil, and ordered the oil-lamps fourteen times to be lit. 16. Having caused (a tube?) to be filled with scented water, he fixed mats at the top (of the Thûpa); (on these) he caused handsfull of blue lotuses to be scattered; this offering was made seven times. 17. Having dug a channel (from the Thûpa) to the Khema pond (which was situated) to the west of the Thûpa, he made there a water offering. 18. An entire Yojana around (the Thûpa) he caused flowers to be planted, and made a flower thicket at the most excellent Mahâthûpa. 19. The prince, having collected flowers covered with opening buds, made a flower thicket fourteen times. 20. Having gathered various flowers, he constructed seven times a flower-pillar with a terrace and an enclosure. 21. He saw ... of various shapes, ornamented ...; the prince made them similar in shape. 22. He ordered chunnam work to be executed at the most excellent Mahâthûpa. Having celebrated the coronation (of the Bo tree?), he held a festival connected with the execution of chunnam work (at the buildings around the Bo tree?). 23. Sakyaputta, the great hero, penetrated the whole Truth near the Assattha tree (and became?) the supreme (Buddha?). 24. Of this Bo tree which stood in the delightful Meghavana garden, illuminating the island, the prince held a coronation and a bathing festival. 25. The Bhikkhu fraternities who bring happiness (to the people), after having spent the rainy season (in the prescribed manner), celebrated the Pavâraṇâ ceremony; (the king) bestowed on them a Pavâraṇâ donation in order to show his liking for the Pavâraṇâ ceremony. 26. He bestowed a donation of sandal wood on the Bhikkhu fraternity, the most excellent assembly. To the most excellent Mahâthûpa he made the donation of a great kettle-drum. 27. ... dancers and acrobats in auspicious attitudes (?), all ... He constructed ... and made a donation of it to the Mahâthûpa. 28. At the full moon day of the month Vesâkha the Sambuddha was born; he celebrated a festival twenty-eight times in honour of this month. 29. Between the two monasteries of the delightful Mahâmeghavana and of the most excellent Thûpârâma he constructed an Uposatha hall. 30. He did many other meritorious acts and distributed rich donations. This prince reigned twenty-eight years.

31. Prince Nâga, the son of Kuṭikaṇṇa, made bricks and other things (?) of costly substances in the most excellent (Ambatthala Thûpa?), — 32. and erected seats for the Dhamma preachers everywhere in the beautiful Ambatthala Thûpa. He made a great offering called Giribhaṇḍagahaṇa. 33. As many wise Bhikkhus were in Lañkâdîpa, he gave a robe to each one of the Bhikkhu con-

gregation, of the most excellent assembly. This prince reigned twelve years.

34. Âmaṇḍagâmani, the son of Mahâdâṭhika, known by the surname Abhaya, caused a well and also the Gâmeṇḍitalâka to be dug. 35. He constructed the Rajatalena (Vihâra). Over the Thûpa, in the most excellent Thûpârâma, he constructed a double canopy made of silver. 36. In the two most excellent palaces of the Mahâvihâra and of the Thûpârâma, he completely constructed treasuries and treasure-caves. 37. He also interdicted the destruction of animal life in the territory of Tambapaṇṇi. This prince reigned nine years and eight months.

38. His younger brother, known as king Kaṇirajânu, reigned full three years. 39. The royal son of Âmaṇḍagâmani, known as Cûlâbhaya, constructed the most excellent Gaggarârâma. 40. King Cûlâbhaya reigned one year. A woman called Sîvalî, known by the surname Revatî, — 41—43. the daughter of king Âmaṇḍa, reigned four months. The son of Âmaṇḍa's sister, Ilanâga by name, removed this Sîvalî and reigned in the town. King Ilanâga, the destroyer of his enemies, having heard the Kapi-Jâtaka, ordered the Tissa and Dûra ponds to be dug. This king reigned six years in the island of Lañkâ. 44. The king called Sîva, known by the surname Caṅdamukha, constructed the Manikârâma (Manikâragâma tank?) near the monastery called Issara. 45. The queen-consort of that king, known by the name of Damilâdevî, bestowed her own revenues from that very village on that Ârâma. This king reigned eight years and seven months.

46. King Tissa, known by the surname of Yasalâla, governed eight years and seven months[1]). 47. King Subha, the son of a doorkeeper, constructed the Subhârâma and the delightful Villavihâra. 48. Likewise he constructed hermit's cells which were called after his own name. This king governed six years over his kingdom.

---

1) According to the Mahâvaṃsa: seven years and eight months.

XXII.

1. King Vasabha constructed in the Cetiyapabbata monastery ten Thûpas, a most glorious deed by which high reward is to be gained. 2. In the Issariya Ârâma he constructed a delightful Vihâra (and) a pleasing and delightful Uposatha hall. 3. He also ordered a large kettle-drum to be made for the most excellent Mucela monastery. Every three years he gave six robes (to each monk). 4. Throughout the whole of Lañkâdîpa he repaired dilapidated Ârâmas. Everywhere he constructed residences and made most precious offerings to the pious (Bhikkhus). 5. In the most excellent Thûpârâma he constructed a relic-chamber; full forty-four times the king held (Vesâkha) festivals. 6. In the Mahâvihâra, in the Thûpârâma, and in the Cetiyapabbata monastery, at each of these places he ordered a thousand oil-lamps to be lit. 7. 8. The eleven tanks (formed by this king were) the Mayanti, the Râjuppala tank, the Vaha, Kolamba, Mahânikkhavaṭṭi tank and also the Mahârametti, the Kehâla and Kâli tanks, the Jambuṭi, Câthamañgana, and Abhivaḍḍhamânaka tanks.

9. 10. He also constructed twelve irrigation canals in order to augment the fertility (of the land). Various meritorious acts he did; he made a wall and a ditch around the town with towers at the gates, and a great palace. He ordered lotus-ponds to be dug at different places in the town, the capital. 11. The most eminent king conducted water by means of an underground aqueduct (to those ponds). This ruler governed forty-four years.

12. The son of Vasabha, known as Tissa, the royal lord, ordered the Ârâma called Mañgala to be constructed. He reigned straightway (after his father's death) three years over the Island.

13. Tissa's son, Gajâbâhukagâmani, caused a great Thûpa to be built in the delightful Abhayârâma. 14. This royal chief constructed the pond called Gâmani, according to the wishes of his mother; this lord (also) ordered the Ârâma called Rammaka to be built. He ruled twenty-two years over the Island.

15—17. The ruler of Tambapaṇṇi called king Mahallanâga caused the Sajîlakandakârâma, the Goṭapabbata in the south, the Dakapâsâna Ârâma, the Sâlipabbata Vihâra, the Tanaveli (Vihâra), and in Rohana the Nâgapabbata (Vihâra) and the Girisâlika Ârâma to be constructed. Having reigned six years he reached the end of his life and died.

18. 19. The son of Mahallanâga, known by the name of Bhâtutissa, caused for the sake of (re-)establishing the Mahâmeghavana garden, a wall fence with towers at the gates to be constructed (around it); this king also founded the Vara-Ârâma (Gavara-Âr.?). 20. Having caused the pond called Gâmani to be dug, Bhâtutissa, the lord (of the Island), gave it to the Bhikkhu fraternity. 21. He (also) ordered the pond called Randhakaṇḍaka to be dug. In the delightful Thûpârâma he constructed an Uposatha hall. 22. This king bestowed a great donation on the Bhikkhu fraternity. He reigned twenty-four years over the Island.

23. His younger brother, well known by the name of Tissa, erected an Uposatha hall in the delightful Abhayârâma. 24. He constructed twelve edifices within (the limits of) the most excellent Mahâvihâra. In the Dakkhiṇârâma he built a Vihâra and a Thûpa. 25. Many other meritorious acts he did in honour of the blessed religion of the Buddha. He reigned eighteen years.

26. The sons of Tissa's own body, two brothers worthy of royal dignity, reigned as rulers three years over the Island.

27. Vañkanâsikatissa reigned three years in Anurâdhapura, a king of proper and meritorious conduct. 28. After the death of Vañkanâsikatissa his son Gajâbâhukagâmani reigned twenty-two years. 29. After Gajâbâhu's death the father-in-law of that king, Mahallakanâga, reigned six years. 30. After the death of Mahallanâga his son Bhâtikatissa reigned twenty-four years over Lañkâ. 31. After Bhâtikatissa's death his younger brother Kaniṭṭhatissa reigned eighteen years over Lañkâdîpa. 32. After the death of Kaniṭṭhatissa his son, known by the name of Khujjanâga, reigned two years. 33. Kuñjanâga, the younger

brother of Khujjanâga, put his royal brother to death and reigned one year over Lañkâ.

34. Having gained the victory (over Khujjanâga), Sirinâga reigned nineteen years in the most excellent Anurâdhapura over Lañkâ. 35. The king called Sirinâga by name made an offering of a garland of costly substances to the Mahâthûpa and erected a parasol over the Thûpa. 36. He constructed an Uposatha hall, the most excellent Lohapâsâda. This prince reigned nineteen years.

37. The son of Sirinâga, the royal lord called Abhaya, gave two hundred thousand silver pieces to the Bhikkhu fraternity. 38. At the most excellent great Bo tree he constructed a stone ledge. This king governed twenty-two years. 39. His younger brother, known as king Tissaka, erected a most excellent parasol over the Abhayârâma and over the Mahâthûpa. 40. In the delightful Mahâmeghavana and in the beautiful Abhayârâma, at both most excellent Vihâras, he constructed a golden Thûpa. 41. Having heard the Gilâna discourse (of Buddha) which was preached by Thera Deva, he gave medicaments for the sick and (constructed) five most excellent residences (for the Saṃgha?). 42. Having seen a portent in the night, (he constructed) the Dassamâlinî Ârâma; near the delightful Bo tree he erected figures formed by lamps.

43. In the reign of that king they proclaimed many wrong doctrines; proclaiming captious doctrines they ruined the religion of the Jina. 44. The king, when he perceived that wicked Bhikkhus ruined the religion of the Jina, together with the minister Kapila subdued those wicked ones. 45. Having destroyed these captious doctrines and caused the (true) religion to shine, he gave (to the Fraternity) the Hatthapaṇṇika (Sattapaṇṇika?) palace and (caused) boiled rice (to be provided) in the Meghavana. This royal ruler governed twenty-two years.

46. Tissa's own son, known by the name of Sirinâga, reigned full two years over the Island. 47. This Sirinâga constructed an enclosure around the great Bo tree and also a beautiful pavilion.

48. (The king) called Asaṅgatissa (Saṃghatissa) fixed golden parasols over the most excellent Mahâthûpa, on the top of the Thûpa. 49. (He also constructed) of jewels a Thûpa of the shape of a flame at the most excellent Mahâthûpa, and in connection (?) with that work he also brought offerings. 50. (Having heard) the Andhakavinda Suttanta[1]), which was preached by Thera Deva, this victorious king ordered rice-milk continually to be distributed at the four gates (of the town).

51. Vijayakumâra[2]), the son of Sirinâga, reigned after his father's death one year.

52. Saṃghatissa reigned four years; he fixed a parasol and goldsmith's work on the Mahâthûpa.

53. King Saṃghabodhi by name was a virtuous prince; this king reigned two years. 54. This victorious king ordered rice-milk continually to be distributed in the delightful Meghavana garden, and in the most excellent Mahâvihâra he constructed a room where food was distributed by tickets.

55. The king called Abhaya, known by the surname Meghavaṇṇa, constructed a stone pavilion in the most excellent Mahâvihâra. 56. 57. To the west of the Mahâvihâra he built a cloister for monks given to meditation. He (also) constructed an incomparable stone altar around the Bo tree and ordered a trench to be made, lined with stones, and a very costly triumphal arch. In the most excellent Bo tree sanctuary he erected a throne of stone. 58. Within the Dakkhiṇârâma he constructed an Uposatha hall. He distributed a great donation to the fraternity of Bhikkhus, the most excellent community. 59. The king, having constructed a royal palace, a great, delightful building, gave it to the Bhikkhu fraternity and then received

1) This discourse of Buddha which contains praises of those who provide rice-milk for the Fraternity, is contained in the Mahâvagga of the Vinaya-Piṭaka, VI, 24.

2) The stanza treating of Vijaya is interposed between two sections which refer to king Saṃghatissa's reign. The confusion seems brought on by an injudicious employment of different sources; I do not believe that we ought to alter the succession of these verses.

it back. 60. In the Meghavana garden the king also celebrated a Vesâkha festival. He reigned thirteen years.

61. The son of Meghavaṇṇa was king Jeṭṭhatissa; this royal lord reigned over the island of Tambapaṇṇi. 62—65. In the most excellent Mahâthûpa he offered a very costly jewel. Having built a palace covered with iron and offered to it that most excellent jewel, the chief of men gave (to that palace) the name „Maṇipâsâda" („palace of the gem"). Having constructed the Pâcînatissapabbata Ârâma, the ruler of men called Tissa gave it to fraternity of Bhikkhus. The ruler of the earth, the chief of men, having ordered the Âlambagâma pond to be dug, held festivals (there) during eight years. This king reigned ten years over Tambapaṇṇi.

66. After Jeṭṭhatissa's death his younger brother, king Mahâsena, reigned twenty-seven years. 67. This king once thought thus: „There are two kinds of Bhikkhus in the Religion (of Buddha); which of them hold the right doctrine and which hold the wrong doctrine, which are modest and which are shameless?" 68. When thinking about this matter and searching after modest persons, he saw wicked Bhikkhus who were no (true) Samaṇas and (only) looked like (Samaṇas). 69. He saw people who were like stinking corpses, and in behaviour like blue flies, wicked persons, who were no (true) Samaṇas and (only) looked like (Samaṇas), — 70. Dummitta and Pâpasoṇa and other shameless men. He went to those wicked Bhikkhus and asked them about the sense (of the Religion) and the doctrine. 71. Dummitta and Pâpasoṇa and other shameless men secretly consulted in order to mislead the pious (king). 72. These wicked, infatuated men taught that (computing) the twenty years (required for) the Upasampadâ ordination from the conception, which has been admitted (by Buddha) in (the story about) Kumârakassapa[1]), is not allowable. 73. The practice of (wearing) ivory (fans)[2])

1) Mahâvagga, I, 75.

2) I have translated this passage according to the indications given in the Mahâvaṃsa Ṭîkâ (see the quotation in the footnote, p. 118), although

which has not been admitted in the story about the Chabbaggiyas, these shameless, idle (?) teachers taught to be allowable. 74. Regarding these and other matters many other shameless Bhikkhus, without a reason, for the sake of their own advantage, taught that (the true doctrine) was a false doctrine.

75. Having performed through his life, in consequence of his intercourse with those wicked persons, evil as well as good deeds, this king Mahâsena passed away (to another existence) according to his actions.

76. Therefore one should fly far from intercourse with wicked men, as from a serpent or a snake, and self-controlled one should perform acts of benevolence as long as his existence lasts.

I do not known any story in the Vinaya mentioning the Chabbaggiya Bhikkhus, which relates to the use of ivory fans. There is in the Khuddakavatthukhandha (Cullavagga, V, 23, 1) a precept which implicitly excludes the use of fans made of ivory („anujânâmi bhikkhave tisso vijaniyo vâkamayaṃ usîramayaṃ morapiñchamayaṃ"). I think that this is the passage alluded to, though the Chabbaggiyas are not expressly mentioned in it; in the short stories which precede and follow this one, most frequently mention is made of the transgressions of the Chabbaggiyas, so that the expression „Chabbaggiyânaṃ vatthu" may have been extended to this passage also, by an inaccuracy which scarcely will be deemed strange.

INDEX OF PROPER NAMES.

(An asterisk indicates that the passage is corrupt or the reading doubtful.)

TABLE OF THE CEYLONESE KINGS
ACCORDING TO THE DÎPAVAṂSA.

Vijaya (reigned 38 years)	9, 28—44.
Interregnum (1 year)	11, 9.
Paṇḍuvâsa (30 y.)	10, 1—6.
Abhaya (20 y.)	10, 7.
Interregnum (17 y.)	11, 1—2.
Paṇḍukâbhaya (70 y.)	11, 1—4.
Muṭasîva (60 y.)	11, 5. 13.
Devânampiya Tissa (40 y.)	11, 4 — 17, 92.
Uttiya (10 y.)	17, 93—109.
Siva (10 y.)	18, 45.
Sûratissa (10 y.)	18, 46.
Sena and Gutta (12 y.[1])	18, 47.
Asela (10 y.)	18, 48.
Elâra (44 y.)	18, 49—52.
Abhaya Duṭṭhagâmani (24 y.)	18, 53 — 19, 10. 23.
Saddhâtissa (18 y.)	20, 1—7.
Thûlathana (1 month and 10 days)	20, 8.

1) 22 years according to the Mahâvaṃsa.

King	Reference
Lajjitissa (9 y. 6 m.[1])	19, 11—13; 20, 9—11.
Khallâṭanâga (6 y.)	20, 12.
Mahârattaka (one day)	20, 13.
Abhaya Vaṭṭagâmani (5 months)	20, 14.
Pulahattha (Âlavatta) (3 y.)	
Bâhiya (Sâbhiya) (2 y.)	
Panayamâra (7 y.)	19, 15; 20. 15—17.
Palayamâra (7 months)	
Dâṭhika (2 y.)	
Abhaya Vaṭṭagâmani (12 y.)	19, 14. 16—20; 20, 18—21
Mahâcûli Mahâtissa (14 y.)	19, 21—22; 20, 22—23.
Coranâga (12 y.)	20, 24.
Tissa (3 y.)	20, 25.
Sîva (1 y. 2 m.)	20, 26.
Vaṭuka (1 y. 2 m.)	20, 27.
Tissa (1 y. 1 m.)	20, 28.
Niliya (3 m.[2])	20, 29.
Anulâ (4 m.)	20, 30.
Kuṭikaṇṇatissa (22 y.)	20, 31—35.
Abhaya (28 y.)	21, 1—30.
Mahâdâṭhika Nâga (12 y.)	21, 31—33.
Abhaya Âmaṇḍagâmani (9 y. 8 m.)	21, 34—37.
Kaṇirajânu (3 y.)	21, 38.
Cûlâbhaya (1 y.)	21, 39—40.
Sivalî Revatî (4 months)	21, 40—41.
Ilanâga (6 y.)	21, 41—43.
Sîva Candamukha (8 y. 7 m.)	21, 44—45.
Tissa Yasalâla (8 y. 7 m.[3])	21, 46.
Subha (6 y.)	21, 47—48.
Vasabha (44 y.)	22, 1—11.
Vaṅkanâsikatissa (3 y.)	22, 12. 27.
Gajâbâhukagâmani (22 y.)	22, 13—14. 28.
Mahallanâga (6 y.)	22, 15—17. 29.
Bhâtutissa (24 y.)	22, 18—22. 30.
Kaniṭṭha-Tissa (18 y.)	22, 23—25. 31.
Khujjanâga (2 y.)	22, 26. 32. 33.
Kuñjanâga (1 y.)	
Sirinâga (19 y.)	22, 34—36.
Abhaya[4] (22 y.)	22, 37—38.
Tissa[4] (22 y.)	22, 39—45.
Sirinâga (2 y.)	22, 46—47.
Vijaya (1 y.)	22, 51.
Saṃghatissa (Asaṃgatissa) (4 y.)	22, 48—50. 52.
Saṃghabodhi (2 y.)	22, 53. 54.
Abhaya Meghavaṇṇa (13 y.)	22, 55—60.
Jeṭṭhatissa (10 y.)	22, 61—65.
Mahâsena (27 y.)	22, 66—76.

1) According to the Mahâvaṃsa: 9 years and 8 months.
2) 6 months according to the Mahâvaṃsa.
3) According to the Mahâvaṃsa: 7 years and 8 months.
4) In the Mahâvaṃsa, Tissa and Abhaya are transposed, and to Abhaya only eight years are given.

BERLIN, printed by A. W. SCHADE.